THE ONLY GAME

THE
ONLY GAME

Roddy Forsyth

MAINSTREAM
PUBLISHING

IN CONJUNCTION WITH

M^{c}EWAN'S
LAGER

All rights reserved
First published in Great Britain 1990 by
MAINSTREAM PUBLISHING COMPANY
(EDINBURGH) LTD
7 Albany Street
Edinburgh EH1 3UG

British Library Cataloguing in Publication Data
Forsyth, Roddy
The Only Game
1. Scotland. Association football, history
I. Title
796.334′09411

ISBN 1 85158 107 3

Typeset in 10/11 Bembo by Bookworm Typesetting Ltd, Edinburgh
Printed in Great Britain by Martins of Berwick, Berwick Upon Tweed

Author's Note

This is not a history of Scottish football. It is an appreciation, an attempt to measure Scotland's contribution to the world of football and to look at our game as an outsider might view it. Readers who require a blow by blow account of their favourite team will not find it here and, in any case, other authors have satisfied that need admirably.

Instead, I have tried to reveal the larger picture and to show how the Scottish game was shaped and, in turn, how the Scots helped to shape football and prepare it to take its place as the world's most popular sport. There is a powerful case for suggesting that if the Scottish working man had taken to rugby, instead of soccer, as his counterparts in Wales did, we might well have seen West Germany play Argentina for the rugby World Cup in July 1990, watched by a global audience of a billion viewers.

The export of a succession of gifted players and managers and the epic, and frequently bitter, rivalry between Rangers and Celtic, were instrumental in shaping the international image of Scottish football until the Premier Division, the rise of Aberdeen and Dundee United and the remarkable sequence of events at Ibrox after 1986, aroused considerable interest abroad, and this outside curiosity has grown steadily in recent years.

The impact of football on a nation of barely five million people is an extraordinary phenomenon. The impact of Scots on football, when the record is scrutinised, is equally compelling. That is the purpose of this book.

ACKNOWLEDGMENTS

A number of individuals and organisations deserve thanks for their invaluable assistance. In particular:

Scottish Brewers, for their generous sponsorship of this book, made possible by the enthusiasm of Tony Belfield and Roger Crossthwaite.

BBC Radio Sport in London, BBC Radio Scotland Sport and BBC Scotland for the use of material recorded by the author over several years.

The *Glasgow Herald* for extensive use of its picture library; Ron Anderson, Harry Reid and Arnold Kemp for their cooperation and above all Bob Tweedie, who worked himself into a melt to find 140 illustrations at short notice.

The Times, for encouragement and forebearance on the part of Tom Clarke, sports editor, and Michael Roffey, picture librarian, for excavating old photographs from the English archives.

The *Sun* for access to their files and photo library, courtesy of Jack Irvine.

The Scottish Football Association and Scottish Football League for help and guidance.

Tony Higgins, for advice on players' salaries and conditions.

Bill Campbell at Mainstream Publishing, who nursed the project for three years.

Hugh, who first lifted me over a turnstile, and Pat, who had to wash the strips, and finally, Marian, for endless patience when her holidays were consumed by proof-reading and deadlines.

Foreword

by DENIS LAW

I'll never forget the first football match I ever heard on the radio. It was 1954 and Scotland were playing Uruguay in the World Cup finals in Switzerland. The match ended Scotland 0 Uruguay 7 – what an awful score to remember, even after all these years. At least it brought home to me that success in international football didn't depend on whether we won or lost to England, although having been on four winning sides against the Auld Enemy I can tell you that it is just about the sweetest pleasure for a Scot, especially when it happens at Wembley. (Remember 1967? We can talk about 1961 some other time.)

There were people around after the Uruguay match who thought that Scotland had nothing more to offer to football at that level and when we didn't make much of a show in the 1958 finals in Sweden, it looked as though they might have been correct. But Scottish players have always been famous for their passion and their skill and the game of football will never be able to do without these two ingredients.

My career was just about to begin in 1958 and I soon discovered just how much English football owed a debt to Scotland. At Huddersfield I played under Andy Beattie and Bill Shankly, at Manchester City it was Les McDowall and at Manchester United, of course, there was Matt Busby and Tommy Docherty. There was Jock Stein, too, when he was caretaker manager of Scotland in the mid-1960s. There can't have been many people who played for Shankly, Busby and Stein and I count myself extremely lucky to have been one of the few.

When you read about them in this book it is hard to believe that there will ever be their likes again. Certainly they all came from a way of life, the coal mines, which has almost vanished in Scotland, and it is even more astonishing to realise that they were all born within a few miles of each other. If you collected the trophies their clubs won under their guidance, there wouldn't be a display case in the world big enough to hold them all.

My old team-mate, Paddy Crerand, calls the three of them – Jock, Bill and Sir Matt – the Great Triumvirate and, as he says, if they had appeared together in the middle of the pitch at Old Trafford to talk about football for an hour and a half, there would have been a capacity crowd to listen to what they had to say.

Look at the players, too. Can you imagine our game without its quota of fiery Scots like Dave Mackay, Billy Bremner, Archie Gemmell, Gordon Strachan or Graeme Souness? Or brilliant footballers like Jim Baxter, John White or Kenny Dalglish? The acid test is to take all the English teams which have won the championship, the FA Cup or a European trophy in the last 25 years and see how many did it without a Scot in their ranks.

You'd be lucky to count a handful, while some of the others had as much as half a team from north of the border. Then there are the Scottish sides themselves. Rangers, Celtic, Aberdeen and Dundee United have all been European finalists while Scotland has qualified for the World Cup finals five times in a row. It is a phenomenal record for a country with a population which is not much more than half that of London, and there isn't another nation in the world of that size with a record which comes anywhere near that of Scotland.

Plus the fact, as you can read here, it is too often forgotten that it was the Scots who really showed the world in the early years how football should be played – with passion and commitment and skill. The passion is still there as we saw in the Grand Slam rugby match at Murrayfield, when Scotland thrashed an England team which thought it only had to turn up to win, and the passion was there in the World Cup match in Genoa when Scotland tore into Sweden and won a thrilling victory.

Passion is nothing without skill, of course, and there are definitely not so many gifted Scottish players around as there were in my time, although I have to say that the same thing is true for most other countries at the moment. Still, there is always the new generation and we shouldn't forget that in the final of the youth World Cup in 1989, a brave set of Scottish youngsters were only beaten on penalties by a very mature looking Saudi Arabian team, so perhaps Scottish football is about to write another chapter in the history of the most popular game in the world.

In the meantime, there is always this book to celebrate Scotland's contribution to football. In my opinion Roddy Forsyth has written the best book about Scottish football to date, and I have seen hundreds of them over the years. Roddy and I covered the World Cup finals in Spain, Mexico and Italy together and we have often sat up into the early hours of the morning discussing many of the incidents and people mentioned in these pages.

It was fun to talk about and as great a pleasure to read. If you enjoy *The Only Game* even half as much as I have done, I guarantee you are in for a football lover's treat.

Best wishes

Denis Law

Contents

Prologue

1978: ON A QUAYSIDE in Buenos Aires a group of children gaze across the waters of the River Plate, busy with tramp steamers, passenger ferries, oil tankers and cargo boats but they are waiting for a vessel to emerge from *beneath* the waters. Realising that there is a British onlooker at hand, they crowd him and demand in Spanish: "Donde esta el sumarino?" – "Where is the submarine?"

They have heard, as apparently everybody in South America has heard, that 40 Scottish football supporters who want to see their team play in the World Cup finals have chartered a Second World War vintage Nazi U-Boat from a French port and have almost completed a three-week journey beneath the hemispheres.

But the onlooker does not know when the submarine will come and the children go back to staring at the greasy waters of the Plate. Later they are joined by a news film crew from Globo TV, the Brazilian network, who tell them that when the U-boat surfaces the passengers will appear on deck to play bagpipes while it cruises into harbour.

★   ★   ★

1985: THE AUSTRALIAN OPEN Championship, one of the four Grand Slam tennis tournaments, has reached the quarter-final stages in Melbourne. Etched in brilliant sunlight on Centre Court at Kooyong, John McEnroe is losing by four games to love against Slobodan Zivojinovic of Yugoslavia and in exasperation at a carelessly dropped point McEnroe bounces his racquet off the baseline.

Most of the spectators audibly murmur their disapproval but one group, on the highest seats behind Zivojinovic, sing a chorus of "Oh, spot the Loony!". These men wear replicas of the dark blue Scottish team jersey and they are taking in the tennis by way of a diversion before the real action, the Australia v Scotland football match which will decide which team goes on to the World Cup finals in Mexico.

"Quiet please!" calls the umpire. "Ach, quiet yersel'!" someone replies from the high seats. When McEnroe actually departs after a whitewash third set, he glares fiercely at the men in dark blue, who are singing "Cheerio, Cheerio, Cheerio! . . ."

★   ★   ★

1986: THE SUBURB OF Neza on the edge of Mexico City has attracted a million incomers in 20 years and they are still arriving from the countryside at a rate of 1,500 every day to live, many of them, in shelters of cardboard and tin in the middle of unspeakable piles of rubbish in the surrounding hills.

Outside the newly constructed municipal stadium, where Scotland, Denmark and Uruguay play each other, a tall red-faced man wearing a T-shirt and kilt is trying to speak to several fascinated locals. Unfortunately, he has lost his voice cheering for Scotland, so he does the next best thing and signs autographs for his admirers.

On Mexican television that evening, a newsreader says that several Scottish supporters have offered to adopt babies whose parents were lost during the earthquake which killed 50,000 people in Mexico City in 1984. Next morning a local newspaper hails the Scots, in a front page headline, as "The Gentlemen of World Football".

★   ★   ★

1928: ON THE EVE of the so-called Wembley Wizards match, which England lost 5–1 to Scotland, the *Weekly News* was moved to comment on odd scenes in the Metropolis: "Now it is rather startling to find such douce buddies as Kirk elders and bank tellers flaunting garish tartan tammies and flying Scottish favours in the Strand on a Saturday morning and possibly going gyte in the afternoon if Gallacher scores a goal at Wembley. In the minds of the public there seems to be some association between putting a tammy over one's head and straw in it."

★   ★   ★

CHAPTER ONE

The Only Game

"The Scots were celebrating their religion – football"
(Sunday Times, 1977)

WALK INTO A pub in Scotland and, if you know anything about football, you'll never talk alone. If you know nothing you can be even better company. You can be a good listener.

No other people has such a sporting obsession, such an extraordinary fixation with a single game, as the Scots with football. When they follow the national team on its travels, the scale of their odysseys may be immense – from the Arctic Circle to Australia in the World Cup qualifying campaign of 1985. Sometimes the migration happens in very considerable numbers, like the estimated 25,000 who turned up in Spain in 1982, and a lot of the spectators in any Scottish football crowd will look as though they had just fled through the heather with Bonnie Prince Charlie after Culloden.

What, for example, were the regulars of a street bar in Malaga to make of the vision which strode into their company and insisted on buying each of them a bottle of San Miguel beer to celebrate Scotland's 5-2 victory over New Zealand in La Roselida stadium earlier that evening? He wore a kilt of red, yellow and green Buchanan tartan complete with leather sporran, white tennis socks, Nike trainers and a replica of the dark blue Scotland jersey. On his head was an orange construction helmet clamped over a red and yellow lion rampant flag which draped down across his neck and shoulders. He looked like a cross between a Highland cattle thief and a Samurai warrior but he was a 28-year-old solicitor from Kirkcaldy, junior partner in a prosperous Glasgow practice, so allergic to the prospect of scorn that he would never have worn the kilt along the main street of his native town in daylight. If anybody had suggested that Harry Lauder represented the typical Scot, our man would have been properly indignant but he was only too happy to disguise himself as a refugee from *Brigadoon* to celebrate a World Cup match in southern Spain.

The Scots do not behave like this for any other sport, even when cause is offered. St Andrews is the spiritual home of golf but when Sandy Lyle won the US Masters in 1988, Augusta was spared an invasion of the 18th green by raiders intent on removing a divot for use as a shrine in a Glasgow garden.

There is, of course, rugby, which is a first cousin in the football family and certainly when Scotland won the Grand Slam in March 1990 at Murrayfield, each home score was resoundingly cheered by crowds at the four Scottish Cup quarter-final matches which were being played simultaneously that afternoon. In Jenners department store in Princes Street, demure and elderly Edinburgh matrons were seen to stab the air in delight with their umbrellas when the public address system announced that Scotland had moved into a 13-4 lead just before half time.

But this demonstration of solidarity with the oval ball code had been

Dumbarton v Queen's Park with Dumbarton Rock in the background. The presence of women in the crowd was not always a civilising element, as a report in an 1882 edition of the *Scottish Athletic Journal* made clear: ". . . a slovenly looking, petticoated and extremely vulgar section of the crowd had answered to the invitation – 'Ladies free'. The language which came from the lips of these ladies was sickening to listen to. The men behaved moderately well, and, in respect of them, it may be as well to forgive the fairer sex in the hope that in future matches they will stay at home."

INTERNATIONAL FOOT-BALL MATCH,
(ASSOCIATION RULES,)
ENGLAND v. SCOTLAND,
WEST OF SCOTLAND CRICKET GROUND,
HAMILTON CRESCENT, PARTICK,
SATURDAY, 30th November, 1872, at 2 p.m.
806
ADMISSION—ONE SHILLING.

cemented by the fact that England were providing the opposition and that most southern commentators had surpassed themselves in conceit and complacency in predicting that the English merely had to turn up and play to strength to win. Under those circumstances, the fiery cross would be put round for a Scotland-England ludo contest. It is only the Scottish football side, though, which can unite the nation in anxiety about a meeting with Costa Rica.

Whatever prompts many thousands of Scots to respond to football in this schizoid fashion, it is obviously not a taste for success. The Brazilians, who can be considered occasional rivals in intensity, have at least passed the game's ultimate test and on three occasions their potent mix of Latin and black bloodlines has seen the World Cup paraded in carnival through the streets of Rio. If Brazil ever fall on hard times the nostalgic Copacabana barfly can at least point to a list of triumphs and sigh for the scores of yesteryear. But where are they for the Scots, whose team has never won the World Cup and which has never even qualified for the finals of the European Championships?

A team without glory, a country without Parliament, a nation without nationality, Scotland exists on the international stage only through sport, and mainly through football. At every international match involving Scotland there will be flags inscribed with the words "Remember Bannockburn" and tartan throngs singing of *Flower of Scotland*, with its references to the War of Independence against England *in the 14th century*. It is as if the Sioux Indians were allowed to enter the world archery championships while their supporters danced in warpaint to celebrate the Battle of the Little Big Horn.

But football would be a dismal business if it only amounted to 11-a-side politics or history replayed between goalposts, and it is often forgotten that the Scottish influence on the game itself was so profound that it transformed the winter pastime of English public schoolboys into the most popular sport in the world. The immense television audience of 700 million who watched the 1986 World Cup final may have been aware that the Argentinian defender with the unlikely name of John Brown, who scored the opening goal against West Germany, had a Scottish great-grandfather, but few could have guessed that Maradona could claim direct descent from James J. Lang, a Glasgow man nicknamed "Reddie" when he played for Sheffield Wednesday in 1876.

One description of Lang, a forward, suggests that he bequeathed his talents straight to the South American. "A muscular little bundle of energy, captivating to watch. First rate at dribbling, Lang raced through defences often finishing with a shot on target." However, the bond which links the two men across the gulf of more than a hundred years is financial, not genetic. Lang, the first-ever professional footballer, was the pioneer who marked out the route which Maradona would follow to become the most highly paid player of a subsequent generation.

As a matter of historical fact, Lang's claim to be the first of a new species was challenged by another Glaswegian by the name of Peter Andrews, a left-sided player who was also gifted with dribbling talents, although less lethal in front of goal where he tended to snap too anxiously at the chances which came his way. Andrews did score one of Scotland's goals in the 2-2 draw with England at The Oval in 1875 and within a year he was on the books of a team called Sheffield Heeley, but while he almost certainly received cash backhanders for his activities on the pitch, he moved to England because his firm sent him to work at their branch in Leeds. Lang, who was a shipyard worker, was hardly likely to find much employment in his line in Sheffield, and it is usually accepted that he moved across to England to play football for money and so he became the world's first professional. It was not a title he welcomed until some years later, because in 1876 it was illegal for teams to pay players, not that the stigma was much of a deterrent to working-class footballers with ability and ambition.

It was also inevitable that the first paid players would be Scots. Even in 1876 they were in exodus across the border and their preference for soccer over rugby was critical to the development of the two varieties of football, which had been rivals for dominance for almost 20 years. Of course, football was never exclusive to Britain or to the 19th century, and in China 200 years before the birth of Christ there was a sport called *tsu chu* – literally *kick ball* – which featured bamboo goalposts and nets. The Greeks and the Romans played versions which were more like the modern handling game of rugby or American football and players were not too scrupulous about how they forced the ball over each other's line to score.

In fact, the most striking feature of football's history through the centuries is the sheer wildness of the game, to the point of serious violence and death. In the 16th century it was described by Philip Stubbes in the *Anatomie of Abuses* as more of "a friendlye kind of fight than a play or recreation, a bloody and murthering practise than a felowly sporte or pastime." Stubbes was a Puritan and his objection to football was mainly that it was played on the Sabbath but his catalogue of players' injuries was scarcely compatible with good health on any other day of the week; broken arms, legs, necks and backs, dislocated limbs, eyes gouged out of their sockets and noses gushing with blood after being battered "uppon hard stones".

In the early 19th century well-meaning individuals, such as Sir Walter Scott, tried to curtain the worst excesses by enforcing simple rules, although inevitably there were critics who thought some of the fun was going out of the game. Scott, like a Georgian version of Elton John, devoted a good deal of energy to his local team, the Men of Ettrick, and he arranged a derby match with the Men of Yarrow, managed by the Earl of Home. This was held to be a great success

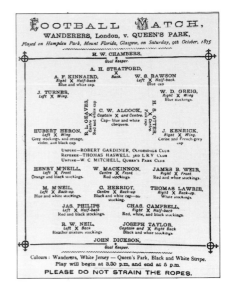

Match card for Wanderers v Queen's Park with C. W. Alcock and Lord Arthur Kinnaird, two of the founding fathers of football, in the Wanderers line-up.

Wanderers v Queen's Park, 1875. Wanderers won the FA Cup the following year while Queen's Park won the Scottish Cup for the third year in succession in 1876. Queen's won this match by a handsome 5-0.

and Scott suggested that the game might become a fixture although he felt that the teams were on the large side with 150 players each. If the introduction of rules was a setback to the more psychopathic enthusiasts, there was still plenty of opportunity for mayhem, as recorded by the anonymous author of a 19th-century poem called *The Football Match*, which described a bounce game played by half a dozen youths on Salisbury plain:

> The ball it being thrown up, my boys, the game it did draw nigh,
> Young William stuck a sharp penknife into young Jackson's thigh,
> Here's health unto these rippling lads, and so the game went on.

However, in 1848 the use of weapons, at least by players, came to an end when 14 former pupils of the great English public schools got together at Cambridge to find common ground between football games being played at Eton, Harrow, Rugby and other institutions. Most of the code they devised, known as the Cambridge Rules, resembled today's football varieties and it was the signal for the start of small-scale tournaments. At an entirely separate meeting in Sheffield about seven years later, another rule book was drawn up which allowed a rougher game and players could use their hands to shove opponents legally.

A move to hammer out some kind of universal game was bound to happen but the attempt fractured over the usual issue of what constituted an acceptable level of physical collision. The issue which disrupted the founding fathers concerned the practice known as "hacking", in which players could tackle an opponent by kicking him on the shin whether he was in possession of the ball or not. This was a charming relic of the anarchic matches at Charterhouse

The result of the Scotland-England match in 1878 would induce stupefaction on both sides of the border if repeated now; the Scots won 7-2.

and Eton, where the youngest pupils were given the job of halting bulkier players by ambushing them in a mob and if the juniors were trampled underfoot or tossed over railings in the process, it was an accepted hazard of initiation into manly society.

When the hero of *Tom Brown's Schooldays* spends his first Sunday at Rugby, he asks his new friend if he can play in the School-house match.

> "Oh but do show me where they play. And tell me all about it. I love football so, and have played it all my life. Won't Brooke let me play?"
>
> "Not he," said East, with some indignation; "why, you don't know the rules – you'll be a month learning them. And then it's no joke playing in a match, I can tell you. Quite another thing from your private school game. Why, there's been two collar bones broken this half, and a dozen fellows lamed. And last year a fellow had his leg broken."

If the most visible reward for schoolboy players was the accumulation of scar tissue, most of those who were not actually hospitalised seem to have believed that such experiences promoted the growth of "character", the mortar of Empire-builders. Public school theorists so frequently compared football to warfare that it is easy to believe that the Charge of the Light Brigade was simply a mass dribble through cannon fire.

Naturally there were those who thought that if football was to become a more fluent activity it would have to go easy on the unarmed combat, an opinion which caused the die-hards to turn caustic. One advocate of the hacking game openly accused his opponents of cowardice and of trying to drain football of its courage and pluck. In a taunt calculated to prod raw nerves he warned the reformers that "I will be bound to bring over a lot of Frenchmen who would beat you with a week's practice." Since the French were the forerunners of Oscar Wilde as model degenerates so far as British opinion was concerned, the remark was virtually libellous. In acrimonious circumstances the new rules were imposed by the Football Association, which had been founded in October 1863. It took only two months for the Blackheath club to decide they could not stomach Association football and they walked out of the FA to offer leadership to those who preferred the Rugby game. It split soccer and rugby but apart from handling, it would be hard to tell them apart.

The breach between the two codes was not so dramatic as the feuding parties supposed. Out with Blackheath went two of the original Cambridge rules, which allowed a player to catch the ball or hold it in his hands and run towards the opposition goal, and the emphasis in soccer was placed on controlling the ball with the feet. The dribblers were now free to run without being dragged bodily to the ground but the game they played would have looked farcical to today's spectators.

The idea of the new sport was that a player should hold on to the ball until tackled when, it was hoped, a team-mate would gather possession and continue to bear down on goal. The thin red line mentality was still dominant, and attacking teams advanced in skirmishing order, with eight or nine players moving forward in close support of each other, while the opposing defenders would cluster round the man with the ball and try to kick it out of his path. The soccer pioneers had been inspired by a textbook called *The Simplest Game*, but technically it was more like a sport for the simple-minded. Even the embryonic version

of rugby had more versatility. The time had come for the Scots to export their revolution.

★   ★   ★

Those who take for granted that modern football is one of England's gifts to civilisation usually believe that Scotland was the first stop on the sport's progress round the world but, in fact, the two countries developed the game at the same time and the Scots appear to have had a more thorough grasp of its possibilities from the beginning. There is a vivid description of an incident in the match organised by Sir Walter Scott at Carterhaugh when a certain Walter Laidlaw picked up the ball and played it to his team-mate William Riddell, lying wide of the mass of players, much as a rugby scrum-half would now combine with a wing three-quarter, or an American football quarterback might try to find a wide receiver. Riddell sprinted clear and he would have scored but for one of the less predictable hazards of the old-fashioned football. A spectator on a horse chased Riddell and ran him down. Still, the account indicates that rugby was a native game in the Borders eight years before William Webb Ellis ran with the ball at Rugby school.

The Edinburgh schools also played football in the early years of the century, and while there was no running with the ball, players were allowed to handle. This was pretty much the same game as was being played at Eton and Harrow and was the forerunner of soccer, although the Edinburgh establishments eventually followed the Rugby tradition after the great divide amongst the legislators and it was their support which gave rugby the edge in Scotland in organisation and popularity in the early years.

Queen's Park had started playing the Association game in Glasgow in 1867 but the club's influence was a long way short of the power wielded by the schools and when Edinburgh Academical FC produced the first Scottish rulebook in 1868, there was no debate about the name of the game. Their work was titled "Laws of Football as played by the Principal Clubs of Scotland" and by football they meant the handling variety. In London two years later, the Football Association tried to outflank its rugby rival by arranging two games billed as "England versus Scotland". The label was an economy with the truth and the Scotland teams were composed of Scots living in London. There must have been a dearth of immigrants because the selectors were reduced to using some individuals whose names *mostly* sounded Scottish. The teams were also short of pit men and blast furnace operators, unless there was moonlighting by the likes of W.H. Gladstone, son of the Prime Minister, or Quinton Hogg, grandfather of one of Mrs Thatcher's Lord Chancellors. Nevertheless, Charles Alcock, the honorary secretary of the Football Association, who organised the games, must have suspected he was in on the start of a rivalry with broad appeal when his showmanship prompted a lengthy newspaper correspondence which ended when the captains of five Scottish clubs issued a challenge to their English counterparts. It was accepted and although neither country was an independent state, the game can be considered to be the world's first international football match. Alcock could not congratulate himself, however. It was the rugby men who would play the world's first football international, in Scotland.

When the rugby players of Scotland and England met at Raeburn Place in Edinburgh, on 27 March 1871, the Scots won by a goal and a try to a goal, but both sides had contributed to the flow of play by giving up hacking off the ball, the habit of tripping a player who was not in possession. The Scots impressed their opponents with the quality of their team-work, which must have been well developed to draw admiration from an England side which contained ten former pupils of Rugby school. The size of the crowd was noteworthy, too. At least 2,000 spectators – perhaps as many as 4,000 – turned up at Raeburn Place and the success of the occasion must have given Charles Alcock hope for his own cherished project. In a letter to the *Glasgow Herald*, calculated to trigger patriotic energies, he had written: "In Scotland, once essentially the land of football, there should still be a spark left of the old fire, and I confidently appeal to Scotsmen to aid to their utmost the efforts of the committee to confer successs on what London hopes to found, an annual trial of skill between the champions of England and Scotland."

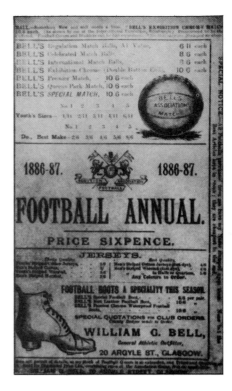

Six months after the rugby contest, the second football international was played, also in Scotland, but this time it was a soccer contest at Glasgow, at the West of Scotland cricket ground in Partick. The scene of this momentous event looks very much today as it did on St Andrew's Day, 1872, when another healthy crowd of 4,000 turned up to see Scotland and England draw 0-0. Although there were no goals, the spectators were excited with the action because the Scots, like their rugby countrymen, were much the better at team-work. There was a much more important development to be seen, however. Although both teams were full of men chosen for their dribbling skills, the Scots had discovered the passing game. It was the birth of a new age, the moment when vision outstripped mere physical prowess. Sixteen years later, a football writer declared: ". . .the introduction of a combination of passing tactics from forward to forward to the discouragement of brilliant dribbling by individual players, so far revolutionised the game that we may fairly say that there have been two ages of the Association play, the dribbling and the passing."

The English had laid down the rules of football, so that the rest of the world could play the game. It was the Scot who transformed football into an art, so that the world could enjoy it.

★   ★   ★

The invention of the wheel was important, but it was the idea of the axle which made it work, otherwise *Ben Hur* would have been an epic tale of gladiators on unicycles. The passing game was the axle of football and it brought time and space into the game's strategy to replace the old scene of random lurches around the pitch, so that every player (apart from the goalkeeper) could offer a threat even when the ball was elsewhere.

The passing game had to come, sooner or later, but it was probably logical that the Scot should have invented it. A people with an unusually well developed aptitude for engineering was bound to be attracted by the *dynamics* of sport, the notion that a game involved science as well as art. It was not an accident that for 50 years afterwards their footballers were known in England and abroad as the "Scotch Professors". Scotland had been the home of golf for 300 years and it must have been obvious to any seasoned golfer that a football player could beat opponents if he chipped or lobbed or simply rolled the ball around the pitch. The dribblers would always be valued for their close control but now the future belonged to the man who could dissect a defence with a single astute pass.

DRIBBLING

The new style of play was immediately seen to be superior, although Scotland were beaten 4-2 by England in the second match between the countries, but the Scots had an excuse for that setback because the selectors could only afford to pay for eight return train tickets and three London players were conscripted to make up the numbers. One of them was H.W. Renny-Tailyour, whose international career ranks as particularly unfortunate, because he had also been in the Scottish rugby team beaten by England the year before, and never played in the national colours at either sport again.

Defeats by England were soon seen to be exceptions to Scottish rule, at least in the soccer code. For almost 20 years after 1873 Scotland enjoyed a spectacular domination over the Auld Enemy, suffering only two defeats and winning most of the annual matches by margins which would induce a stupefied daze north of the border nowadays . . . 7-2 in 1878, 6-1 and 5-1 in 1881 and 1882. When Ireland and Wales joined in the international series, they offered even more fuel for northern self-satisfaction when they were hammered routinely with scores such as 10-2 and 8-0.

The first Scotland players must have felt like Napoleon's soldiers in their early campaigns; it was mainly a matter of turning up to collect yet another battle honour from a defeated neighbour. The Scottish Football Association's annual *Handbook* became a litany of self-congratulation and in 1879 was able to declare: "It is with great pleasure your committee have to report that another season has passed without a single defeat to mar our brilliant record. It is now six years since an international was lost."

Such effortless superiority was not duplicated on the rugby field, where the English showed an aggravating tendency to avoid crushing defeats and even to come out of the first decade of internationals with a greater share of victories, a contrast which went a long way towards confirming to most Scots that soccer was much the more rewarding form of football. In addition, the Scottish Football Union, which governed rugby in the north, found itself in persistent dispute with the Rugby Football Union over rules and results and there was frequent animosity between the two parties, so that when Scotland scored a late and contentious equalising try against England in 1881, it was in character for the English President to remark that ". . . the Scotch team was strong, their strength being in umpiring." Three years later, another match between the two countries came to a full stop for half an hour while the players and officials became involved in a fierce argument about a try scored by an English player while the Scots had pulled up for what they thought had been a foul. This controversy extended to the point where the Scottish Football Union announced: "Scotland was willing to have the dispute terminated, but not by an unconditional surrender to England."

Since the Scots, like the Irish, were (and still are) allergic to the idea of surrender to England, unconditional or otherwise, rugby was clearly losing ground in the struggle for affection north of the border. Its strongholds were in the great Scottish schools, mostly in Edinburgh, where Edinburgh Academy, Merchiston and Loretto dominated, and in the Borders, but these local struggles could not become the national pattern. There was no innate reason why rugby, which was adopted by Welsh miners and shipyard workers, should not also have become the sport of the Scottish working classes, a development which might well have given it ascendancy over soccer as the games were spread to the rest of the world through

the British armed forces and merchant fleets. But in Scotland the
Borders did not have the population to offer rugby a solid enough
platform to sustain it as a national sport while the Edinburgh adherents
who ruled its destiny were loth to carry rugby to the industrial
workers, largely because it was apparent from the earliest days of
mass interest in organised games that the day of the professional
sportsman was at hand. Outside the Borders, rugby became the
preserve of the professional classes, men who were attracted to the
sport because of its social overtones rather than its earning-power
and who were frequently accused of excluding talented Borderers
from the national side to the benefit of their own former school
cronies.

The reactionary nature of rugby's governors in Scotland was vividly
advertised by J. Aikman Smith, the autocratic secretary of the Scottish
Rugby Union, when he was asked in 1928 why Scottish players did
not wear numbered jerseys in international matches. "It is a Rugby
match, not a cattle sale," was Aikman Smith's cutting retort, which
he did not see fit to soften merely because he happened to be replying
to King George V. This was the same mentality which perceived
nothing wrong in the bill for 7/6d which was sent, in 1918, to Jock
Wemyss of Gala and Edinburgh Wanderers for a Scotland jersey he
had failed to return after his first cap in 1914. The fact that he had
overlooked the matter in his haste to enlist for the First World War,
during which he lost an eye, was not thought to be a pardonable
excuse.

These attitudes were hardly likely to appeal to the Scottish working
man, temperamentally inclined to a belief in his own right to argue
the toss with anyone, and even the Scottish Football Union had to
recognise the reality of a changing world when it changed its name,
in 1924, to the Scottish Rugby Union. Most Scots had decided long
before then that soccer was the more satisfying form of football and
that football was the only game for them.

★ ★ ★

The industrial Scot, the collier, the shipbuilder, the boilermaker was
the foundation of the advancing game north of the border and south
and his aptitude for the game may have been due, in some measure, to
an understanding of teamwork bred by the kind of close co-operation
required to meet the demands of pit owners and yard gaffers. Such men
had the physical and mental hardness which was a tempered version of
the "pluck" so valued by the English public schoolboys who had given
the game its first framework.

When shinguards were introduced in 1884, they were the invention
of Sam Widdowson of Nottingham Forest and it is entertaining to
speculate that the idea grew in his mind during his only experience of
international football, when he played against Scotland. What could
not be devised in England during the early years was the tactical
awareness of the Scottish player, but what the English could not
invent they could import, a trend which was to accelerate as the
appetite for football expanded in both countries.

For a while there was an overlap between the gentleman player,
who saw the sport as a leisure pursuit, and the career footballer,
whose livelihood came from the game, albeit illicitly at first In 1884,
Accrington, an English club with a taste for Scottish talent, were
impressed by the skills of Frank Shaw, a forward with Pollokshields

Athletic, who combined fine close control and dribbling ability with the gift of good distribution. To sweeten their approach they suggested an annual salary of £120 but they had to wait for their reply. When he eventually responded, Shaw advised the Accrington committee that he had not been able to give the matter his attention until "my return from a fortnight's cruise amongst the Western Isles, on my yacht".

James Lang, already mentioned as the world's first acknowledged professional player, had a more typical background of maritime vessels. He worked in a shipyard in Clydebank before he moved to Sheffield Wednesday, where he had the nous not to mention that he had lost an eye in a yard accident. He went to some lengths to conceal the fact so that opponents would not discover that he literally possessed a blind side, but if Lang's claim to be the first paid footballer probably rests on his willingness to admit the source of his income ahead of others whose claims may have had similar substance, he remains a fitting symbol for those in the game who declined to see the cash which had begun to flow towards the accomplished player.

Lang and his compatriots remodelled the sport in England where the native game was built on a team formation of seven – sometimes eight – forwards supported by full backs who played in the rugby tradition of supporting attackers. The backs reinforced the attacking surge by picking up loose possession and driving on towards goal.

The early Scottish sides were not exactly born of the fortress mentality, with six players employed up front, but the two flanking players were given a shuttle role and dropped back into midfield when the need arose, and they were reinforced by two traditional backs, played behind the forwards, as well as two deep-lying defenders whose beat was much closer to the goalkeeper. In modern language, this would represent a formation which varied between 2-2-6 and 2-4-4 and it was not long before the shrewder tacticians realised that teams were better balanced if yet another forward was withdrawn into a semi-defensive position to create the familiar 2-3-5 formula – two full backs, three half backs and five forwards – which remained the basis of football strategy for half a century.

If the Scottish player was ahead of the game, the native administrator trailed behind those in England. The Football Association was founded almost ten years before its Scottish equivalent but the Scottish League was born within two years of the Football League for the very practical reason that, as soon as professionalism was legal in England, the southbound migration became a haemorrhage which had to be staunched before the game in Scotland was bled white of its finest talent.

Ironically, the Football League was the creation of one William McGregor ("predictably a Scot", as an English commentary records drily), a Perthshire draper who bought a shop in Birmingham near the Aston Villa ground. McGregor joined Villa, although not for athletic purposes, as he later admitted when he revealed that he had only ever played football on a single, unsuccessful occasion. "I tried it once when I was very young and had to take to bed for a week," said the man whose vision and timing as a football administrator were wonderfully matched to a sport in which the organisation had begun to collapse.

Football in 1888 attracted unprecedented crowds but the explosion in spectator interest was threatened by the fact that clubs arranged

William McGregor, the founder / 23
of the Football League.

fixtures entirely to suit themselves and were quick to call them off if conditions seemed unfavourable to their chances. Supporters found grounds locked against them without notice and clubs who wanted to fulfil fixtures were embarrassed by opponents who failed to turn up and left them with a wage bill for players who had not been employed. When it was suggested that players should forego their pay in the event of a cancelled fixture, the ominous tone of antagonised Scottish voices inclined most club treasurers to write the notion off as a non-starter.

To McGregor, musing amidst his bustles and stays, the solution was startlingly obvious. He composed a letter which was sent to six clubs, including his own Aston Villa, in which he observed:

> Every year it is becoming more and more difficult for football clubs of any standing to meet their friendly engagements, and even arrange friendly matches . . . I beg to tender the following suggestion as a means of getting over the difficulty. That ten or twelve of the most prominent clubs in England combine to arrange home-and-away fixtures each season. I would take it as a favour if you would kindly think the matter over . . . and should like to hear what other clubs you suggest.

McGregor had given the football universe its shape, although at first it was formed in a local constellation with six Lancashire clubs, three from Staffordshire and the others from the counties of Derby, Nottingham and Warwick, and his idea proved so attractive that two important candidates, Sheffield Wednesday and Nottingham Forest, had to be turned down for the opening season. Since there were no professional teams in the south, the Football League started as a northern affair and consequently it drew a substantial number of employees from Scotland to the point where some teams were composed almost entirely of Scots. The first League goal was scored by Jack Gordon (nationality inevitable), a member of the Preston North End team known as The Invincibles, who had won the FA Cup in 1889 without conceding a goal and who, for an encore, became the first champions in 1890 without losing a game.

Preston's manager, Major William Sudell, was an open admirer of Scottish players and habitually trawled the seemingly inexhaustible shoals of northern talent for new recruits. Sudell and his Scots were legendary for their relentless confidence, although they overreached themselves spectacularly when they won through to the FA Cup final of 1888 and asked if they could be photographed with the cup before the match, because they would be dirty afterwards. The match referee, Major Francis Marindin, was moved to ask, quite reasonably as it turned out: "Had you not better win it first?" The airy confidence of the Preston players was punctured when they took only one of the ten chances they created, while West Bromwich Albion made two and scored both, a feat which entitled them to meet the Scottish Cup winners Renton in a match billed as "The Championship of the World". The game was played in a raging snowstorm from which Renton emerged as world champions.

An Englishman with footballing talent often became a stranger in his own land simply by stepping into his team's dressing-room, as witness the Liverpool side which played the club's first-ever League game in September 1893 with ten Scotsmen and a goalkeeper called McOwen, whose surname disguised the fact that he had been born a native. McOwen's inclusion was a significant advance from an

English point of view, because the very first Liverpool team, seen in a friendly against Rotherham, consisted of 11 Scots, who lined up as follows: Ross, Hannah, McLean, Kelso, McQueen, McBride, Wyllie, Smith, Miller, McVean and Kelvin. The selection read like a Glasgow street directory because the first Liverpool manager, John McKenna (an Irishman, despite his name), had acquired 13 players during a productive trip to the city in 1892. In the 1985-86 season, when Liverpool won the League and Cup double, they again fielded teams without an English player, although the Scottish contingent was reduced to a mere four individuals.

Other teams were similarly full of emigrant Scots, in particular Sunderland, known as the "Team of all the Talents", title winners in 1892, 1893 and 1895, who usually took the field with a token English player in their line-up, perhaps to offer hope to local lads without any claim to the tartan. Something must have happened, possibly in the blizzard at Renton, to antagonise West Brom against imports from north of the border, because it is alleged that they never used a Scottish player between 1905 and 1937, a circumstance so unlikely it suggests a deeply rooted prejudice. When West Brom beat Derby Junction 3-0 in the semi-finals of the FA Cup in 1888, the referee (Major Marindin again) asked them whether they had any Scotch Professors in the side, and when told they did not, presented them with the match ball in recognition of an achievement against overwhelming odds.

West Bromwich aside, the southbound flow continued to pour into William McGregor's League, and even 50 years later it was said that unemployed supporters in Preston were in the habit of meeting each train from Scotland in order to see who might be playing for North End the following Saturday. As late as 1956 Accrington Stanley, having learned not to offer contracts to yacht-owners cruising in the Hebrides, fielded several teams composed only of Scots.

If the Football League had ever imposed a quota restriction on imports, as Scottish supporters devoutly wished it would, the game in England would have been deeply impoverished, although it must be said that the experience of playing in a highly competitive league also worked to the benefit of Scottish footballers, sharpening their skills in a manner unavailable on most of their home grounds. William McGregor could not have foreseen that the organisation he founded would be imitated throughout most of the world in the next century and beyond, but he had a shrewd idea of what his inspiration had achieved by the end of the 19th century, when he wrote:

> I really believe that the game would have received a very severe check, and its popularity would have been paralysed once and for all, if the league had not been founded. I am not saying that football would have died, because football will never die. Even if the time should come when it ceases to be the highly organised sport it is today, it will still be the pastime of the juveniles, because it is not easy to conceive the introduction of a game which will prove its superior.

Before we move on from William McGregor he must also be given credit for another achievement. Aside from being a pillar of the Birmingham Football Association he was also one of the driving forces behind Aston Villa, who were established as an institution in the English game with five championship wins in the 1890s and two FA Cup wins, one of which brought the double to Villa Park. When McGregor appraised their performance afterwards, he was

Hampden Park for the
Rangers-Hamilton Academical
Scottish Cup final in 1935.
Rangers won 2-1.

not shackled by undue modesty. "For brilliancy and, at the same time, for consistency of achievement," he declared, "for activity in philanthropic enterprise, for astuteness of management and for general alertness, the superiors of Aston Villa cannot be found."

Villa reached the apex of their success on 26 May 1982 when, having qualified as champions of McGregor's League to play in the European Cup, they beat Bayern Munich 1-0 in Rotterdam to take the trophy to Birmingham. It would surely have afforded the genial draper from Perthshire particular pleasure to know that three of the victorious team – Des Bremner, Ken McNaught and Allan Evans – had followed him on the trail from Scotland, to be rewarded with a view from the highest summit in European club football.

★   ★   ★

Question: What did the thief and the Lord High Commissioner to the General Assembly of the Church of Scotland have in common?
Answer: They both got an FA Cup to keep.

The life of Arthur Fitzgerald Kinnaird was short of colour in about the same way that the Aga Khan lacks the price of a cup of tea. He has been described as a character straight from the pages of Dickens but he was more like something from a novel by Thackeray or Trollope; in fact, the image which remains to us is almost more vivid than Trollope himself, which is saying something when one considers that for Trollope a typical day consisted of rising at seven and writing 2,000 words until nine, when he set off for his job at the Post Office, an activity which he combined with foxhunting three days a week. On his slack days, Trollope used to play cards until the small hours, but he was a sloth compared with Kinnaird.

The Hon. A. F. Kinnaird, who was born in Kensington but who qualified to play for Scotland because of his parentage and the fact that he owned an estate in Perthshire, first played football at Cheam and Eton schools before he made his mark as accomplished player at Cambridge University, where he took an MA degree as a graduate of Trinity College. He had been a sprinter at Eton and extended his athletic interests at Cambridge, where he was chosen to represent the university at tennis, fives (an indoor ball game played with gloved hands or sticks) and swimming. By way of diversion, he entered and won an international canoe race staged at the Paris Exhibition in 1867 when he was 21.

The following year Kinnaird was elected to the Football Association Committee and went on to become one of the game's most accomplished administrators, so much so that he is considered one of football's three founding fathers, the others being Charles Alcock and Major Marindin. Kinnaird played in the games which led to the establishment of the annual fixture between Scotland and England. When the first official international was played in 1872, it was essentially a club contest between Queen's Park and 11 Englishmen who played for Kinnaird's team, Wanderers, but he won his single Scottish cap the following year, as one of the three London residents called in to make up the numbers when the Scots could only afford the rail fares of three of their players.

It was in the FA Cup that Kinnaird was to set a combination of records which is unlikely ever to be surpassed. He played in more FA Cup finals than anyone else, a total of nine, five of which

Lord Arthur Kinnaird, famed for his red beard and athleticism.

GLASGOW FOOTBALL TEAM.—FEBRUARY 14TH, 1880.

Glasgow team in 1880, made up of players from the city's principal clubs for representative matches against Edinburgh and others.

brought him winners' medals. His first appearance was in 1873 when Wanderers beat Oxford University and although the result gave him great pleasure as a Cambridge man, Kinnaird regretted that the final had not featured Queen's Park, who had beaten Oxford in the semi-final, but who were confounded yet again by the railway companies' insistence on cash for journeys from Glasgow to London.

Kinnaird also turned out for Old Etonians and reached the final with them twice in succession, in 1875 and again in 1876, when they were beaten by Wanderers, but he guessed more successfully in the following two seasons when, as a Wanderers player, he was again in Cup winning sides. At the start of the 1879 campaign he was back with Old Etonians, an astute move on his part because they beat Wanderers 7-2 in the first round and went on to take the trophy. He was the personification of the gentleman footballer but the day of the revolution was at hand and Kinnaird must have scented change when Old Etonians met the northern side Darwen in the fourth round of the tournament.

The public schoolboys were cruising in a 5-1 lead with 15 minutes left to play at Kennington Oval when Darwen dazed them with four goals before full time. Etonians refused to play extra-time, a ploy which might have put the northerners out of the Cup by default, because like Queen's Park they had no spare cash for repeated trips to London, but a public subscription was got up and Darwen returned for the replay which ended in a 2-2 draw. The third match put Etonians through by a handsome margin of 6-2 but Darwen's performance caught the newspaper's attention and their resistance was credited to the Scottish players, Fergus Suter and James Love, who had first come south with Partick Thistle on tour. The pair were persuaded to stay

Scotland team for the annual international with England in 1880. The Scots won 5-4, Ker scoring three, and Baird and Kay one apiece.

INTERNATIONAL FOOTBALL MATCH,
SCOTLAND *v.* ENGLAND,
PLAYED AT GLASGOW, 13TH MARCH, 1880.

SCOTCH TEAM.

J. A. Allan,   J. Nicolson,   A. Rowan,   R. W. Neill,   D. Hamilton,   J. Kaye,
Caledonian.   Vale of Leven (Umpire).   Caledonian.   Queen's Park (Capt.)   Parkgrove (Referee).   Queen's Park.

C. Campbell,   J. M'Pherson,
Queen's Park.   Vale of Leven.

A. M'Lintock,   J. Smith,   G. Kerr,
Vale of Leven.   Edin. University.   Queen's Park.

M. M'Neil,   J. M'Gregor,   J. C. Baird,
Rangers.   Vale of Leven.   Vale of Leven.

on and it was widely suggested that they were in the habit of finding money in their boots after they had taken their post-match baths.

Kinnaird, however, went on to another three finals with Old Etonians, who lost the first to Old Carthusians in 1881 but were winners against Blackburn Rovers at Kennington Oval in 1882, on which occasion the spectators called for an encore. Kinnaird obliged by standing on his head in front of the stands to immense applause. He was back at Kennington for the following but this time it was the game which was to be turned on its head because Etonians lost to Blackburn Olympic and the cup moved north, where it remained until the turn of the century when Tottenham Hotspur brought it back to the capital.

Kinnaird's contribution to the tournament was remarkable even for the days of the gentleman player and he was the only man to have appeared in consecutive finals for different teams until Brian Talbot played for Ipswich and Arsenal exactly a century later. He had cut a distinctive figure, playing in long white trousers with a quartered cap and was instantly identifiable because of his magnificent long red beard, all of which, combined with his athletic ability, made him a hero to the crowds who increasingly flocked to football in the 1870s and 1880s. He was often mobbed by supporters before cup finals and on one occasion they unhitched the horses from his coach and dragged it, with Kinnaird saluting them, to the players' entrance.

Although he reached no more Cup finals after 1883, he played on for a further ten years and only decided to retire at the age of 46. His favourite position was half back but he was famously versatile and played almost every other role for Wanderers and Etonians. He was a phenomenon of Victorian sport on and off the pitch and went on to become the first President of the London FA and Treasurer of the FA itself before he was elected President in 1890, a position he held until his death at the age of 75 in 1923. When he was not playing football or administering its fortunes, he filled in with an active career in Parliament where he took his seat as Lord Kinnaird, and a spell as President of the YMCA as well as a period when he acted as Lord High Commissioner to the General Assembly of the Church of Scotland.

The Football Association publicly advertised its debt to him in 1911 when it presented him with the FA Cup to keep in recognition of his services to the game, although it was not the original trophy he had held aloft as a five times winner because that had been stolen in 1895 from a bootmaker's window in Birmingham, where it was being exhibited by the holders, William McGregor's Aston Villa. Instead, they gave him the second FA Cup and replaced it with the third and present trophy. And so it was that a thief and Lord Kinnaird each came to possess an FA Cup of their own.

★　　★　　★

Without Arthur Kinnaird, James Lang and William McGregor, football would certainly have been impoverished and might easily have lost the momentum which was to carry it on to its unrivalled position as the world's most popular sport. It was anything but a foregone conclusion in the early days of organised football, which first emerged in the English-speaking countries, that the soccer code would ultimately become the dominant version.

The explosion of interest in football was a result, in Britain, of the Saturday half-holiday which gave industrial workers a free afternoon on a day not traditionally reserved for religious observation. By coincidence football had begun to organise itself at roughly the same time and so the demand for a spectator sport which could focus local ambitions and rivalries was immediately met. The winter games of

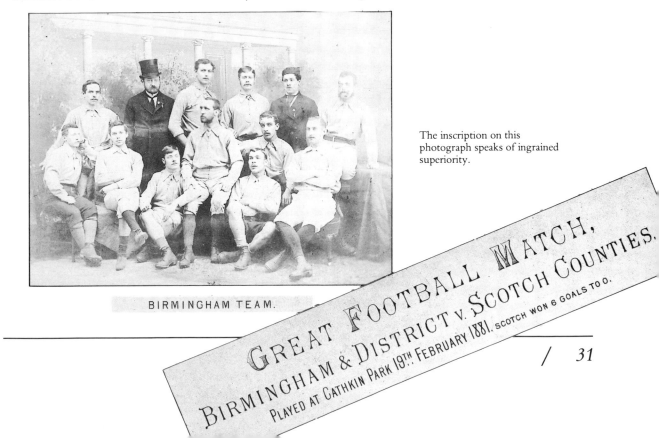

BIRMINGHAM TEAM.

GREAT FOOTBALL MATCH, BIRMINGHAM & DISTRICT v. SCOTCH COUNTIES. PLAYED AT CATHKIN PARK 19TH FEBRUARY 1881. SCOTCH WON 6 GOALS TO 0.

The inscription on this photograph speaks of ingrained superiority.

public schoolboys which were originally intended as activities outwith the cricket season were adopted by workers apparently at random, so that the Rugby Union version was particularly popular in the Welsh coalfields as well as the rural Scottish Borders. When rugby's governing bodies refused to sanction professionalism, a breakaway union was formed in the north of England to play the game known as Rugby League, played with 13-a-side instead of 15.

In the United States in 1880 American football was devised to meet the needs of the Ivy League universities who required a common game to provide regular fixtures and the sport they invented was a mixture of soccer (which permitted the forward pass) and rugby union (in which handling and scrums are allowed) played by teams of 11 men. Canadian football, based on rugby union but with 12-a-side, began earlier than American football but developed more slowly. Similarly, in the southern hemisphere soccer failed to overcome the challenge of rugby union (in New Zealand) or Australian Rules football, another hybrid bred from rugby and Gaelic football, imported to Australia by Irish gold miners and played 18-a-side.

In Britain Arthur Kinnaird, the greatest of the early soccer heroes, was an obvious contributor to the first rush of enthusiasm for the new game of Association Football but when the sport became tactically sophisticated and financially rewarding it was James Lang and his fellow professionals, the Scotch Professors, who inherited Kinnaird's mantle and transformed football on both sides of the Border. And when the structure of organised professional football was in danger of collapsing under the weight of its own success it was McGregor, the draper, who saved it.

Other countries, the United States especially, were keen to export their national pastimes but Britain had the advantage of a vast Empire scattered throughout the globe and served by the world's most immense maritime fleets. The men who crewed these vessels planted their games in every port of call and as the enthusiasm for team sports caught hold in each country, Association Football had the advantage of established tactics and practical organisation which could be imitated immediately.

It would be parochial to suggest that others could not have taken the parts played by Kinnaird, Lang and McGregor, but in establishing football theirs was the decisive and dramatic impact. Their achievements have inevitably dimmed with the passage of time and they scarcely exist at all in the popular imagination. They have also been absorbed into the persistent English perception of football as a purely native game but although its principal developments often took place in England, we have seen that in its fragile infancy the sport looked to Scotland for its nourishment, to be revived with a potent draught. If England claims to be the mother of football, Scotland is the rightful father.

★　　★　　★

Of course, as the world inherited football it was inevitable that Scotland's share in the game's advances would diminish. Nevertheless, the Scots continued to set standards which would not be surpassed, especially in their staggering public commitment to the game. Geographically Scotland might occupy a splinter of an offshore island but in 1900 Glasgow was the third-biggest city in Europe after London and Paris and within its boundaries it contained the three largest football

stadia in the world – Ibrox, Celtic Park and Hampden Park and it was at the latter, the national stadium, that phenomenal crowds were to be accommodated, reaching astounding peaks in the 1930s.

At the height of the Depression in 1933, Hampden admitted 134,710 spectators without the benefit of tickets to witness Scotland's 2-1 defeat of England. Two years later the official attendance at the same fixture had fallen to 126,693 but there were scenes of dangerous chaos outside the ground and it was thought likely that over 200,000 fans had crammed themselves into the stadium. When tickets were introduced for the 1937 Scotland-England international, 150,000 briefs were sold although 453 ticket-holders apparently failed to make it through the turnstiles because the official crowd figure is recorded as 149,547, which stood as a world record until overtaken by the 199,850 total registered at the specially constructed Maracana Stadium in Rio de Janeiro 13 years later. The fanatical devotion to football in the west of Scotland at that time is further emphasised by the fact that on the Saturday afterwards 146,433 paid to watch Celtic and Aberdeen contest the 1937 Scottish Cup final at the same venue.

Successive safety restrictions on crowd size saw Hampden's capacity cut by the summer of 1989 to 73,000 and the announcement later that summer by FIFA that, in the wake of the Hillsborough disaster, matches designated as high-risk fixtures – such as World Cup qualifying games, European tournament ties and domestic collisions like Celtic v Rangers – would not be watched in future by substantial numbers of standing spectators, meant that Hampden was now literally a relic of a remarkable but bygone era, and the SFA turned its attention to the pressing need to provide Scotland with a national stadium fit for the 21st century.

At the other end of the scale Scotland contains the smallest town

Clyde v Falkirk in the early years of the century. McTurk is the Clyde goalkeeper, Morrison and Gilligan (in dark shirts) his defenders.

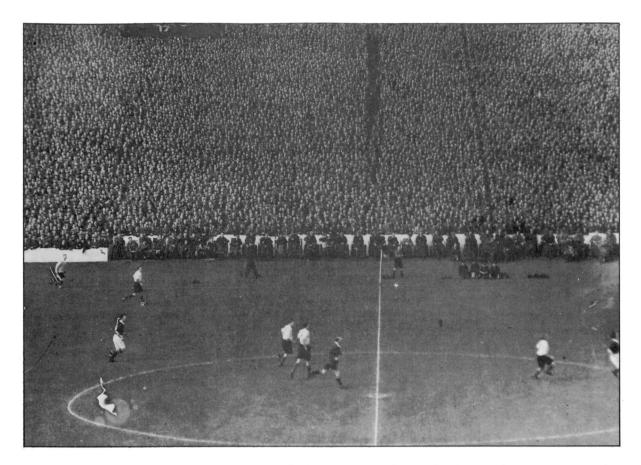

Hampden crammed in the 1930s. The stadium set European crowd records with 149,547 for Scotland v England and 146,433 for Celtic v Aberdeen, both games taking place in a single week in 1937. The attendances given are for customers counted through the turnstiles. Many thousands more entered by other means.

in Britain to field a senior professional side, Brechin City's ground at Glebe Park is bucolic by comparison with Hampden, and its boundaries are marked on one side by an impressive hedge and on the other by a tiny stand behind which can be found a number of working stables.

It was at Pittodrie, Aberdeen's ground, that the manager's dugout was first devised, an innovation which permitted team bosses a close-range view of 22 pairs of stockings and allowed them to give the standside linesman the benefit of their impartial advice.

Needless to say, Scottish aptitude for colonisation played a major part in planting the game's roots across the world. Henry Madden, a Glaswegian, was manager of the Czechoslovakian club Slavia for 33 years from 1905 and his admirers erected a statue to his memory in Prague. In Uruguay his fellow countryman John Hurley was responsible for the introduction of the traditional Scottish style of play at one of the country's foremost clubs, Penarol, and he subsequently became the dominant figure in Uruguayan football for over half a century. He also found time to oversee the fortunes of Argentina's River Plate Club. In 1902 the Scottish tea millionaire Sir Thomas Lipton instituted the oldest South American international competition when he presented the Lipton Cup to be played for by Uruguay and Argentina. Sir Thomas also attempted to inaugurate a World Cup tournament in the early years of the century, but the planet was not ready for such an advanced idea and it took a further two decades before the first World Cup was played, appropriately enough in Uruguay.

Outside Hampden in 1926.

Blackburn Rovers, who beat
Queen's Park 2-1 in the FA Cup
final at Kennington Oval in 1884.
Queen's scored two goals which
would have been allowed in
Scotland, where the off-side rule
required only two defenders
between the ball and the goal:
English rules required three.
Queen's Park were also aggrieved
that Blackburn fielded four
professionals, as payment of
players had not been sanctioned
in Scotland. Ironically, one of
Blackburn's paid stars was Fergus
Suter, formerly of Partick Thistle
and Darwen. Suter is third from
the right in the back row, with a
moustache.

As football's popularity grows in China the possibility exists of an Oriental entry in the Scottish Cup since Shanghai Engineers were registered as a member club of the Scottish Football Association towards the end of the last century. The national associations of New Zealand, seen in the 1982 World Cup finals in Spain, and Canada, represented in the 1986 Mexican finals, were both directed by Scotsmen and the award of the 1994 finals to the United States was in large part the responsibility of Ernie Walker, who in his capacity as SFA secretary was the guiding light of the three-man FIFA committee whose task was to decide between the Brazilian, Moroccan and American bids to host the ultimate soccer tournament.

The Americans, meanwhile, cannot complain of inadequate opportunities to learn how football should be played in the classical style. When the Scotland coach Andy Roxburgh was asked to attend the United States Coaches' Convention in Washington in 1988 he was gratified to see a special award in the Soccer Coach of the Year category go to Jimmy Mills, a former resident of Clydebank. When the two Scots spoke after the awards ceremony Roxburgh was perplexed to discover that while his compatriot was naturally pleased by such recognition, he had not been offered as much coaching work as he would have liked in the previous few months. Nothing could better illustrate the typical Scottish male's lifelong devotion to soccer. When he received his Coach of the Year trophy Jimmy Mills was 92 years old.

—WELL DONE MAC!!—

CHAPTER TWO

"Hungry, Hungry Boys"

"After whisky, footballers have been the favourite and most expensive export from Scotland to England."
(Jimmy Guthrie, *Soccer Rebel*, 1976)

DURING THE FILMING of a series of television interviews at Old Trafford, Paddy Crerand was asked to draw on the experience of a career with Celtic and Manchester United to conjure an image of the typical Scottish player. Crerand, a fairly representative sample of the breed, paused in concentration and then replied: "He would have great natural ability. He'd fight King Kong and at the same time he'd have a button that he could press and destroy himself." There was a further moment or two of silence before Paddy added, anxiously: "Was that all right?"

It was better than all right. In a couple of brief sentences Crerand had summoned a dozen visions of the archetype – Law, Baxter, Johnstone, Souness, Bremner . . . a line stretching back through Woodburn to the days of Hughie Gallacher and Alex James, a collection of footballers whose extravagant talents were as often as not coupled with a striking degree of wilfulness to the extent that, even in Scotland, where perversity of nature can seem to be a genetic inheritance, they were well qualified for the role of folk heroes.

For the best part of a century after the first professional players appeared, the popular image of the Scottish player at his most effective usually placed him as an inside forward, the engineer responsible for steering his team into attack and steadying the craft when conditions got rough. This notion, which contained a good deal of observed truth, was partly a legacy of the social conditions which prevailed amongst the adult male population in Scotland until well after the Second World War. Born of a race with a tendency to be smaller than average in height, the Scottish working man was not likely to stretch his inches working at the coal-face or foundry but he was inclined to be as tough and durable as the boiler plates hammered into shape in the Clyde Valley steelmills from which he very often emerged.

Such men usually had the capacity to apply themselves assiduously to the football skills which offered a passage from harsh manual graft to paid athleticism, so that their close control on the ball became a prized asset. Not long before he died in 1987, Tom Fagan, chairman and general factotum of Albion Rovers, as authentic a working man's club as it is possible to discover, offered a revealing insight into the abrasive social climate of industrial Lanarkshire some 60-odd years previously.

> The miners were hungry, hungry boys and the only way they could get away from where they were, to get out of the pits, was through football, and they could get on to playing for ten pounds a week which was a fortune then. Full time . . . my God! When I was in Whifflet as a

Gallacher, visibly ageing, his career on the downturn with Derby County.

BOBBY ROBSON

Bobby Robson, former England player and manager of Ipswich, then of England and now manager of PSV Eindhoven.

"First and foremost, the Scottish player is an individual, a great little technician, very adept and very clever but I suspect in some cases they are their own worst enemies. I think they're masochists, they destroy themselves and I've often tried to diagnose why that should be because over the years I've got to know lots of them and when I was manager at Ipswich I had three cracking Scottish boys, but I wouldn't have wanted any more than that. And that typifies what I'm saying about them. They're great in small numbers in a football club, very tenacious, hard so-and-so's who want to win, but I don't think they sometimes know how they do win.

"I know how they lose, though. Remember when they came to Wembley in 1961 and thought England didn't have a team, were going to win 4-0 and stroll home? It ended up 9-3. I got the first, actually, and it was a good day for us. People blamed Haffey, the Scottish goalkeeper, and maybe he dropped a couple but he wasn't responsible for nine. The Scots didn't know how to defend that day. They all wanted to attack but you can only attack if you've got the ball and so they got thrashed. "To be fair, I think they've learned from that because people have come into the Scottish game and said 'Hey, just a second – we produce wonderful players and we

young man, there was 150 people lived in our back court and we used to play football against the Watsons, the ones that owned the building.

In 1926 during the miners' strike my father ran the Soup Kitchen Cup and I played against the Bellshill Endurables. I'm no' goin' tae tell you what they were, but they were Orange, and they met me in the pit the following week and gave me a doing. Aye, good days right enough . . .

The Soup Kitchen Cup was probably not a milieu foreseen by Lord Arthur Kinnaird when he mused with fellow Etonians on the likely spread of the game, but the kind of footballer who could accommodate the rigours of such tournaments was unlikely to be intimidated too easily in other circumstances. Hughie Gallacher, born in Bellshill in 1903, was a case in point, a man whose horoscope must have been dominated by temper, rising, and a conjunction of planets spinning in reverse. Even a casual survey of his life reveals a personality forcing relentlessly against the grain.

Gallacher was not merely a Protestant by birth, although that alone should have been enough to cast his destiny in a region fermenting with sectarian bigotries; he was the son of Ulster parents who were members of the local Orange Lodge, yet he married a Catholic lass from Bellshill, a move which can hardly have made for tranquil family gatherings around the senior Gallachers' hearth. In later years, Hughie played for the Scottish League against the Irish League in Belfast and typically disdained warnings to be cautious when he decided to visit friends in the city after the match. He was less sanguine when a bullet narrowly missed his head and ricocheted from the street wall behind him. There were subsequent suggestions that it was a deliberate near miss arranged by Irish fans who took exception to the skills he demonstrated against their team but the fact of a Catholic wife cannot have amused the local Protestant activists.

The divisions in Gallacher's character had a powerful impact on those who came within his orbit, such as the youthful Matt Busby who, when an unknown player, was invited by the established star to train with him. Bob McPhail, later an inside forward with Rangers, played alongside the temperamental Gallacher at Airdrie and found that opponents were not the only ones who felt the whip of his tongue.

> Nobody got on well with Hughie Gallacher. I remember him giving me a row for scoring a goal. Jimmy Reid crossed one and I headed it in and Hughie said to me: "You'd no right to be there – that's my job."
>
> He was a strange mixture. He could be very dapper and would come properly dressed to Airdrie in the morning to do his training, but if you went down in the afternoon to Bellshill you would see him sitting at the corner with his feet up, a personality for Airdrie and then another one for the miners and the people that he lived amongst.

The circumstances of Gallacher's signing for Airdrie were macabre, as he recollected some years afterwards when he wrote: "Imagine my surprise when the car drew up at an undertaker's office near Airdrie Cross . . . and there in the vicinity of wreaths and other mournful paraphernalia I signed the documents that really put my foot on the ladder of fame." His signing-on fee was a fiver and when he was handed the note by Jock Weir, an Airdrie director, he asked if it could be exchanged for a weightier equivalent in silver coins.

Airdrie's gain channelled Gallacher into a football career at a stage in his life when he might have tried his skills in the boxing ring, a common enough option in Bellshill which produced as many men who were useful with their fists as with their feet. The volatile Gallacher was later known to combine the two arts and he could shift his energies into bitter feuds in the middle of matches, a trait which greatly encouraged less skilful antagonists in opposing defences.

When the inevitable move to England arrived, Airdrie's five pound investment produced a £6,500 return, then a record fee, for his transfer to Newcastle United where he immediately secured devotion from the Tyneside faithful by scoring two goals and laying on another in a tingling battle with Everton, for whom the formidable Dixie Dean scored one of the 37 hat-tricks he achieved in his career. The contest also threw into sharp relief the divergent models of footballer manufactured on either side of the border with Dean, a clean-cut locomotive of a player in contrast with the tricky Gallacher who, although he would have made light-welterweight as a boxer, was a diminutive five feet six inches for which he compensated with a sprint start off the mark and an ability to turn inside a tight arc as a consequence of his low centre of gravity.

Gallacher regularly disrupted tall defences with a remarkable ability to launch himself towards high balls and his versatility remains vivid in the memories of those who watched him perform at the height of his career with United. Raich Carter, a prodigiously gifted England inside-forward in his own right, was prepared to state unequivocally that Gallacher was the greatest centre-forward who ever played football which, with due allowance for hyperbole and the development of a more demanding modern game, is an assertion which should indicate that Hughie could play more than a little.

With the symmetry of a Greek tragedy, however, the torments of Gallacher's private life multiplied in inverse proportion to the display of his footballing gifts. His temper was volcanic enough when provoked on the field but a taste for the bottle produced ugly and violent scenes when he socialised around Newcastle. His marriage to the girl from Bellshill, marred by the death of their first child, quickly foundered and although he reached the altar again with a Gateshead

don't win anything. There's just got to be a reason for that.' I think that discipline and teamwork is coming into Scottish football more than it's ever done, certainly since the 1978 World Cup in Argentina.

"If we had a British team we could be a world power for certain but I wouldn't like it and it wouldn't half be an awkward situation to be manager of that side. There's enough pressure already without people in Scotland saying that there should be seven Scots in the side, people in England demanding seven English and others asking why there are only two from Northern Ireland or three from Wales.

"Souness could have played for any country in the world. If Dalglish had been a Brazilian he would have played for Brazil, no question about it. The Scots have produced as many and as good players as anybody in the world. Full stop. No need for me to say any more."

Gallacher outside a London tearoom during his spell with Chelsea. The photograph is undated, so Gallacher's misdemeanour is unclear. He was suspended on several occasions, by his clubs and by the Football Association.

Hughie Gallacher on the day of his marriage to Hannah Anderson of Gateshead, his second wife.

Gallacher in Newcastle colours.

girl he imperilled his second union by a too obvious penchant for flirtation.

With a touching belief in the therapeutic powers of responsibility, the United directors made him team captain, but he had no reserves of will to help him withstand the physical assaults which most opposing teams employed against him as part of a lamentable but sadly effective strategy. After United won the championship in 1927 the team began to break up again and a slide down the table was halted within a precarious point of relegation. Anxious to rebuild their squad, the St James's Park board, without consulting Gallacher, came to terms with Chelsea on his transfer to London.

The Scot was bitter at this turn of events, having no desire to leave the north-east, but he turned the situation to his financial advantage in a prolonged negotiation with both clubs which took the best part of a day to complete. Judging by Gallacher's subsequent account of his part in the discussions, they must have resembled one of the more chaotic scenes in a Buster Keaton movie.

> I had bounced up half a dozen times, put on my bowler and marched homewards. First Chelsea officials pulled me back, then it was Newcastle's turn. Everyone had lunch in the same room, the Newcastle folk in one corner with me seated amongst Chelsea officials at a nearby table. Afternoon came and went. So did tea time. Then, at last . . . Newcastle received a record £10,000 fee.

The deal which took Gallacher south marked the start of his decline as a player but there was no sign of that when he returned to Newcastle with Chelsea three months later. A massive crowd of 68,586, even more impressive for being assembled on a midweek afternoon, crammed into the ground to set a record which will not be surpassed.

The following year an enthusiastic crowd of northern supporters assembled to welcome him back for another Chelsea-Newcastle fixture but Gallacher had become involved in a more serious encounter with the London constabulary, and his only public appearance that day saw him fined ten shillings in the West London Police Court on a drunk and disorderly charge. Derby County bought him for £3,000 and he stayed there for two years before moving to Notts County for £2,000, and the melancholy decline continued when he was transferred to Grimsby Town in January 1938 in a deal worth £1,000, followed pathetically quickly inside five months with a shift to his final club, Gateshead.

He had been a prolific performer, scoring 386 goals in 544 games for seven clubs in a career which bridged 18 years and he averaged more than a goal a game in 20 internationals for Scotland. On two occasions he scored five goals while wearing a dark blue jersey, once against Northern Ireland in 1929 (a record for a Scotland player in a single game) and once against the Irish League.

He appeared in charity matches for another 15 years but on 11 June 1957, he committed suicide by throwing himself under the York-Edinburgh express train hours before he was due to appear at Gateshead Magistrates Court on charges alleging assault and maltreatment of his 14-year-old son. In a letter he left for the coroner, Gallacher wrote: "If I live to be a hundred I'd never forgive myself for having struck my son." His decapitated body was found on Dead Man's Crossing at Low Fell, grimly appropriate co-ordinates for the end of a tormented life.

But the memory of his footballing gifts, preserved for half a century by many who saw him play, deserves a gentler epitaph, to be found in the Tyneside children's song:

Do you ken Hughie Gallacher
The wee Scots lad?
The finest centre-forward,
Newcastle ever had . . .

★ ★ ★

Football presents special difficulties when it comes to an assessment of how great players of past eras might have adapted to the demands of the modern game. The cricket historian has the supreme advantage of detailed statistics which yield a fairly precise notion of the pace of a game played at any time during the last century as well as the state of the wicket, the overhead conditions and so on, all made possible because the game is so concentrated and repetitive in its format. Similarly, the American obsession with yardage and catches received or missed allows their football achievements to be freeze-fried for future recollection.

If the career of Alex James is reduced to numerals it practically evaporates from the imagination. He made only eight international appearances for Scotland and his collection of honours with Arsenal – four league championship and two FA Cup medals – is more than respectable but rather short of legendary. Yet James was not merely the popular conception of the Scottish footballer of his day, he rivalled Harry Lauder as the clearest image of a Scotsman available to the general imagination.

James, like Hughie Gallacher, was fond of gangster movies and dressed in the mode of Cagney.

Of course, it is part of the transient nature of football that its most satisfying flourishes are truly available only to those spectators in physical attendance (a fact not altered by the advent of slow motion TV replays) and since the great Scottish players have often preferred decoration to demolition, their gifts deserved a more ornate memorial than the deceptive simplicity of a scoreline. But no such structure exists and we depend on the eyewitness accounts to recreate the shape of their contribution.

In the case of James, one or two people who might have been expected to know their business were willing to offer powerful testimonials. Dennis Compton, who looked as though he would make a first-class footballer with Arsenal until cricket intervened, wrote in his introduction to a recent biography of the Scot: "Alex was the greatest ball player I've ever seen yet what impressed me most was the apparent effortlessness and naturalness of his play."

Before his death in 1987, Hugh Taylor, the doyen of Scottish football writers, told the author of this volume that he had not seen a player to exceed James for his combination of close skill, vision and distribution, although from the candidates who had emerged from Scotland he estimated Jim Baxter and Kenny Dalglish as serious rivals.

The relationship between Alex James and Hughie Gallacher fascinated and puzzled many of their contemporaries and even at this distance an extraordinary duality seems to have governed their careers and personalities. The records are not conclusive about their relative physique; James may possibly have been half an inch taller (or, to be more exact, less diminutive) and Gallacher's fighting weight was

James selected for Scotland, an arrangement which was to be short-lived.

perhaps three pounds lighter, but they could have stepped into each other's clothes with comfort, the more so since both were dapper dressers in the style of James Cagney, a pair of stocky little dandies.

If their wardrobes were interchangeable, their characters were in radical contrast. Gallacher, moodily switching from courteous charm to abrasive confrontation with bewildering suddenness, was the antithesis of James, who was prepared to drift agreeably on the tide, although he was perfectly capable of manipulating its flow to suit himself. Accounts of their early friendship sometimes read like biographies of the juvenile Jekyll and Hyde but there was not the symmetry about their developments that subsequent mythology suggests.

One history of Newcastle United, otherwise excellent, touchingly depicts Gallacher and James as boys together "kicking a ball round a lamp post in a Glasgow slum". If this is true they must have been making round trips of 20 miles to play their street games, because both of them came from Bellshill where devotion to local rivalries was on a Sicilian scale, as many an unfortunate referee could testify after officiating at a junior or amateur derby which ended as a Donnybrook. Nor was either man a product of the slums, although industrial Lanarkshire was not in danger of being mistaken for the Garden of Scotland.

The James household in Caledonian Buildings in Mossend consisted of one bedroom and a kitchen which was also used as a living-room and which contained bed recesses, curtained off. The toilet was outside in the yard but if the facilities were functional they were not impoverished by the standards which prevailed in the Central Belt and which persisted into the 1970s in some areas. In any case, with three sons and two daughters variously contributing wages the James family was never near the breadline. Alex's father Charles was a Victorian parent, disinclined or possibly unable to view football as a worthy activity for his son, and he frequently took the back of his hand to a boy who in later years recalled that his elder brother Charlie went to enormous trouble to balance the antipathy of Mr James senior with sympathy and encouragement.

Throughout his life Alex James displayed a notable ability, away from the football field, to let others shift for him, a tendency which combined with a stubborn resistance to authority if he felt that its ends were not his interests. It is unsurprising to discover that before he became a full-time player James found it difficult to concentrate his mind on any other form of employment. At the age of 16 he worked in a nearby steelworks owned by the Beardmore company who also ran the enormous and impressive Parkhead Forge, close to Celtic Park, and it may have been the Beardmore connection between the two areas which encouraged Protestants like James and Gallacher to travel on Saturdays to Glasgow to watch Celtic, when their allegiance would more naturally have been given to Rangers.

The two youths were exposed to a particularly fine Celtic side where they found in Patsy Gallagher a prototype for their own subsequent careers. Patsy, known as the Mighty Atom, was the same height as his Bellshill admirers, though he was considerably lighter, a disadvantage for which he compensated with express courage against opposition bent on intimidation or injury. Hughie Gallacher was able to apply the lessons learned from his namesake more quickly than his companion could, although their juvenile footballing careers had proceeded in tandem and both graduated to the acolyte's role of lugging the Bellshill Athletic kit hamper to the railway station for a reward of half a crown.

Two months after he left school, Hughie Gallacher had played for Scotland's junior international football side and was signed by Queen of the South, from where he proceeded to Airdrie and the career related earlier in this chapter. James, the younger of the two and nothing like so accomplished a goalscorer, found progress more elusive and he was obliged to continue with his unconvincing attempts to earn a living outside the game.

He lost his first job as a clerk with Beardmore after taking part in a diversion which involved filling a beer bottle with acid and high explosive and then bolting for cover before the lethal combination exploded. One day the mixture failed to ignite and with a remarkable absence of common sense James came out of hiding to give the bottle a thorough shake. Predictably, it blew up and drove a slice of glass into his cheek where it left a lifelong scar, although the damage would have been worse if he had failed to pull the glass out instantly before his face was seriously disfigured by the acid.

He was sacked from a subsequent job with the local railway company as well as from a number of other posts and football seemed unlikely to provide a secure alternative because, improbable as it may now seem, he was playing for a local juvenile side, Brandon Amateurs, at centre-half. Even allowing for the fact that Scots were smaller then than at present his selection in such a position seems a capricious act. Still, it eventually profited James because the centre-half, alternatively known as the pivot, was the link between defence and attack and it was in this role that James learned the apprentice arts of distribution in the middle of the park.

Because he was short of inches he was not thought of as professional material and he later confessed that the spell with Brandon was the low point of his career as a player, aggravated by the fact that Gallacher had attracted the attentions of several senior clubs. However, James was at last picked up by Orbiston Celtic, a junior side from the mining hamlet which was Matt Busby's home. Orbiston was known to visiting teams as Cannibal Island because of the intimidating atmosphere of matches played there and as Busby noted in his memoirs, teams with the confidence or poor judgment to beat Orbiston Celtic on the village pitch usually had to make a run for it at the final whistle. "They might leave with two points," Busby recollected in a dry aside, "but never with shoes and trousers."

There could hardly have been a less promising nursery for James's skills but his small stature brought out an unlikely protective strain in his team-mates which effectively shielded him from the worst aggression of visiting teams, although when Orbiston Celtic were away from home he was obliged to develop the evasive arts of the swerve and dummy which became his trademark in later years. The recipe only required the addition of experience, which came with a move to the Glasgow junior side Ashfield and his first senior contract with Raith Rovers after he was noticed by one of the club's directors, Robert Morrison, who was a disciple of Bobby Walker, a forgotten figure now but a greatly admired inside-right for Hearts and Scotland before the First World War.

Morrison realised that he had discovered Walker's successor and promptly entered into lengthy signing negotiations with James, who revealed how thrawn he could be when money was concerned before agreeing to join the Fife team. It was to prove a stormy passage for the club, whose new signing walked out and returned to Bellshill when the Raith manager was misguided enough to advise him to change his style on the field and it became evident long before the end of James's three-year stay in Kirkcaldy that he was not temperamentally suited to the functional regime of an outfit which was forced by financial stringency to value the artisan rather than the artist.

By and large, though, he enjoyed his time in Fife, which offered him a solid platform for his entry into English football in 1925 when Preston paid £3,000 (causing Robert Morrison to resign from the Raith board) and it happened at a crucial stage of football's evolution because that summer FIFA changed the offside rule so that two, rather than three, opponents had to be between a player and the goal. For a couple of seasons there was a flood of scoring, which had been the legislators' intention, but it dried up with the introduction of a tactical change which saw the centre-half withdrawn from midfield to a position between the two full-backs in a 3-2-5 formation. There is no certainty about who devised the idea of the third back, but the evidence falls in favour of Bob Gillespie, the Queen's Park and Scotland centre-half, as the man who was seen to express it before any other player. Half-backs were told to offer the full-backs defensive cover while the inside-forwards dropped off their own attack line to receive clearances from their defence and switch the team into a forward momentum.

Arsenal with the Cup in 1930. James is seated to the right of the trophy.

It was a situation made for James's particular talents but spectators were not happy with the conversion of forwards into midfield players and at Preston they expressed their annoyance by throwing missiles at their own team. He was unlucky, too, to be in a side whose attackers were not prolific scorers and in a Second Division where brawn and pace were rated higher than more incisive skills.

What James could do given the opportunity was brilliantly demonstrated when he scored two goals in Scotland's famous 5-1 victory over England in March 1928 but Preston refused Scotland's request to make him available for an international with Wales later in the year and his bitter anger with the Deepdale board led ultimately to a transfer to Arsenal where the new tactical arrangements were to be perfected by the Highbury manager Herbert Chapman.

Chapman had constructed a formidable defence at Highbury but until James's arrival the team lacked a midfield trigger for their attacks, although his impact was delayed by the Arsenal strategy of pulling the inside-forwards deep into their own half for additional cover to frustrate advancing opponents, a ploy which meant that the little Scot was often caught too far downfield to be able to turn play around effectively. Eventually, he was deployed in the left midfield channel and another inside-forward, Cliff Bastin, shifted to the left wing to complete the arrangement which would make Arsenal the most formidable team in England in the early 1930s.

They were the benchmark by which other teams were measured and James was the key to their dominance. At Highbury he won four championship medals, three of them consecutive, and he was twice in a victorious FA Cup final side. In his first final, against Huddersfield in 1930, he dictated the course of the match, strutting and feinting through the middle and creating an audacious opening goal with a free kick distributed so rapidly to Bastin that the opposing defence was hopelessly scattered when the ball was returned for James to swerve his shot around the flailing Turner. He manufactured the second decisive score seven minutes from time, releasing Ted Lambert with leisure to place the ball around the advancing goalkeeper.

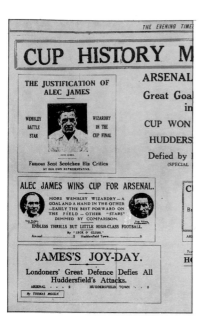

By common consent, the 1930
Cup final belonged to James.

The final belonged to Alex James by general consent and his was the genius which carried Arsenal towards their annexation of the title in 1931, 1933, 1934 and 1935. Chapman had perceived that James was a dynamic mixture of unorthodox and the acute and the Scot was allowed a free run of midfield which he exploited so thoroughly that he can be regarded unarguably as the first exponent of the modern brand of football. Arsenal's success was widely mocked and held in contempt for being boring and lucky, the usual reward for football's pioneers, but James was a paragon of entertainers and his presence in the Highbury side put them ahead of Rangers, their only real rivals in British club football which, at that time, was still the pinnacle of the world game.

If his gifts were not rewarded with a substantial number of Scottish caps, it was partly because he competed for his position in the national side with Bob McPhail of Rangers and the Motherwell inside left George Stevenson, in a period when Scotland's international calendar usually consisted of three or four matches. It did not help his cause that he called off from the 1933 collision with England on the grounds that he was unfit, only to play for Arsenal on the same afternoon and help them to a decisive win over Aston Villa, the principal contenders for their crown. He was not forgiven north of the border for this failure to rally to the flag and was never selected for Scotland again.

James was not the sort of man to pine for his country or the prospect of lost honours. He rarely returned to Bellshill and made little issue of his nationality, although he never lost his very marked Lanarkshire accent. Nevertheless, his vast contribution to the development of football was a distillation of the Scottish game at its most creative. He was short of pace and weak in the air and he scored comparatively few goals for Arsenal but he compensated for his disadvantages by cultivating a panoramic tactical sense and insisting that team strategy should be expanded to accommodate it. His contradictions were entirely typical of the Scottish player but unlike many of his compatriots he was able to resolve them, which is why his appeal was significantly greater in England than in the land of his birth and why, in the last analysis, Scots felt that the mercurial Gallacher was more representative of their race.

★   ★   ★

Just as Gallacher and James were bound together in the public imagination of their era, another pair of supreme talents emerged during the 1960s to receive the adulation of a dazzled public on either side of the border. In the folk memory of Scottish football the names of Law and Baxter are inseparable yet they were never in the same club and they played for Scotland together on a total of 22 occasions, by no means a sizeable figure, but one which consisted of 13 Scottish victories against seven defeats and two draws.

Hidden within the statistics is the more telling information that they combined against England four times and were winners on three occasions, their single experience of defeat being administered three months before England won the World Cup in 1966; even then the Scots were only beaten by the odd goal in seven, a setback which they repaid with interest the following season when they travelled to Wembley to offer the world champions a lesson in the possibilities of arrogance.

At a time when regimentation appeared to have eclipsed flair in

Denis Law as Bobby Moore bows the knee at Hampden.

football, Baxter and Law personified swagger, the trait which most appeals to the Scottish supporter. While Alf Ramsey's players were jeeringly referred to as robots, nobody could have presented a greater contrast to the notion of the regimented team man than Baxter, jersey invariably flapping outside his shorts and stockings rolled down around his ankles to reveal his disdain for the protection of shinguards, or Law (another man for the loose jersey), prowling the edge of a penalty area waiting for the moment when he could unleash the unmistakable blond head at a cross hanging between a posse of wrong-footed defenders.

Both were east-of-Scotland natives. Law, the younger of the two by five months, was born in Aberdeen where his father was a trawlerman on the North Sea boats, although the boy discovered a profound aversion for the maritime life after he was taken along on a short offshore trip on a day of bitter cold. Like Alex James, he was the youngest of a large brood, in this case consisting of four boys and three girls, and as James had done before him, he learned the art of allowing others to take care of life's repetitive or dull tasks, as the many friends and associates who have spent hours at airports searching for Denis's lost luggage can testify.

In appearance he was also the runt of the litter, afflicted by a squint which forced him to wear corrective spectacles, but he was able to play football by keeping his right eye closed for the duration of a match, a habit which he sustained for several years afterwards, and his competitive instincts were sharpened to compensate for his physical disadvantage. Law's headmaster once wrote to his mother to ask if

the boy should be permitted to take part in football. Mrs Law replied: "Yes, Denis can play" – which must go down as a masterstroke of understatement.

Soon after his 15th birthday he was approached by Archie Beattie, a scout for Huddersfield, whose brother Andy was manager of the Yorkshire team, and the boy joined on amateur forms.

Law's recollections of the period suggest that he was an insular soul because when he was installed in the club's boarding-house, which was run by a chain-smoking lady by name of Mrs Clark, he was perplexed to discover that the numerous other apprentices lodged there were actually English, a possibility that had apparently never occurred to him, but he was able to settle into his own career fortified by an operation which at last achieved the feat of pointing both his eyes in the same direction.

His ambition was already clearly focused on a rapidly rising path and he made the first team at the age of 16, scoring in his second game, against Notts County. A month later Andy Beattie retired and Bill Shankly took over at Huddersfield. Shankly's extraordinary managerial techniques, examined elsewhere in this volume, had a predictable impact on Law, who was selected for Scotland's game against Wales at Ninian Park on 18 October 1958 to become the youngest player to turn out for Scotland since the 19-year-old Bob McColl in 1899. Scotland won 3-0 and Law was credited with one of the goals, although he admitted later that a clearance had hit the back of his head to beat the Welsh goalkeeper Jack Kelsey. He would score another 29 goals for Scotland, many of them with the correct side of the head, and set a record equalled by Kenny Dalglish 25 years later.

The man who gave him his chance in a dark blue jersey was Matt Busby, who offered Huddersfield £10,000 to take Law to Manchester United, although as he admitted later: "I wasn't sure where I would have put him because I had so many good players, young players, at Old Trafford, some of whom were killed in the Munich disaster. So I had to give up the idea of Denis Law. Fancy having to give up the idea of Denis Law!"

In March 1960 Huddersfield's foresight in holding on to their principal asset was rewarded when an approach from United's city rivals Manchester City resulted in Law moving to Maine Road for a new British record fee of £55,000. But for the player and his new club there were to be collisions, in the first instance over the methods preferred by the City trainer Jimmy Meadows, an advocate of stamina-building routines which did not appeal to the wilful Law, who had acquired an appetite for ball work under Shankly's guidance.

Nevertheless, his aptitude for breaching convention was stimulated in October 1960 when he was chosen to play for the Football League against the Irish League at Blackpool. The Football League for the first time selected Scottish players to represent it and were repaid with two goals from Law in a 5-2 victory. In April 1961, however, Law angered Manchester City by choosing to play for Scotland against England at Wembley when his club was involved in a League match with West Ham which would have a significant bearing on City's chances of avoiding relegation to the Second Division. As matters turned out City managed a 1-1 draw while the Scots collapsed in the course of 9-3 hammering at the hands of England, the worst defeat in Scotland's history and so demoralising that half of the team, including Law, were dropped for the next match.

Despite his preference for country over club City tried to induce him to extend his stay at Maine Road with a contract which would have given him £4,000 a year, reflecting the recent abolition of the maximum wage for footballers which had been held at £20 a week, but Law was seduced by the prospect of much larger gains from Italian football which then, as now, was offering handsome sums as bait for British players. Inter Milan proposed a signing-on fee of £5,000 with bonuses of £100 a point, an immense reward for a player whose international career was still in its infancy.

But Italian football was decidedly not cavalier, unlike Law's attitude to contracts; hardly had he signed an agreement to join Inter when he was offered – and accepted – identical terms to play for Torino. The additional attraction was the presence of Joe Baker who had joined Torino from Hibs and Law flew to Turin insisting that his signature on the first agreement was worthless because Manchester City had not reached any agreement with the Milan club over his transfer – unsurprisingly because he had not bothered to inform City of the negotiations.

For the second but not the last time in his career Law had set a transfer record, on this occasion as the first British player to break the £100,000 barrier, but there were unforeseen drawbacks, too, as Law recently recalled.

> Joe and I had a lovely apartment overlooking the River Po and for the 1960s it was really big time, although I used to come home and take back a bottle of HP sauce which looked great in the middle of the table with the spaghetti. I could speak English and Joe could speak Scottish and everything around us was perfect, especially the people, who couldn't do enough for us. And the training suited me because it was all work with the ball. But the football was awful. Whenever we lined up for a game and looked at the opposition we could see two men ready to mark Joe and two on to me and, of course, our team played the same way as well but it was rubbish. It really was rubbish.

The two players fuelled numerous headlines because of incidents off the pitch, most of them relatively harmless, but on one occasion their

between the two countries; the Englishman assumes that nobody dislikes him while the Scotsman wouldn't be happy without an enemy. I think that gives Scottish players an extra edge when they come down here intent on showing the English what they're made of.

"But I look upon Scotland as part of the British Empire, as it were, and when I was a kid I used to look at all the pink on the map and say, 'Isn't that marvellous! We own all that.' It's gradually receded as the years have gone on but I hope that Scotland's still with us as well as those marvellous players – some of the finest you could get, really."

Denis Law shoots as the 'Rest of the World' attack England during the FA centenary celebration match, Wembley 1963.

"Denis once kicked me at Wembley in front of the Queen in an international. I mean, no man is entitled to do that, really."
(Bobby Robson)

"Denis wouldn't think twice about giving you one. You would tackle Denis and all of a sudden it was like a needle in the side – whack, take that one! You had gone to make the tackle but you were the one who ended up hurt."
(Emlyn Hughes)

"Denis didn't need a lot of handling. Now and again he used to create and I used to have to say, 'Now what's all this carry-on about?' But, above all, he was interested in the success of the club."
(Sir Matt Busby)

"I went for a fifty-fifty ball with him and I thought I'd take it easy because Denis was my big pal. Christ, he nearly killed me. And I says, 'Den, what are you doing?' 'No friends on the park, son,' he says. 'The only friends I've got are in these red shirts for Manchester United.' So that was a lesson I learned and kept throughout my life."
(Billy Bremner)

wayward tendencies almost proved lethal when Baker bought a new car, a powerful Alfa Romeo Julietta Sprint which he took into the mountains for a test drive. The pair stopped for drinks and a meal and returned to Turin where Baker, suddenly faced with a roundabout, took it on the left in the British fashion. The car struck the kerb and overturned, very nearly killing both men.

Baker was kept on a drip for six weeks but although Law escaped with slight injuries he was finished with Italy. The manner of his return to Britain was characteristic. Torino were drawn against Napoli in an Italian Cup tie, the winners of which would play in the next round on the same date as a friendly between Scotland and Uruguay at Hampden Park. As the Cup tie proceeded, Torino's coach became convinced that Law was not exerting himself to his limits (Law's recollection: "I'm not saying I didn't try – because if you're a pro footballer . . .") and eventually instructed the referee to send the Scot from the pitch, an incident which prompted the club to ban their wayward import for a fortnight.

Law had previously revealed to Matt Busby his desire to return to Manchester to join United, but when he completed his club suspension he was informed by Torino that they had reached agreement on a transfer to Juventus. Law responded to this alternative plan in his usual fashion. He took a taxi to Milan (paid for by his agent, Gigi Peronace, a detail usually omitted in Law's version of the story) and flew to Britain where he defied Torino to carry out their threat to ban him from football. He correctly calculated that the Italians would not waste their investment and in July 1962, for the third time in two years, Law was the subject of a record-breaking transfer deal when United paid Torino £115,000 to make him the most expensive player bought by a British club.

He had found his spiritual home, for which, according to the man himself, he was prepared to sacrifice cash advantages. "I was like everyone else in that I would change my job for better money but the difference was that in Italy I didn't enjoy it so I really did come back for far, far less money. Well, Matt Busby being a Scotsman, what was he going to give me anyway? I think I got two pairs of boots out of it."

If boots were part of the transaction which took Law to Old Trafford, they must have been golden. At last he had found the context which would permit his style to flourish within the constraints of teamwork and he embarked on what he was to describe as the best years of his professional life, although the United jigsaw was not completed until the arrival of Paddy Crerand from Celtic in February 1963. Ironically, it was at this point that United might have brought Denis Law and Jim Baxter together at Old Trafford, a possibility which held a powerful attraction for Busby.

At that time we had both Paddy Crerand and Jim Baxter in mind and we were trying to think about what was best for us as a team. We all knew Jim was very talented but eventually I felt that Pat was the one we really needed, a player who created by taking his time but who had a lot of strength in him, too. Denis actually had a hand in Pat Crerand's transfer because he was very keen on Pat and so that was how it came about.

With Law and Crerand later augmented by George Best, there was a potentially explosive streak of Celtic temperament in the United side, but Busby was judicious in the mixture of stick and carrot he used to

Law inhabits the Scottish dream – scoring against England at Wembley.

control his more fiery players and Law's jumping jack energy was encouraged in an attack which gave each of the forwards freedom to play instinctively. It was a policy which was swiftly rewarded and within a season of Law's arrival at Old Trafford, Manchester United had won the FA Cup, beating Leicester City in the final. On 25 May 1963, a bright and sunny day at Wembley, United took the lead within 15 minutes when Crerand offered Law a close-range opportunity to beat Gordon Banks. The lead was doubled by another import from Scotland, David Herd, and although Leicester scored through Keyworth, a further Herd goal settled the issue.

Law had entered a magical passage in his career. Earlier in the season he had equalled the achievement of Hughie Gallacher (Airdrie, Newcastle, Chelsea and Derby) by being capped for Scotland while playing with four different clubs. He scored a hat-trick in the Scots' 4-3 defeat by Norway in Bergen shortly after his FA Cup final appearance and went one better against the unfortunate Scandinavians when they came to Hampden in November, an occasion which saw him score four times in a 6-1 victory. His venomous finishing was recognised on yet another level when the Football Association celebrated its centenary with a match between England and a Rest of the World Select, in which Law was included. Inevitably he scored against England in a 2-1 defeat.

There were to be two championship medals in his time at Old Trafford, although he was desperately unlucky when a long-term injury cost him his chance to grace Manchester United's European Cup victory over Benfica at Wembley. His career at Old Trafford came to an end in 1973 when he was handed a free transfer by yet another Scottish manager, Tommy Docherty, and he moved back across Manchester to rejoin City. In a finale which was entirely compatible with the melodramatic tenor of his career he scored his final professional goal against Manchester United at Old Trafford with a backheeler which appeared to have relegated his former club to the Second Division although, in fact, results elsewhere ensured

Paddy Crerand and Jim Baxter,
mates and partners for Scotland.

they would have gone down in any case. His farewell appearance for Scotland followed soon after, when he played in the 2-0 victory over Zaire and it was fitting that he should have departed the scene during the World Cup finals.

If the alphabet of his achievements, begun in Aberdeen, was satisfyingly concluded against Zaire, Denis Law is securely fixed in the football pantheon as the supreme example of a Scottish centre forward. Just as his Manchester United teammate Bobby Charlton exemplified the English vision of a clean-cut, personable sportsman, so Law was the very image of the Scot as hit man, combative, swashbuckling and wickedly effective. As Bill Shankly put it: "He would have died to have won. He would have kicked you to have won. He had a temper and he was a terror – a bloody terror, with ability."

★   ★   ★

Perhaps the most extravagantly gifted player ever to be seen in a Scotland jersey was Jim Baxter. His skill was comparable with that of his contemporary, George Best, and like the Irishman his talents were poised upon a self-destructive streak which he carried around with him like a private version of the San Andreas Fault. He used his talent as security for a mortgage on the good life and when he was required to draw on the reserves of fitness which might have sustained his career for another few years he found he had left himself with nothing in the bank.

He was finished with football at a criminally early age, retiring to become a publican shortly after his 30th birthday, but the brief flare of his achievements was so vivid that his play has remained unforgettable to anyone fortunate enough to see him in his swaggering, strutting prime. He was by instinct an entertainer and he had the grasp of timing and revelation which are the hallmarks of the showman. When Rangers were attracted by the precocious talents he displayed at his first senior club, Raith Rovers, Baxter knew what he could offer in return.

> Without being bumptious, there are things nobody can teach you. You've either got the cheek and the arrogance or you haven't and if it isn't inside you nobody can manufacture it. I played with the Scotland under-23 team when I was at Raith Rovers and I was treated like a second class citizen because I wasn't with Rangers or Celtic or Hearts. I said to myself that if ever I got a chance of that cherry I would bite it and have a good go at it. So I had a good go at it. When Rangers came for me I just took it from there and told myself "You're on stage now – at Ibrox, Parkhead, no matter where – you're on stage." So I gave them what I had.

What he had was a talent which expanded to fill available space, style coupled with an apparently total absence of self-doubt. Like Alex James, who operated in the same area of the park, he was short of pace and he could never be accused of bonecrushing interceptions, but providing the correct arrangements were made around him, as they were at Ibrox, he could be practically invulnerable.

> I had a lot of help from great players when I was with Rangers and I would have to say I didn't appreciate them until I went down south. There was Ralph Brand, sharp as a tack, Ian McMillan, a very clever

The master of spin and flight.

JIM BAXTER

"Jim didn't have a left foot, he had a golf club. It was a two-iron, four-iron, eight-iron, wedge. Whatever the distance, whatever the weight, he could drop it spot on. If he had applied himself there might not have been a better player in the whole wide world than Jimmy Baxter. He was just sheer genius."

(Bobby Robson)

"A pass from Baxter was like a guided missile. I always wanted to give England a right good thrashing and the only time we might have managed it was in '67 but Baxter started tipping the ball up and all that stuff. A very good performance though."

(Denis Law)

"Liverpool played Sunderland while Jim was there and it was one of those awful, stinking dirty days they have up at Sunderland. We came off at the end of the game with a win, but what a battle it was, and there was Jim as though he'd been out for a Sunday stroll. They'd been giving him the ball all afternoon and he had almost won it for them but there was not a stain on him – jersey and shorts immaculate. A fabulous, fabulous player."

(Emlyn Hughes)

"An ability like that is a gift from God because guys can work all their lives and never be able to play like that. George Best had it, Jimmy Johnstone had it and Jim Baxter had it but I think sometimes when you get it easy you don't really appreciate it. We all feel abused when we watch it being wasted because we all want to see that kind of talent. That's why we got annoyed at him for not using it to the best of his ability."

(Pat Crerand)

player who never got the credit he deserved, Willie Henderson, a marvel at 18 and like a rubber ball so that when he was kicked he was just up and away past his marker. And when you think about the way the team was built, it was strange. Eric Caldow and me were on one side and Harold Davis and Bobby Shearer were on the other. On our side we couldn't tackle a fish supper but Harry and Bobby were out looking for bodies. So when Celtic played us they all wanted to be at outside right."

While Baxter was with Rangers, Celtic players often wanted to be outside the ground during Old Firm matches but nothing he did during a Glasgow derby equalled his displays of arrogance whenever England provided the opposition. He had an extraordinary mastery of the spin and flight of a football and an elegance of touch which meant that he frequently appeared to impart energy to the ball where another player could do nothing more than kick it. When Baxter composed a sweeping pass it would swing to its target with the grace of a carpet bowl drifting on to the jack. He shared with Franz Beckenbauer of Bayern Munich and West Germany a capacity to banish urgency from the heart of an intense contest so that the moves he orchestrated became a precise extension of his own leisurely tactical approach.

Understandably, the English were less inclined to view his caprices in international matches as a rhapsody in dark blue but for Scots traumatised by the 9-3 thrashing administered at Wembley in 1961 it seemed not so much that he turned the tables as that he spun them with outrageous ease. A new aluminium and glass roof had been added to Wembley by the time of the 1963 international but instead of keeping the lid on the raucous Scottish army assembled on the terracings below, it simply served to bounce their celebratory anthems around the stadium.

The circumstances were ripe for a Scottish fiesta – a profound desire to redeem the humiliation inflicted two years earlier, a team reduced to ten men within five minutes after Smith's reckless challenge broke Caldow's leg, and Baxter on his Wembley debut, primed to glide across turf which looked as though it had been manicured to save him the least fraction of unnecessary resistance. Caldow's injury reversed the left flank deployment around Baxter, who now found Davie Wilson withdrawn from the outside left position into the full back berth vacated by the stricken Rangers defender.

Baxter had never scored two goals in a game before that afternoon, nor had he taken a penalty kick. Soon after Caldow was stretchered from the pitch the slim Fifer beat England's new goalkeeper, Gordon Banks, with a rising left foot drive and within a few minutes Scotland were awarded a penalty kick which the Scottish captain, Dave Mackay, instructed Baxter to convert.

"Eric had been the captain but he was off and Dave, being the kind of guy he was, just grabbed the ball and said, 'Stick that away, Jim.' I didn't want to disappoint him, so I just stuck it away – two nothing, first penalty taken at Wembley, no' bad, eh?" is Baxter's succinct reprise of the moment which saw Gordon Banks topple to his right as the ball swept into the net beyond his left arm. The Rangers winger, Willie Henderson, watching as his team-mate coolly picked his spot beyond the goalkeeper, was moved to remark that Baxter's only concern was whether to put the ball in off the crossbar or to get it to bounce back to him off the rear stanchion.

In fact, Baxter's mind was exercised by even less likely possibilities of Scotland's domination. Having succeeded in scoring twice on his

A taste for the high life ultimately grounded Baxter's prodigious talent.

Wembley debut he began to ponder the chances of a hat-trick and decided that there was no rule to say the necessary three goals had to be put behind Gordon Banks. When Bryan Douglas reduced the margin with an English goal in the second half Baxter was forced to abandon his notion, but not before he had succeeded in disturbing his own goalkeeper, Bill Brown, by letting him in on one of the more bizarre plans to be hatched in an international arena.

> If we had made it 3-1 I wanted to go to the photographers behind our goal and ask them how long there was to go and if there had been a minute left I would have scored a goal through my own net to say, "There's a hat-trick." I wanted to do that but Bill Brown said, "You're not on." Bill will tell you. He thought I was kidding but when he realised I wasn't he nearly fainted. I would have done it, too, just for a laugh. Aye, that would have been good, wouldn't it?

Whether Baxter truly meant to beat his own goalkeeper for amusement will never be known for certain but it would have been an act of defiance rather than a gesture of superiority. Baxter was allergic to constraint and reserved his greatest contempt for those he perceived as functionaries or yes-men, of whom there were one or two at Rangers, the kind who thought his jersey should be tucked neatly inside his shorts, in keeping with the club's conservative image. Baxter

JIM BAXTER

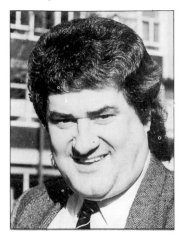

Jim Baxter was born in Hill of Beath, Fife, on 29 September 1939. Upon leaving school he spent a brief spell as a cabinet maker in Dunfermline before working in the pits at Fordel Colliery. From Crossgates Primrose he moved on to part-time senior football with Raith Rovers in April 1957 and to Rangers three years later. Sometimes listed as an inside-forward, sometimes as a left-half, he was essentially a left-sided midfield creator of enormous class. He is enshrined in the memory of a grateful Scottish audience for his display of disdainful superiority at Wembley in 1967, when England suffered their first defeat as world champions, beaten 3-2 by Scotland.

"They were world champions and they were full of themselves – you'd better believe that – and if you remember, it was a makeshift Scottish side. I think Jimmy Johnstone fainted or jumped off the train at Edinburgh or something. But we were a good workmanlike side, everybody playing for one another and things began to go for us and we were so much on top it was unbelievable. People said we could have gone and emulated the 9-3 win England had in 1961. I said: 'Take the piss oot o' them – never mind bothering about 9-3.'

"Ah, we were laughing, Denis and I and Billy Bremner, we just had a great laugh with wee Alan Ball running about daft. He was the hero of the World Cup and Bremner said we should call him Jimmy Clitheroe after the wee comic with the short trousers and the squeaky voice. So I kept calling him Jimmy Clitheroe and trying to give him nutmegs and he was going

looked and laughed at such dignitaries and inevitably set himself up as a target for retribution, much of it on a tiresomely petty level. In later life he insisted that he was not as awkward as many believe.

> I didn't like their regulations and rules and this thing about playing for the jersey. I loved Rangers and I still love them yet but playing for the jersey is a lot of nonsense and I think they've realised it now. My attitude was that if you do your job you get away with cheek but if you don't produce what's wanted you don't get away with it. It's as simple as that.

Rangers were well aware that they were incubating a personality which did not sit comfortably with their dour tradition. After Rangers played Real Madrid in a European Cup match in Glasgow, the Spanish team's legendary Hungarian Ferenc Puskas requested Baxter to act as guide on a tour of the city's nightlife, preferably with some kind of dalliance as part of the proceedings. Improbably, the pair ended up at a party in Drumchapel, not one of the city's more select localities, where arrangements were made for Puskas to enjoy some time alone with the lady of the house in the privacy of her kitchenette, an encounter which proved to be wholehearted on both sides. Asked afterwards by a reporter how the distinguished visitor had enjoyed his evening in Glasgow, Baxter laconically replied: "Nae wonder they call him the Galloping Major. I can understand it now."

Baxter's attitudes inevitably brought him into conflict with Willie Allan, the autocratic secretary of the SFA, the collision occurring after Rangers beat Celtic 3-0 in the 1963 Scottish Cup final replay. When the final whistle went, Celtic's captain Billy McNeill sportingly threw the match ball to Baxter, who promptly left the field with it, ignoring the referee's request that he should return it. Inside the Rangers dressing-room the players agreed to present it to their gifted inside forward Ian McMillan, who was about to retire from the game, but the incensed Allan announced to newspaper reporters that the SFA would take steps to have the ball returned to them before what he referred to as "the law of the jungle" carried Scottish football into anarchy. The Rangers manager Scot Symon sensibly sent the Association a duplicate ball to conclude a ludicrous chapter.

Rangers, however, were unwilling to make any gifts to their star player when he decided that his earnings should be brought into line with the kind of wages he might expect from one of the better English clubs, in effect a rise of a hundred per cent or so. His five years with the club had coincided with a substantial accumulation of honours, a total of three championships, three Scottish Cup and three Scottish League Cup winners' medals but Rangers felt unwilling or unable to raid the kitty and Baxter was transferred to Sunderland for £80,000 in May 1965.

He had passed the high point of his club career and was to play at Roker Park and subsequently with Nottingham Forest, in teams which were not equipped to take advantage of his supreme vision which was, in any case, being rendered decreasingly effective by his pathological dislike of training. He combined a growing taste for hard drinking and gambling with a devotion to the female cause. These extra-curricular activities debilitated him so that on his return to Ibrox in 1969, he carried an obvious paunch which indicated only too clearly that his second spell with Rangers would be short-lived.

In fact, it ended with the indignity of a free transfer the following year. What might have happened had he been subjected to the wisdom of a Busby or a Stein can only be conjecture, although it is fairly certain that the combination of his departure to Sunderland and the advent of Stein as manager at Parkhead set back Rangers so seriously that they were unable to overhaul Celtic for almost a decade. By his own admission it was woeful self-neglect which put him out of the game.

> It's the easiest thing in the world to get fit if you're young but I was lazy and always wanted to be opposite and then eventually I found that I was missing a yard and that ordinary players were able to put me out of the game. And I felt that was it, time to stop, and I gave up at 30 years of age. It was a crime, really, because I should have been there for another five years but I wasn't fit and I'd lost enthusiasm for the whole thing.

Such a prodigal and casual disposal of genius which ranked him as truly world class is perhaps the most vivid example of the self-destructiveness which so often seems to haunt the greatly gifted Scottish player but Baxter's incomparable abilities have not been lost to the future. The 1967 Wembley meeting of England, unbeaten since their World Cup victory a year earlier, and a Scotland team intent on exorcising their own failure to reach the tournament's finals, was captured on film.

There are two moments which reveal Baxter's utter command of the proceedings, as he literally sauntered through the match, taunting the English with their inability to win possession. In one scene, he stands on the halfway line with not an opposition player in the Scottish half. His stockings are bunched around his ankles as he takes a pass from Bremner and toes it straight back with his right foot. Bremner returns the ball and Baxter, with the most minimal of effort, curves it off the outside edge of his left boot towards the supporting Gemmell.

Later he appears on the opposite flank to orchestrate another number, this time on the maddened Alan Ball, who is bumped casually out of the way as he lunges to intercept. Baxter then sets off down the wing, keeping the ball off the ground with his left foot for four strides until, at last, he chips it forward on to the chest of Denis Law, loitering in the home penalty area. Looking back on this performance years later, Baxter admitted to a single regret. "There were no pockets in my shorts or I would have done it all with my hands in them."

*   *   *

No survey of the Scottish player can overlook the winger, although in any activity other than football it would have been easy enough to do exactly that; the winger always got a seat at the front in team photographs otherwise he would have had to climb on a colleague's back to get into the picture. He inhabited an outcrop of the game which has always seemed a particularly Scottish domain although England produced two of the very greatest exponents of wing play in Stanley Matthews of Blackpool and Preston's Tom Finney. Interestingly, Finney's schoolboy idol had been Alex James but he grew up too small to be given a beat in the midfield like James and was switched out to the wing.

A generation of schoolboys were inspired by the vision of Alan Morton, nicknamed the Wee Blue Devil after a pressman picked up a remark made by an English supporter during his side's 5-1 defeat by Scotland at Wembley in 1928, when Morton created three of the

hairy – the man was going potty. Billy gave him pelters all right and Denis – well, of course, Denis was arrogant, you know? 'Go away little man,' and all that. Aye, we had him potty.

"They were frightened to come and take the ball off us. If you could go back you would hear us laughing at them, kidding them on. We were never in any danger of losing that one. I played twice at Wembley and we won twice and it was fantastic for the fans because it's their pilgrimage. Every two years they put down their half quids or their pounds or whatever it may be and they go down there and to get a victory is great for the players but it's terrific for the fans if you can rub salt into the wounds.

"But I never said to myself 'Oh, I'm Scottish.' I never did the Bill Shankly thing. It wouldn't have bothered me to have been a German or an Italian. If I'd been born in Berwick instead of Beath I'd have done it to Scotland if I had been picked. Aye, simple as that."

Gordon Smith, the Hibs cavalier.

Willie Henderson – "like a wee rubber ball" according to Jim Baxter.

Scottish goals. Morton was another man familiar with the coal-face but he was a mining engineer, not a pitman, and he was shrewd enough to learn his craft with Queen's Park where a player who attracted an offer from a professional club was permitted to accept the whole of the transfer fee, paid as a weekly wage during his first year.

When he moved to Ibrox in 1920 Rangers inherited a prodigy. At five feet four inches he was another in the succession of small-made Scottish players of his era but he was well-proportioned, with muscular legs which he used to drive himself past defenders who lacked the agility or balance required to thwart his sudden changes of direction which in any case were notoriously unpredictable. He had a devastating turn of speed and as if that were not enough he could score from positions which would have confounded a Brazilian.

One of his characteristic ploys was a right-angled turn on the byeline which produced a hanging cross dropped at the back post for a waiting team-mate to head in on goal. All good things did not come to him naturally, however, and although ultimately he could use both feet well he had been obliged as a schoolboy to work hard to bring his left foot up to the standard of his more favoured right, the reward for which was a reputation as the greatest left winger Scotland has ever produced.

The other side of the park was the realm of a series of remarkable wingers, such as the refined (and at five feet nine inches, unusually tall) Gordon Smith of Hibs, who could score goals as well as create them, with over 300 to his credit in a Scottish League career of 23 years which ended in 1964, a period which saw him overlap with Rangers' Willie Henderson, known familiarly to the Ibrox legions as Wee Wullie, whose speciality was to beat opponents on the rim of the pitch, no matter how diligently they tried to deny him space against the touchline.

Perhaps he was unaware it existed; Willie was famously myopic and during one intense Rangers-Celtic match at Ibrox he drifted across to the dugouts and enquired how much time was left to play. Unwittingly, however, his query was directed towards the opposition bench where the Celtic manager Jock Stein entered into the spirit of the occasion and obliged with an answer. Henderson, whose hearing seems to have been defective as well as his vision, replied: "Thanks, boss", to hilarity amongst the Celtic contingent.

Jock Stein was not always afforded so much amusement by the extraordinary individual who inhabited Celtic's own right flank but his persistence with Jimmy Johnstone was an unsung achievement of his considerable career, and one which Stein himself recognised when he suggested that his efforts might have been responsible for keeping the wee man in football for five years more than might otherwise have been expected from a personality who was as rumbustious as Jim Baxter.

Johnstone was yet another product of Lanarkshire but, like the area itself, by the time he reached his peak, he was an extension of the past rather than the future of football and was possibly the last man who played the game by himself. This is not to diminish his contribution, which could be mesmerising, especially on the occasions when he simply devastated opposing defenders like the English international Terry Cooper, who spent a miserable evening attempting to contain the wee man as he ran amok during the second leg of Celtic's European Cup semi-final with Leeds in 1970.

But he was not amenable to being part of anybody's game plan and his relationship with football was essentially that of a man with a private obsession. When he was 12 years old he was galvanised by the gift of a book which described how Stanley Matthews had refined his skills with relentless practice and the youthful Johnstone promptly climbed over the railings of St Columba's School in Uddingston to begin a course of night classes in solitary magic.

> I used to go into the playground and I practised for hours and hours on end, running with the ball, sprinting, twisting and turning. There was a wall about a hundred yards long and as I went up and down I played one-two's off it and then when I went home I would put milk bottles down and go in and out of them for another hour or two.

If anyone could have constructed a map of Johnstone's meanderings during one of his more expressive performances for Celtic it would have looked like a page from the *Book of Kells*, the margins full of fantastic curlicues. It was precisely this quality of decoration which at once made Johnstone the delight of the fans and the despair of other players, including his team-mates, who were often at one with the opposition in their inability to foresee where his bewildering switches of direction would take him next. The usual disadvantage of watching football on film is that the camera is unequal to the pattern of a game as a whole, but when future generations witness Johnstone spinning through a swarm of defenders they should not find it too hard to guess that in his own mind he was really just back amongst the milk bottles.

At five feet four inches (apparently the standard height for Scottish wingers) he looked like Mickey Rooney allowed to play with the big boys but the fringe of red hair on his bullet head also signified a temper which was never seriously repressed and which simply invited less favoured opponents to put the boot in. His courage, however, was not in question, as former Celtic team-mates, such as full back Jim Craig, willingly testify.

> The wee man deserves a great deal of credit for his sheer bravery because he would go at a player, be chopped brutally, receive a free kick and go at the same player again, knowing what was coming. It takes a very brave man to do that because he drove at players very quickly and if he was brought down in full flight he could receive some very nasty blows time after time.

Johnstone was clearly adored by the Celtic support partly because in appearance he was such an improbable athlete, as if he had stepped straight out of the Parkhead Jungle and on to the pitch, the punters' dream made pallid flesh. He had the irreverence and instincts of an urchin and could rouse Jock Stein to impressive wrath, as when he hurled abuse at the Celtic bench while being substituted against Dundee United in 1968, causing the enraged Stein to pursue him up the tunnel. Another incident which saw the Celtic manager provoked beyond endurance occurred in Buenos Aires in 1967 as Celtic were preparing for the second leg of their world club championship encounter with Racing Club. Stein, fearful that the Argentinians could disrupt his team off the field, warned the players that it was possible that the locals might insinuate attractive women into their rooms. There was a pause as this information was digested, broken at last by Johnstone's cheery announcement that "I'm in room 616 if any of youse don't want

JIMMY JOHNSTONE

"It was a Friday and we were playing Rangers next day so we had a five-a-side match to get some practice. Wee Jimmy came along that day and joined in and we couldn't get the ball off him for 20 minutes. We all stopped and I was looking at Davie Provan and Frank McGarvey and Danny McGrain and thinking this isn't supposed to be happening because we're practising for a big game. He was there for 20 minutes with the ball, sitting on it, doing everything with it. I've never seen an exhibition like it. Unbelievable he was."
(Charlie Nicholas)

"We were playing a tour game in the National Stadium in Vienna and Jimmy disappeared off the park just like that and came back on ten minutes later. I said, 'Wee man, what's happening, where have you been?' 'Oh,' he said, 'bursting for the toilet. I just had to go.' It was the best disappearing trick I ever saw."
(Tommy Gemmell)

"Celtic played in Alfredo di Stefano's testimonial match in the San Bernabeu stadium in Madrid and Jimmy was superb. Even when he was falling over the ball he was taking two or three people down the wrong road. But what sticks in my memory was that he had arranged to take a holiday in Spain with his family after the match and because he had a terrible fear of flying he arranged for a taxi to take them 400 miles and charged it to the club. Only Jimmy would get away with that."
(Bertie Auld)

"We were playing Celtic and I said to Jimmy, 'How many times can you keep the ball up?' He said, 'Och, about four or five hundred if I put my mind to it.' I said, 'Well, I can keep you up for the same amount.' So we might have had a circus act if he could have kept the ball up and I kept him up at the same time. But he was a magical player and we used to have a lot more laughs when we played each other than people realised."
(John Greig)

Jimmy Johnstone congratulated by Celtic goalkeeper Evan Williams after he had tormented Leeds and, in particular, Terry Cooper – the 1970 European Cup semi-final at Hampden.

yours . . .", followed by the player's undignified departure while Stein lunged across the room in pursuit.

He had been a ball boy with Celtic and was so thoroughly bound up with the club that when the time came for him to move on to Sheffield Wednesday, destiny insisted that his game would atrophy in less familiar surroundings. As a Scotland player Johnstone earned 23 caps, a total which did not reflect his abilities. It was restricted in part because he was often injured or suspended and partly because Rangers' Henderson was accumulating 29 caps in the same position at the same time. Johnstone was never able to tie his international place down for a sustained period, his most extended run in 1974 coinciding with the notorious incident at Largs when he chose to push out from the Clyde coast in darkness in a rowing boat equipped with only one oar, a ploy which ended in the lifeboat being called out to rescue him from the riptide. It was an overblown episode but characteristic of a man whose mortal fear of flying did not prevent him spending part of his post-football career acting as front man for a company specialising in air holidays.

His amalgam of courage and aggression, style and insecurity, provided vast entertainment as well as deep frustration. As Hugh McIlvanney memorably observed of the wee man: "He added substantially to the gaiety of nations off the field too, didn't he – especially the maritime nations . . ."

★　　★　　★

The number of claims that this player or that player is world class perpetually exceeds the total of those individuals who actually qualify for such a description but in the 1980s Scots were able to suggest that two of their own might fit comfortably into any of the great national teams. Kenny Dalglish and Graeme Souness emerged as professional footballers in the most resonant sense with playing careers which overlapped, and reached their peaks, at Liverpool. Around the axis of their time together at Anfield the progress of the two men has been curiously symmetrical, Dalglish making his name with Celtic before heading south and Souness concluding his playing days with a remarkable move to Ibrox, there to become player-manager of the other half of the Old Firm. As it happens, either Glasgow side might have been able to claim both players as former pupils.

Dalglish, the older of the pair by two years, was brought up in one of the high-rise council blocks overlooking the Albion, Rangers' training ground, a couple of hundred yards from Ibrox itself, and his father was a long-standing Rangers supporter whose affection for the club had been passed on to a son who kept photographs of his favourite players around the house, as Celtic's assistant manager Sean Fallon discovered when he called to discuss the possibility of adding the younger Dalglish to the Parkhead strength. Both parties knew that Rangers were aware of the teenager's potential and were expected to make a move before long, but the timing of Fallon's visit added significant weight to his overtures because it was 1967 and Celtic had just won the European Cup. With the pragmatism which was subsequently to be associated with the Dalglish name, it was decided that an apprenticeship under Jock Stein was entirely acceptable.

There can be no question that Dalglish displayed an impressive appetite to learn his craft. Celtic farmed him out to Cumbernauld United so that he could earn a trooper's scars in the junior ranks and

Scrutinising his native game: Dalglish at Tynecastle.

Stein would have let him linger there for two seasons but at the end of his first term he asked to be made a full-time professional. Stein declined, only to find Dalglish back at his office door with his father as a reinforcement, upon which it was agreed that the youth could be called up. The manager must have been gratified to discover his judgment proved fruitful just over a year later when Dalglish made his first-team debut as a substitute against Hamilton Academical; he started for the first team the following season and at the beginning of the 1969-70 season he scored seven goals in two rounds of the Drybrough Cup.

The moment of truth for the Dalglish household came when Celtic encountered Rangers in a League Cup tie at Ibrox and were awarded a penalty kick which Dalglish was instructed to take; no division of loyalties was evident as he sent Peter McCloy the wrong way in the Rangers goal.

Stein employed him variously in midfield and as a striker and he was a natural in either role, blessed with a positional sense which permitted him to create play with the searching pass to a well-placed colleague or to finish a move with his apparently innate whiplash reactions in front of goal. When the situation called for it he could summon his close control to carry him past defenders on the dribble, usually to finish with a powerful shot on target, but his supreme attribute was the ability to dictate the pace of a contest while bringing other players into the game.

Kenny Dalglish

His Scotland career began in one of the rare full internationals to be played outside Hampden when Scotland met Belgium at Pittodrie and Dalglish, aged 20, was sent on as a substitute by Tommy Docherty during Scotland's 1-0 victory in a European Championship match in November 1971. Docherty said of him some years later: "There are people who tell me he's a yard short in pace. I say to them that he's ten yards faster upstairs." A further 101 appearances for Scotland were to follow and he equalled the record set by Denis Law by scoring 30 international goals, the recollection of some of which can still thrill the senses.

One of these, in another European Championship tie with Belgium in Brussels in 1982, was a breathtaking demonstration of expertise which saw Dalglish take charge of the ball on the right edge of the Belgian penalty area to sway past two markers and lob Pfaff as the goalkeeper left his line. A player of more homely talents would have treasured the moment but when Dalglish was invited to reflect upon it five years later he was not inclined to dwell on the aesthetics. "Obviously, I remember it," he said, "but the biggest thing I remember about that night is that we lost 3-2 so when you put it into proportion it counts for nothing really."

Such disinclination to take consolation from glorious defeats is a characteristic which sets Dalglish aside from the mass of his countrymen but he can hardly be accused of wallowing in his triumphs either. Graeme Souness, whose midfield role with Liverpool and Scotland afforded him a close view of Dalglish in action, was witness to many shimmering examples of his fellow Scot's ability to transform the mundane transaction of a contest into an exceptional currency.

I saw him score that goal in Brussels, coming in from nowhere and pushing it around the keeper from the right but it was almost Kenny's trademark to do that and he did it against Spain at Hampden before the

Dalglish with Liverpool, 1986.

Mexico World Cup finals and in a match against Ipswich that I played in. But I will always remember him scoring a goal against Aston Villa one day when we were struggling at home in the league. It was a shot from about 30 yards, which is one thing, but this shot was aimed through someone's legs. Now you ask him about it and he'll say, "Well, that was luck." But I was there, I was with him, I was behind him and I saw it. But Kenny says it was just luck.

To paraphrase Gary Player, the more Dalglish practised, the luckier he got, to the tune of over a hundred goals in the Scottish League and again during his spell in England. He appeared in three consecutive World Cup finals, in West Germany, Argentina and Spain, and could have made it four but he declined, because of injury, to be included in the squad for Mexico in 1986, a decision which greatly perplexed the then Scotland manager Alex Ferguson, who said: "I was so taken aback I had to jump in the car and go for a drive. I needed time to think about a replacement." Steve Archibald was given the thankless job of filling in for Dalglish but in truth there was no other player of the stature of Dalglish available to the Scots, who stood greatly in need of his services in their final ill-tempered group match against Uruguay which ended in a 0-0 draw when a single goal would have carried Scotland through to the next stage of the finals for the first time. For Dalglish himself there was the consolation of a League and Cup double in his first season as player-manager of Liverpool, a coup which suggested, rightly as events proved, that he was likely to be as formidable a presence in charge of the club as he had been on the park.

He greeted his elevation to the role of manager with habitual candour. "Whether I'm good or bad remains to be seen but when I started as a professional footballer I didn't know whether I was going to be good or bad at that either. My ambition is just the same – to do my best and be honest and realistic enough to step aside if I'm doing a bad job." By the end of season 1988-89 it appeared that would not be too seriously troubled by self-doubt; only an injury-time goal scored by Arsenal against Liverpool in the climactic closing match of a troubled season deprived the Anfield club of three consecutive championships and prevented Dalglish from becoming the first manager to win the English League and Cup double on two occasions.

Like a shark which makes repeated close passes at its target, Dalglish again steered Liverpool within touching distance of the double in 1990, winning the championship comfortably but faltering in bizarre circumstances in an FA Cup semi-final against Crystal Palace, a team which had endured a 9-0 hammering by Liverpool earlier in the season. Still, the many Scots whose hearts and minds were with Dalglish as he strove for the unprecedented feat had the consolation of knowing that in 1989 the championship had been placed in the custody of another compatriot, George Graham, while in 1990 the FA Cup had been annexed by Manchester United under Alex Ferguson.

The script for Graeme Souness's playing career was that of Dalglish in reverse. He trained with Celtic as a schoolboy, moved south to play for Spurs, Middlesbrough and ultimately Liverpool before a brief spell in Italy with Sampdoria was ended with his appointment as player-manager of Rangers, with whom he experienced Scottish League football for the first time. The temperament of the two men has always stood in radical contrast, with Dalglish an acme of rectitude compared with Souness, who regularly appeared to act as a magnetic pole for trouble assembling in his vicinity.

According to his own account, the most memorable event of the time he spent with Celtic came when he was chased along London Road in Glasgow by a couple of local hooligans, one of whom spiced the pursuit by brandishing a sword. After signing professional forms with Spurs, he twice ran away from White Hart Lane and returned to Scotland and on the second occasion the London club suspended him indefinitely, a move which caused the Scottish MP Tam Dalyell to table questions in the House of Commons about the affair. He returned to Spurs but a move was inevitable and it carried him on to Middlesbrough where Jack Charlton was appointed manager shortly afterwards, just as Souness returned from a hard-drinking Mediterranean holiday. Charlton, with his usual diplomatic turn of phrase, wrote later: "I had a big problem with Graeme when I took over . . . I had to get it through to him that if he did not screw the nut, he'd be a bum for the rest of his life."

Young Souness, a Spurs player in 1972, but not for long.

Souness at his peak at Anfield.

GRAEME SOUNESS

"I can earn a great deal more money by playing football outside Scotland than I could in Scotland. But I'd still like to be player-manager of Rangers one day. I'll settle for manager. Jock Wallace, watch out . . ."
(*Graeme Souness, 10 September 1985*)

"Some people thought I was a soccer mercenary and Ibrox was just a stepping-stone to something else. I think I've proved them wrong today."
(*Sounesss after joining the Ibrox board, 23 November 1988*)

"I'm pleased with the two points but it was just a Premier league game, same as any other."
(*After the 1-0 victory over Celtic, 31 August 1986*)

"The longer I'm with Rangers the more I realise how important the games against Celtic are. It's more than just two points."
(*After the 5-1 victory over Celtic, 25 August 1988*)

"It would be nice to win the European Cup being manager of Rangers, wouldn't it?"
(*While a Sampdoria player, 10 September 1985*)

"I'm very disappointed. If we had not lost Terry Butcher with his broken leg, I truly believe we could have won the European Cup this season."
(*After quarter-final defeat by Steaua Bucharest, 16 March 1988*)

Charlton's methods were effective, so much so that his successor at Ayresome Park, John Neal, was able to deflect one bid from Liverpool for Souness before the Anfield club returned with a second and successful offer of £352,000 in January 1978 to set a record for a transfer deal between two Football League clubs (their acquisition of Kenny Dalglish from Celtic six months earlier for £440,000 was a record move between British clubs). The move was the last of three purchases by Bob Paisley of Scottish players who were to have a decisive impact on the fortunes of a club which had already won the European Cup in 1976-77, the other being Alan Hansen, signed from Partick Thistle for £100,000.

Of the trio, Souness was the hard man and, although he has continually insisted that he did not use excessive force as a player, there has always been a well-defined ruthless streak in his make-up which displayed itself in challenges which carried aggression beyond acceptable limits, the tackle which saw Siggi Jonsson stretchered from the pitch in Reykjavik during Scotland's World Cup qualifying tie with Iceland in May 1985 being a case in point. Liverpool did not hire him as a hatchet man, however, and it was at Anfield that he found the proper stage on which to display his capacity to impose his presence on the contest, winning and distributing possession from midfield to great effect and periodically driving forward from the middle of the park to add potency to the team's fast-breaking attacks.

Scotland were to employ him in a similar manner and it remains a matter for regret (not least by Ally McLeod), that he was not introduced into the Scots' farcical World Cup campaign in Argentina until the concluding match with Holland which produced their only victory in the South American finals. Souness emerged from the fiasco with credit and went on to represent Scotland in the concluding stages of two further World Cup tournaments, in Spain and in Mexico, where his last appearance for his country came during the Scots' very creditable 2-1 defeat by West Germany. Having never played league football in Scotland, he was not particularly popular with the Hampden crowd and when Scotland played the USSR in Malaga in 1982, requiring a win to move into the next stage of the World Cup finals, he was jeered by the Scottish support for much of the match, a

phenomenon which came to an abrupt end when he scored a splendid goal in the dying moments of the game.

Souness was not likely to be too aggrieved by such displays of ill-favour. He was capped on 54 occasions in addition to his selection for Scotland at schoolboy, youth and under-23 levels and he left Liverpool with a most imposing honours collection comprising three European Cup, five championship and four League Cup winners' medals. In any case, his unforeseen arrival at Ibrox as player-manager in April 1986 guaranteed an extraordinary profile in the Scottish domestic game.

The volatility inherent in his character was apparent when he made his Scottish league debut for Rangers against Hibs at Easter Road in August 1986, to be sent off after only 34 minutes for a nasty tackle on George McCluskey which precipitated a brawl involving 20 players, leading ultimately to an SFA disciplinary inquiry which saw him banned for five games. He was to be dismissed once more that season, during an ill-tempered match with Aberdeen at Pittodrie which had immense significance for Rangers, who required a single point to secure their first championship for nine years (which they achieved in a 1-1 draw despite his absence) and he was shown the red card for a third time at the beginning of the following season on yet another high octane occasion, in this instance a Celtic-Rangers match at Parkhead.

He continued to collide with the SFA disciplinary committee in his incarnation as a manager, being banned from the dugout for a handful of games towards the end of the 1988-89 season after berating a linesman about stoppage time added on during a Dundee United-Rangers match at Tannadice but he defied the prohibition in full view of the SFA hierarchy during Rangers' Scottish Cup semi-final with St Johnstone at Parkhead shortly afterwards, for which he was suspended for the whole of the following season, a decision which fuelled substantial aggravation between Rangers and the ruling body of Scottish football. He employed himself as a substitute for Rangers in the Scottish Cup final of 1989, which ended in a 1-0 defeat by Celtic, after which he declared he had made his last appearance as a player. However, in the manner of the Dalai Lama he was to manifest himself on other occasions, bidding farewell to the crowd when Rangers celebrated a world record 40th championship in their final home match of the 1989-90 season against Dunfermline. Then for a friendly meeting with Dundee at Dens Park in August 1990 he appeared in the position described by the match programme under "Trialist".

If this could have been construed as an understatement of his position, it was clear that in one way or another he was set to extend his impact, offering students of football in Scotland further opportunities to observe a gifted, highly motivated and contradictory personality on parade in their own domain.

$$\star \quad \star \quad \star$$

Football in Scotland has always been principally the game of the working man and most of its professional practitioners remain exactly that, although they are commonly imagined to be separated from their audience in lifestyle and wealth. The extremes of personal income in the Scottish game are so far apart as to have practically no relationship with each other so that, for example, Rangers' best-paid player in 1990 earned at least one hundred and fifty times more than his equivalent at Stranraer or Berwick. Perhaps 20 per cent of the total number of Scottish players earn considerable salaries and – particularly since the arrival of Graeme Souness at Ibrox – some are wealthy and even rich by contemporary standards.

Most Premier Division players fall into the category described by Paul Sturrock of Dundee United when he says: "The average full-time player does not do badly out of the game but that really means he is earning the same kind of money as, say, a worker on the North Sea oil rigs or maybe a factory worker with good overtime and certainly not the kind of cash that people can take from golf or tennis without ever reaching the higher levels of their sport." Many part-time footballers in Scotland do better than their full-time equivalents if they have another job and if their combined salaries are taken into account but it was possible very recently to discover a part-time Premier Division player with no other source of income, whose earnings from football were so low that he was actually earning a poverty wage.

For most of the game's history a Scottish player, even one blessed with a genius for the game, was not lavishly rewarded for staying at home and had no guarantee that he would do particularly well from a move further afield. Hughie Gallacher generated £23,000 in transfer fees, a very large sum in his day, for the clubs which bought and sold him, but his personal share of that income amounted to no more than £60 in signing-on fees and his total earnings over 11 years almost certainly did not exceed £6,000. Alex James did rather better out of his playing days and Arsenal were able to arrange an extra-mural job in Selfridge's which generated an extra £5 a week, but had he not died in middle age in 1953 James would have entered a period of personal financial stringency. During his first period with Rangers Jim Baxter earned between £35 and £45 as his weekly basic at a time when players with a fraction of his talent could command twice that sum by playing in England.

The freedom of players to negotiate their own contracts, introduced in Scotland in 1980, greatly improved the position of the Scottish footballer and helped to stem the drain of talent into England. Another important factor had been the advent in 1976 of the Premier Division, which increased competitiveness and, inevitably, the rewards for success. The effects were felt most dramatically in the club whose mid-table placings had been comfortable enough in the old First

Division, but who were now threatened with relegation if they suffered any prolonged spell of poor form. This meant that in the late 1970s a club like Hibs was paying its players more or less as much as their equivalents at Rangers or Celtic.

In the 1980s Aberdeen, under Alex Ferguson, moved to the top of the Scottish wages league, with the best basic salary in the Premier Division which the Pittodrie players were able to supplement handsomely with bonuses for domestic and European success so that earnings of £60,000 were not uncommon. The lesson eventually penetrated into the boardroom at Ibrox, culminating in the audacious deal which brought Graeme Souness to Glasgow in 1986 and his arrival meant the end of the low basic wage which for so long prevailed in Scottish football. Rangers at last exerted their enormous financial strength – probably the most substantial in Britain – not only to import expensive and prestigious players but to pay them comparable salaries.

In order to minimise tax liabilities, players' contracts have become more complex and it is not always possible to compare like with like because signing-on fees are spread across two or three years and there are less quantifiable variables such as housing loans, agreements on testimonial matches and bonus and pension schemes which are now inseparable from the top players' negotiations, but it is safe to say that Rangers' more valued players have been able to command upwards of £2,500 a week, while a squad player can count on taking home £30,000 in annual gross salary. When the club's annual report was published in 1990, one individual was reported to have earned between £270,000 and £275,000. It was not, as was widely believed, Graeme Souness, who was the next highest earner at just under £215,000. It was, in fact, Maurice Johnston who also had the benefit of a signing-on fee of £1 million, to be paid in instalments over four years. A Rangers player can also expect the club to pay the equivalent of ten per cent of his salary into a personal pension fund. In the face of such unprecedented changes across the city, Celtic were forced to upgrade their financial structure so that when an influential and popular figure such as Paul McStay renewed his contract at Parkhead, he could look forward to earnings equivalent to an annual salary of £150,000. A full-time Celtic reserve was on around £200 a week in 1990.

Dundee United pay a comparatively low basic wage, many players taking home only £250 a week, but a lucrative bonus scheme is operated at Tannadice which can treble earnings in a good year and the club is generous in the matter of signing-on fees and testimonials for long-standing employees, who also benefit from an attractive pension scheme. Players who choose to stay with United throughout their career are rewarded with a share of the fees paid for colleagues who are transferred to other clubs. In addition, United offer the longest average contracts of any Premier Division club.

The revival of Hearts in the mid-1980s brought an upgrading of salaries at Tynecastle and players such as Dave McPherson and John Robertson, in his second spell with the club, were looking at a weekly wage of £1,000 including bonuses, while at Easter Road earnings for Hibs' players tended to be lower – £25,000 basic for the likes of Andy Goram, Paul Kane and John Collins – but enhanced by a rewarding bonus system. Dundee's first team are paid in a bracket which extends from £12,000–£20,000 annually while at St Mirren remuneration has been more variable because of an erratic bonus structure but the salary scale is not radically different from that of Dens Park.

Motherwell, with the smallest attendance figures of the regular

Paul McStay, Celtic's best-paid player at the beginning of the 90s.

Premier Division clubs, are predictably also the lowest payers, with junior employees on a salary of £8,000-£9,000 and established players closer to the £17,000 level, while Dunfermline and Falkirk pay in the region of £9,000 to £12,000. It is, however, important to understand that many of the clubs mentioned here pay most of their players through bonus schemes which can greatly expand the range of individual pay packets. When Dunfermline won promotion to the Premier Division at the end of season 1988-89 an East End Park player who had taken part in all 39 matches of their First Division campaign would have been rewarded with a £6,000 enhancement of his salary. Most clubs in the First and Second Divisions do not pay out during the close season of around seven weeks and a player at, say, Clyde will get a £30 match fee, to be doubled when a bonus is applicable.

In the Second Division, where Porsche is not the familiar brand name in stadia car parks, we move into the realm of the hardy souls who command £15-£25 a week and even £12, in the case of Albion Rovers prior to their elevation to the First Division. Considering that someone on the payroll at Stranraer or Berwick is liable to have to put in 12 hours a week travelling to matches, often played before minuscule crowds on filthy winter days, there must be a deep suspicion that, at this level, playing (and paying to attend) football satisfies some unfathomable personal need. There is more money to be made from a junior club with a decent support in Ayrshire or Fife and even the urchins who "watch" spectators' cars around Parkhead can come away with as much as £50 apiece on big match days for refraining from the practice of demolishing windscreens.

A survey of the earnings available to players in Scotland cannot include the value of sidelines such as personal appearance fees or perks such as free cars or clothes donated by club sponsors. In addition, even full-time players do not attend at their grounds for what would be considered a normal working day but it is only fair to record that many, if not most, Premier Division players spend a very considerable amount of time performing charity work, and they have the unenviable duty of attending a relentless round of supporters' club functions.

The player who sells his skills in Europe can move into the millionaire bracket if he is able to command a handsome signing-on fee and lucrative annual earnings, Steve Archibald being an obvious example. When the transfer system is revolutionised in 1992, scouts for European clubs will become a familiar sight in Scotland, and offers of £200,000 on agreement of a contract will become commonplace for players whose skills would have been considered unremarkable by the men of two or three generations past, who saw football as their single hope of rescue from the corrosive darkness of the pits.

They could not have guessed that in the Scotland of the 1990s football would be an infinitely more productive industry than coal-mining or that the successors of the hungry, hungry boys would become the inheritors of fortunes so casually dispensed in the name of the simplest game.

CHAPTER THREE

The Gaffers

"John – you're immortal now!"
(Bill Shankly to Jock Stein, Lisbon 1967)

THERE used to be a saying in Scotland that if you wanted a footballer you only had to shout down the nearest mine shaft. The jest could have been broadened to point out that when the hoist drew its blackened, peering cargo to the surface it was equally likely to carry one of the game's future field marshals. The pits were permanent night schools of adversity which produced such graduates as Bill Shankly and Jock Stein, while the teenage Matt Busby was about to emigrate to the United States to escape underground labour when football intervened. The three most eminent Scottish managers – "the great triumvirate", to use Paddy Crerand's phrase – were men whose toughness was authentic but who enlarged rather than constricted the lives of those around them. Their background in the colliery districts matters because it unifies the success of three men of disparate temperaments whose reputation as winners was sanctified by their loathing of cheats, a characteristic which is not to be confused with a disdain for the exploitation of any ambiguity in the rules of play or in the psychology of an opponent.

Jock Stein and Bill Shankly.

If a football manager is not a despot his players will consume his authority like termites. Nothing in a dressing-room shifts faster than blame, even if it is unspoken, and the manager is compelled to be the ultimate arbiter of responsibility or his command evaporates. He knows that although his players depend upon him for advancement they can as easily lose him his livelihood. His instinctive grasp of psychology and the will to apply it to delude players and tell them the lies they need to hear, his ability to be ruthless with those who cheat him or cheat themselves, keep him apart from the dole queue no matter how firm his tactical grasp of the game may be. Busby, Shankly and Stein between them employed a diversity of management styles which proceeded from their own individualities but the common denominator was a remarkable effectiveness.

An oblique look or quizzical word of reproach from Busby could pierce like a rapier, as Bobby Charlton was able to testify years later. "Other managers used to come to discover his secret because he was a man of great influence. I watched this for a few years and then I realised it was nothing that he could teach them, it was just his personality, the way that he communicated himself. It couldn't be copied because it came from the heart. He worried about you, he encouraged you and he was also a very, very tough man, not physically getting hold of you to tell you off, but tough and very strong in the way he used his words. When I went on the field, if I was playing very badly I couldn't get him out of my mind. I was always thinking, he's not going to be pleased with this, whereas if I played well I always thought maybe I'll get the nod of approval today."

Every player who was around Old Trafford in the 1960s echoes

Charlton's opinion, a testimonial reinforced by Paddy Crerand, an individual not easily intimidated on or off the field. "You know, I never heard Matt Busby swear. You can imagine what like it is in a football dressing-room with 20 or 30 fellows and sometimes Matt would come along, maybe having heard somebody swear, and he'd walk in and I tell you the place would be like a cemetery because nobody would admit to doing anything like that. Nobody would speak."

If players at Old Trafford found it difficult to get a word out, their counterparts at Anfield had to endure the opposite problem. Bill Shankly inhabited a magnified world and was not tormented by doubts about the power of exhortation or the capacity of his coalcutter voice to transmit terse demands for utter devotion to the cause of Liverpool. In attempting to come to grips with what he did at Liverpool – what he did *to* Liverpool, more like – sports writers sooner or later tended to see him as evangelic or Messianic, terms which were in Shankly's case peculiarly accurate. There was a distinctly biblical undertone to many of his pronouncements, a definite tang of the Old Testament prophet, and it was never more evident than when he recounted the circumstances of his appointment to the manager's job at Anfield: "It was '59, early in the season, October. We were playing at Huddersfield Town and two people from this club walked down the slope, and asked if I would like to go to Liverpool. It was as blunt as that. And a few months later it came to pass." It took him three years to remake the Anfield team in his own image and carry his tribe of supporters into the promised land of the First Division where they unleashed a brand of fanaticism unprecedented in England.

The power of the crowd was hardly unknown to Jock Stein and he was to mobilise its resources on more than one occasion, but he was always much more wary than Bill Shankly about incitement of the terracing legions because he understood that Glaswegians gathering in serious numbers were not usually in need of a substantial rise in temperature to reach their flashpoint. In part, too, Jock Stein's caution reflected a secluded region of his character, an innate reticence which sat strangely with the expansive public man. Denis Law, who played under Shankly at Huddersfield, Busby at Old Trafford and Stein with Scotland, was particularly well placed to observe their divergent natures.

They all had that acid you require to be a good manager and each of them had that great knowledge of the game which you need to be truly successful. Shanks was the extrovert, wasn't he? "You are the greatest player in the world and although you think you aren't playing well, I'm telling you that you are the greatest" – that was Bill's way and while a lot of people who played for him got capped deservedly, he also got some players international appearances for their country when they really didn't merit the honour, because every team he was in charge of was the best in the world. And he had Bob Paisley as his deputy, the extrovert and the introvert.

Matt was not flamboyant like Bill but he was always in charge. There were people outside the club who might have thought that he was soft because he was quiet-spoken or gentle-mannered but his players knew better than to try and cross him because he was tough all right. The partnership at Manchester United was Matt Busby and Jimmy Murphy, an introvert and an extrovert. Jock Stein was a bit of both, which not many people would have guessed looking at him from the outside, but he could be very outgoing and he could turn in on himself, too.

Maybe he had the best of both worlds because he was certainly a very self contained man.

Sir Matt Busby at the funeral of Jock Stein, 1985.

All three men came from within 20 miles of each other in the major epicentre of the Scottish game. Busby, the oldest, was born in Orbiston, the Cannibal Island village of Alex James's youth, on 26 May 1909. Before he reached adolescence his family suffered grief of immense magnitude when his father was killed by a German sniper on the Somme and three uncles also met their deaths while serving with the Cameronian Highlanders in France. With the male side of the family virtually obliterated and the prospects for her son bleak in the recession of the twenties, Busby's mother decided that they would join her sisters and sisters-in-law who had already emigrated to the United States and they applied to be included in the migrant quota.

So great was the longing to escape the rigours of post-war depression in Britain that the quota could take as long as nine months to process and the teenage Busby began his stint as a collier, playing football for Denny Hibs in his spare time. Within a few games of his first appearance for the Stirlingshire side he was approached by a Manchester City scout who persuaded him to travel south for a trial match and the English club followed up their interest by returning to Scotland soon afterwards. On this occasion Busby was treated to

MATT BUSBY

Matt Busby, later to be knighted in recognition of his services to football in general, and Manchester United in particular, revitalised his playing career when he switched positions from inside-forward to half-back in 1931. Three years later, in the Manchester Guardian, *the distinguished cricket writer Sir Neville Cardus offered a lyrical appreciation of Busby's talents:*

"At best Busby has no superior as an attacking half-back. It is his bewildering footcraft which delights the crowds. His crouching style may not be pretty but the control is perfect, the effect akin to conjuring. His dribble is a thing of swerves, feints and deceptions. Few opponents are not hoodwinked by his phantom pass. Even the real one is nearly always masked. It skids off to the right when one could swear it was destined for the centre. Busby scorns the obvious. His passes not only look good, they sound good. There is that same healthy thwack of leather that means a scurry in the outfield in a cricket match.

"Busby is not sound in defence. A lack of speed he cloaks in shrewd positional play, so that he intercepts more often than he tackles, but it is a flaw in his armour. Some would find another in the spirit of adventure which will not be repressed even in front of his own goal . . . Sometimes he does dare-devil things that make the directors feel old before their time. But who would have him different? He laughs equally at his blunders and his triumphs, which of course is the privilege as well as the proof of a great player. He would be a certain choice for that select eleven of Footballers Who Obviously Love Football – and that is the highest praise of all."

a meal in the Glasgow restaurant owned by the Celtic manager Willie Maley, during which the City representatives suggested that he should give up the pits and play in Manchester at the handsome salary of £5 a week in winter (£4 in summer) for a season, after which, if he was still so inclined, he could cross the Atlantic.

The deal which was struck proved to be good news for Manchester City and fateful for Manchester United, but it disappointed Celtic who had also decided to sign him up only to discover that they had made their move fractionally too late. Although Busby's mother wept when she heard the news, she admitted after a subsequent visit to America that her son had saved her from a new life in a country which would not have suited her temperament. He, meanwhile, was smoothly incorporated into a distinguished City team as an inside forward but discovered his vocation in 1931 when he was switched into an attacking half back role, allowing him to apply his particular gifts of positional awareness and instinctive distribution. In 1933 City reached the 1933 FA Cup final and were beaten by Everton but the following season amidst a spectacular thunderstorm at Wembley they took the trophy with a 2-1 win over Portsmouth.

Busby remained at Maine Road until 1936 when he moved across the north-west of England to Liverpool and stayed at Anfield until the outbreak of war when his services were accepted by Army Physical Training Corps. Towards the end of the war Liverpool offered him the chance to return to Anfield on a five-year contract but the Manchester United directors invited him to apply for the vacant post of manager at Old Trafford and he was duly confirmed in the post in February 1945. The United chairman James Gibson had been particularly impressed by Busby's ideas on how football should be played as well as the man's patent integrity and he persuaded his fellow directors to ratify his choice. It was an inspired appointment although at that time Gibson was less concerned with dreams of championships than with the more pressing problem of keeping his team alive.

United had been a mediocre club for years, overshadowed by Manchester City before the war and almost destroyed by the Germans on 11 March 1941 when an air raid on the Trafford Park area reduced Old Trafford to a smoking skeleton of a stadium. When Busby arrived in September 1945, a month after he was demobilised, the club was in serious danger of capsizing completely under the weight of a debt of £75,000, including an overdraft of £15,000 which could not be extended, and it was purely through the persistent generosity of James Gibson in advancing cash that United narrowly avoided liquidation. It was a disheartening prospect and United were unable to play at Old Trafford until 1949 but even during the homeless years when they were obliged to play at Maine Road there were clear signs that Busby was likely to move more than his team from one city ground to the other and in four of the first five seasons of League football after the war United finished in second place.

Their fluent attacking habits were rewarded by an FA Cup victory in 1948 when they beat Blackpool 4–2 after a run of six victories made more decisive by the fact that United could not play a tie at their bomb-damaged home. While Old Trafford was reconstructed with painful slowness the team signalled Busby's philosophy on their way to Wembley, scoring 22 goals and conceding only eight, half of which were scored by Aston Villa in an astounding tie in Birmingham when Villa scored 14 seconds after the kick-off, only to trail 5-1 at half-time before finally succumbing to a 6-4 defeat.

As the players began to take the strain of success they attracted sizeable crowds which relieved the club of the burden of debt which had acted as a drag upon it for so long. It is not true to suggest – and Busby himself never said otherwise – that he had nothing at all to work with when he returned to Old Trafford, because there was a nucleus of promising players whose development was interrupted by the hostilities, but the 1948 Cup-winning side was a prototype of the team he would later nourish and it illustrated his talent for blending individuals into a formidable unit, often by switching them out of their usual positions to reveal unsuspected gifts, as he himself had been moved from inside-forward to creative half back when he was a City player.

Busby was also far-sighted enough to realise that a club which could breed its own talent would serve itself well in several ways apart from spending unnecessarily on the transfer market. In this he was greatly assisted by Jimmy Murphy, who had been recruited by Busby while both were at the end of their wartime service, and between them the pair overturned the custom of regarding players as a kind of underclass to be ignored by management and first-team members alike. The effect of Manchester United's methods was to attract promising boys like Bobby Charlton, who said: "When I was young I felt that if I could make it at United I could make it anywhere." The club had strong Roman Catholic traditions and the staff were helped in their scouting missions by church officials throughout the country but there was never any question of excluding other sources of potential and as the regiment of hopefuls began to accumulate they were nursed through a hierarchy of reserve teams in order to temper their talent.

United were not in the business of hoarding junior footballers. Even when young players looked the part they were scanned and then re-scrutinised for the qualities which would express Busby's concept of the game as it might be played, a triumph of grace over pedestrianism, a command to begin the dance. In his first year in charge of the reserves Murphy saw his protégés sweep to their League title with an emphatic margin to spare. He accepted Busby's congratulations and then informed him that not one of the players who had taken the title had the special ability which they sought. Gently but definitely, a new officer corps was reared to take their places.

In 1952 Manchester United took the First Division title for the first time since 1911 but although the Old Trafford support saluted the achievement to the start of a new era the club had yet to pass completely through the junction between a side of several veterans modulated by Busby's technique and a team home-bred to fulfil the manager's vision. Midway through the following season United lay at the foot of the table alongside Manchester City, but Busby and Murphy were certain of the virility of their maturing cadets, an assurance which was first demonstrated in a friendly at Kilmarnock. Half a dozen youngsters – Jackie Blanchflower, Eddie Colman, Duncan Edwards, Wilf McGuinness, David Pegg and Jeff Whitefoot – were drafted into the team. The result of a 3-0 victory and Busby experienced the satisfaction of a man who has glimpsed the future momentarily unravel in front of him.

In 1956 United won the championship again, this time finishing 11 points ahead of Blackpool and Wolves and the following season the distance between them and the trailing pack was almost as wide

February 1958. The wreckage of the Manchester United plane is scattered across Munich airport and with it the promise of the Busby Babes.

with Tottenham and Preston nine points adrift. The intimidating virtuosity to be found at Old Trafford was emphasised when they came tantalisingly close to capturing the League and Cup double for the first time in the 20th century with an appearance at Wembley against Aston Villa but they lost the final in literally painful circumstances when McParland of Villa charged Ray Wood in the United goal and fractured Wood's cheekbone. Having accounted for the goalkeeper, McParland scored two goals to give Aston Villa a record seventh Cup win with a 2-1 victory.

United returned to Wembley a year later and lost once more, this time to Bolton, but even if Manchester United had taken the trophy home the silverware would have reflected a requiem rather than a celebration. Half of the 1957 Cup final team had been killed in the Munich air disaster three months before, a catastrophe which very nearly claimed Busby. The United party was on its way home from a famous result, a 3-3 draw with Red Star Belgrade in Yugoslavia which put them into the semi-finals of the European Cup for the second year in succession. Their plane had made a refuelling stop in Germany but although the landing was uneventful enough on a runway treacherously smeared with ice and slush the pilots were unable to haul the aircraft back into the air. Two abortive attempts were made before the fatal third, when the plane lost power beyond the point of no return, ploughed on through the perimeter fence and smashed into a house beyond.

Busby realised that something was wrong a fraction of a second before the fuselage began to shred under the impact of the collisions and he raised both hands to protect his face just as he lost consciousness, to be thrown out into the snow still strapped to his seat. The United right-back Bill Foulkes had also been thrown clear without serious injury; he walked back towards the stricken aircraft and found his manager feebly attempting to push himself off the ground. Harry Gregg was on hand and it appeared to Foulkes and the goalkeeper that Busby was unlikely to survive. They massaged him in an attempt to keep his circulation in action until help arrived and he was taken to the Rechts der Isar Hospital in Munich, critically ill with a crushed chest and broken foot.

Twenty survived of the 43 on board the flight. Eight players, eight journalists, two aircrew and two other passengers were killed and in the span of a few seconds the dazzling Manchester United team which Busby had envisaged and shaped, and which was still on the rising curve of its development, had been destroyed. For days the manager hovered on the verge of death until particle by particle the tangible strength of his spirit pulled him back into life. It was more than a month before he could be told of the deaths of his young men – Byrne, Bent, Colman, Jones, Edwards, Pegg, Taylor and Whelan – or that he had lost confederates like Walter Crickmer, the club secretary, trainer Tom Curry or Bert Whalley, the team coach.

Whalley had been sitting in the next seat to Busby when the crash occurred and he occupied the place normally filled by Jimmy Murphy who had been with the Welsh international team at a World Cup qualifying match with Israel in Cardiff. The loss of so many friends, colleagues and pupils would have consumed the resilience of any lesser man but Busby, whose childhood had been disfigured by bereavement, possessed internal resources of a transcendent quality which enabled him eventually to resume his career at Old Trafford. The trauma of Munich was never to leave him, however, and when was in his late seventies he conceded that the memory was as fresh in his thought as it had been almost 30 years earlier.

> It was such a terrible event that it wanted a lot of getting over and I took a long time to do that. I still recount the situation periodically and I remember that when we returned to playing in Europe I was taking the team overland and by ship and sea and the more I thought about it the more I knew it couldn't go on. I said to myself: "Matt, you'll have to face this sometime, you'll have to do it. You can't have these lads travelling all day one way and then all the next back again." So I decided I'd take a flight and I went to Rotterdam alone, to test myself, to see if I was able to fly. I went to Rotterdam and stayed the night and after I got over this terrible ordeal and flew back, I felt I knew that we had to start travelling by air again. And, of course, we did from that day on.

If there was an abiding irony about the Munich disaster it was the fact that the crash occurred on the team's return from a fixture in the infant European Cup, a tournament which had not earned the approval of the Football League. The League management warned United not to take part with the vague threat of punitive consequences if they persisted, but with the backing of his chairman, Harold Hardman, Busby insisted that international club football could not be ignored and the early and invaluable experience United accumulated on their trips abroad would in all probability have carried the team on to considerable success at this level had the air crash not intervened.

In 1960 a poignant insight into the mixture of profound regret and sustained vision which occupied Busby's energies was revealed when he wrote in the *International Football Book*:

Busby emerges from hospital in Munich.

> I should like to see the honours in England won by a pure footballing side, the sort of team that concentrates on ball skills above all else. Such a team could inspire the other ninety-one clubs. But for the air disaster I like to feel that others would now be copying United to the benefit of the whole League.

The ultimate triumph – Matt Busby, flanked by Paddy Crerand and George Best after the 1968 European Cup final victory over Benfica.

Along with Bill Nicholson of Tottenham Hotspur, Matt Busby remained faithful to his creed and was justified by the rise of a new Manchester United side whose swashbuckling play was one of the principal gratifications to be had from English football throughout the 1960s, a decade which saw them win two League titles, finish as League runners-up, capture the FA Cup in 1963 and reach five consecutive semi-finals. And there was, perhaps a decade after it might first have been installed at Old Trafford, the European Cup in 1968.

The players who survived the Munich disaster had been borne on a tide of national sympathy to the FA Cup final of 1958 but their achievement in reaching Wembley had been in many ways a trick of the light. In reality the team was too shattered to offer significant resistance to Bolton and one effect of their 2-0 defeat was a sense of anticlimax, a feeling that important business had somehow been left unfinished. Ten years later, the European Cup at last offered an opportunity for the circle to be completed although it seemed that once again United's ambition had foundered on the rocks of the semi-finals. When Real went 3-1 ahead in the return leg at the San Bernabeu Stadium there were few in the crowd who would have bet folding money against the Spanish champions. But goals by Sadler and Foulkes put United through to face Benfica in a final to be played at Wembley in what was to all intents a home game for Busby's side.

Like Bolton ten years earlier the Portuguese players were entitled to a measure of sympathy because they were well aware of the size of the emotional investment which was carried by their opponents. Still, the Portuguese were also popular because in Eusebio they possessed one of the dazzling talents of the era and who had impressed everyone who saw him play when the World Cup finals had been staged in England two years previously. United, meanwhile, were without Denis Law who watched the match from the hospital bed to which he was confined after an operation to remove cartilage from a degenerating right knee. It was a cruel deprivation for a player who should have been able to savour the crowning moment of a dazzling career.

In the event, United almost stumbled in front of the tape when Charlton's opening goal was cancelled out ten minutes from time by Graca's header and in the final three minutes Eusebio waltzed through the defence to deliver two venomous shots which were breathtakingly parried by Stepney. From the way both teams slumped exhausted on to the baize turf at the end of 90 minutes it appeared that neither had the strength to fight on but when the half hour of extra play began, it was United who turned out to have unsuspected resources of morale and stamina. A dribble and shot from Best, a Kidd header and a glanced head flick by Charlton put the tie out of Benfica's reach although Stepney was required to make one further acrobatic save before the trophy was confirmed as United property.

United reached the semi-finals again the following year and were desperately unlucky to have a Law goal disallowed by a referee who did not see that it had crossed the line against AC Milan in the second leg at Old Trafford. The Italians hung on to achieve a 2-1 victory and they beat Ajax Amsterdam 4-1 in the final in Madrid while United were left to nurse their belief that they would in all probability have defended their prize successfully.

Busby announced his retirement eight months after the defeat by AC Milan and, as if the vital supply of inspiration had been switched off, Manchester United began a slow decline as a footballing power. He remained as general manager and one of his former Busby Babes, Wilf McGuinness, was appointed to succeed him at the age of 32. The father figure of football could not be replaced by an untried man of half his age and McGuinness was relieved of his post after 18 months. His successor, the self-absorbed Irishman Frank O'Farrell, lasted only the same length of time. There were many who believed that Busby's physical presence at Old Trafford inhibited men of lesser confidence and this cannot be refuted, but he was aware of the problem and attempted to solve it by inviting Jock Stein to take over at Old Trafford. Although Stein was initially keen – and the imagination can only speculate what the pair might have achieved together – the Celtic manager was bound by deeply rooted ties which caused him to remain in Scotland and deprived Manchester United of possibly the only other figure who could have inspired players to joyful zeniths as Busby had done.

With hindsight it is clear that Busby's apogee arrived on that balmy May evening at Wembley in 1968. From the grief of his childhood and the void of the pits he had fashioned an integrity and resolve which carried him through the lacerating trauma of Munich. To recreate Manchester United as a team devoid of caution and replete with adventure should have been inconceivable, but he did it and the European Cup was his reward. When he was knighted for his services to football there were those in Scotland who felt that Jock Stein, as the first British manager to win the trophy, had been slighted by the Establishment, but in truth the honour accorded to Busby was recognition of a life lived to fulfilment long after the point when it might have given way to understandable despair or demoralisation.

Bob Shankly.

His achievement was admirably summarised by Bobby Charlton when he said, soon after Sir Matt's 75th birthday:

He had a vision of what Manchester United should be, which is one of the great clubs of the world, and they are the most attractive team in the world whether or not they are top of the League. What he set out for United to be communicated itself to the players and it communicated itself to the people who followed the club. Nobody at Old Trafford underestimates his contribution to Manchester United. He's in the brickwork.

★   ★   ★

When Tommy Docherty made his first international appearance for Scotland against Wales in 1952 he received a telegram from Bill Shankly – a man he had never met – which read: "You're now the best wing half in the world and when you pull the Scottish jersey over your head the lion will grow twice the size it is on the jersey. Just run about – the jersey will take care of the rest."

That message was vintage Shankly. His capacity for inspiration frequently provoked the cliché that he was larger than life and so he was, but what was infinitely more important was his capacity to remake life to seem larger to others. Perhaps he needed greater space than most people because he was brought up in a family with ten children, five boys and five girls, in the Ayrshire village of Glenbuck just inside the county boundary with Lanarkshire. Glenbuck had a population of around 700 in 1913 when Shankly was born, and even then it was in decline as it became increasingly difficult to work good quality coal from the local mines. It is commonly said that Shankly's father was a miner but, in fact, John Shankly began as a postman before working for the rest of his life as a bespoke tailor, not that he was overburdened with commissions in a village where alterations to clothes were more economic for customers and tailor alike.

Bill Shankly did serve his time as a collier working at a nearby pit top where he had to empty loaded trucks and sort out the stones from the coal, earning extra money on Sunday by unloading wagons of dross at sixpence a ton. By his own account he was capable of shifting two wagons of ten tons each while working alone but within six months he was sent to a new loading job at the pit bottom where he tasted for the first time the fetid atmosphere of a badly ventilated shaft.

In his autobiography he wrote, using the clipped sentences in which he habitually spoke: "We were filthy most of the time and never really clean. It was unbelievable how we survived. You could not clean all the parts of your body properly. Going home to wash in a tub was the biggest thing. The first time I was in a bath was when I was 15." After two years underground Shankly found himself redundant when the pit closed along with most of its neighbours, forcing the Glenbuck men to commute to whatever mines were still being worked in the vicinity. He went on the dole but he was not obliged to live on its pittance for more than a few months before he was signed by Carlisle United, the first fulfilment of the destiny which he believed awaited him.

Football appears literally to have been in the blood of his lineage. On his mother's side his uncle Bob played for Rangers and Portsmouth, where he became chairman of the club, and his uncle William played for Preston and Carlisle, where he was made a director. Alec, the eldest

Shankly boy, played for Ayr United but his career was truncated by the First World War, when he served with the Royal Highland Fusiliers while Jimmy, four years younger, was a centre-forward signed by Carlisle and transferred to Sheffield United for what was then a sizeable fee of £1,000 before moving to Southend United. The middle brother was John, who went to Portsmouth and then Luton where he was the club's leading goalscorer until a strained heart muscle limited his prospects, although he returned to Scotland to play for Alloa before reversing the customary footballer's route by going down the pits.

And then there was Bob Shankly. He played for Falkirk for 17 years and then he became manager of the club, where he achieved substantial gains which for a long time ranked him as the most successful of the brothers. He also guided Dundee to a League championship as well as a European Cup semi-final in 1963, a fact which permits Dundee to rank alongside Glasgow as the only two cities in Britain which have provided two semi-finalists in the champions tournament. Bob subsequently went on to manage Hibernian before making his final move to Stirling Albion where he became general manager and a director. Bob Shankly's period at Stirling overlapped with Bill's tenure with Liverpool thus giving rise to the curious circumstance of one Shankly at Annfield and the other at Anfield.

Bill Shankly in 1937.

Bill Shankly started his playing career at Carlisle under the supervision of the trainer Tommy Curry, who was to lose his life in the Munich disaster, and he was nursed into the team by the manager Tom Hampson whose ministrations had the effect of shaping the player into a prospect which attracted the attention of scouts from Preston, a club which had fallen on lean times. After initial hesitation he moved to Deepdale in 1933, still a teenager, to fill the right-half berth. He was on Preston's books for a total of 16 years and, as he pointed out from time to time, the team was promoted to the First Division in his first season at Deepdale and relegated in 1949 when he left. The summit of his playing days was reached in 1937 and 1938 when Preston reached the FA Cup final in successive years, beaten 3-1 by Sunderland on the first occasion but 1-0 winners with a George Mutch penalty kick in extra time against Huddersfield the following season.

Shankly had also played at Wembley two weeks before the Huddersfield match, when he made his debut for Scotland against England. He required no motivation for the collision beyond what he had already absorbed at primary school in Glenbuck, as he related in his autobiography:

Bill Shankly, lord of the Liverpool dance, 1964.

> At school we were brought up on tales of Bruce, Wallace and Burns. They were the greatest. Our village was the greatest. Our school was the greatest. And the English were vilified. We thought England was our enemy and the English were poison.
>
> Later on, when I became an international footballer, I was like all Scots when confronted by England, the Auld Enemy. We tend to revert to being savages for ninety minutes on those occasions. We become Wallace and Bruce and Sir James Douglas – the Black Douglas – when we put on the blue jersey. I've always wanted to win every game but when I played for Scotland against England the pride was there. Passion was always there when I played, but the pride was unbelievable.

Scotland won 1-0 on that occasion with a goal from the exuberant Hearts forward Tommy Walker, although Shankly was the victim of a vicious tackle by the England hard man Wilf Copping whose lunge

BILL SHANKLY

"Liverpool was made for me and I was made for Liverpool."

"I am a working man and I went amongst my own kind."

"Anfield is my memorial."

"If I was harsh with people, then those people deserved it."

"Above all I would like to be remembered as a man who was selfless, who strived and worried so that others could share the glory and who built up a family of people who could hold their heads high and say: 'We're Liverpool.' "

"I think it's more than fanaticism. It's a religion with them. The thousands who come here to worship . . . it's a sort of shrine."
(On the Liverpool supporters)

"Aye, Everton."
(To the barber who asked him "Anything off the top?")

burst the Scot's stocking and inflicted a cut leg. Next time he played against England, at Hampden Park, the result was less happy and the winning goal in a 2-1 victory for the visitors was scored when Stanley Matthews lobbed the ball over Shankly's head in front of goal: "Tommy Lawton was at the near post and as he smashed his shot I heard him say, 'Get in, you so-and-so.' I could hear the sound of the rain swishing off the net as the ball hit it. It was like a lump of cement in the stomach. If I'd had a gun I would have shot him. Terrible it was."

A man who could hear raindrops fall from the net at a packed Hampden was surely possessed of acute faculties and the five caps he won by 1939 would certainly have been supplemented but for the outbreak of the Second World War, in which he served in the RAF. However, he was able to guest for Partick Thistle who paid for him to have an operation to repair his right knee, damaged while he was playing with Preston. He returned to Deepdale after his demob and in 1949 he began his managerial career as he had begun his senior professional days, at Carlisle.

Shankly had already formulated much of his management philosophy and in judging whether a player was good enough for a team of his he looked for equal measures of ability and courage as well as stamina, resolve and will to win. He took a course which qualified him as a masseur and he relentlessly acquired information about sports injuries so that he could assess the fitness of his players. In practice, he might ignore players who were injured, or else badger them relentlessly while they lay on the treatment table in an attempt to coerce them into an agreement that their disability was no obstacle to putting in a full 90 minutes. There was a ritual quality to these bargaining sessions which Emlyn Hughes, his captain at Liverpool, cherished afterwards.

"I had a lot of problems with my ankles and I would go in on a Sunday morning with an ankle blown up like a football, all red, yellow and green, and Bob Paisley would strap it up, give me hot and cold baths, ultrasonic treatment and all the rest. Then Shanks would open the door and you'd see a little wisp of hair come round the corner. Then he would come back in, sidle into the room, look at the ultrasonic machine, touch this, touch that and eventually he'd end up at the end of your bed and it would start, like this:

Shanks: How is it?
Hughes: Bit sore, boss, but it's not too bad.
Shanks: Is it as bad as when you did it?
Hughes: Well, I only did it yesterday afternoon, boss.
Shanks: I know, but you've had a night's sleep on it. Is it better?
Hughes: Not a lot.
Shanks: Do you think you can walk on it?
Hughes: I think I could walk on it, boss.
Shanks: Well, if you can walk on it you could maybe jog on it?
Hughes: Yes, maybe I could jog on it.
Shanks: Well, if you could jog on it, maybe you could do some training.

"And he would get you to say things you didn't want to say and you'd have to be put in a cart to get to training. This was because he never had a day's illness, he didn't smoke, didn't drink and he used to do all the training himself. I remember when we got in at the end of training and he walked in and said: 'You know something, boys – when I die I want to be the fittest man ever to die.' It was magnificent stuff."

Shankly amidst familiar scenes as the Cup returns to Liverpool.

Between Carlisle and Liverpool he honed his techniques at Workington, Grimsby Town and Huddersfield. When he at last arrived at Liverpool the club was in a depressed state, a league behind their confident city rivals and near neighbours Everton. Shankly first addressed the backroom staff and told them they could stay, providing they gave him loyalty. It was a far-sighted gesture because his audience on that first occasion included Bob Paisley and Joe Fagan, both of whom would ultimately succeed him in the manager's chair.

Most of the players were less fortunate and within a month he had compiled a list of two dozen players he felt were not up to the standards he was about to set and none of them remained a year after his arrival. Building a new team turned out to be vastly harder than discarding the old one because the club directors had got out of the way of spending the kind of cash which was necessary to acquire top-class players. One chance was missed early when Shankly wanted to buy Jack Charlton from Leeds United and offered £15,000 for him. Leeds held out for more but although the difference in the two clubs' estimation was not large, there was no increase in the offer from Liverpool. Leeds were not then the power they were to become under Don Revie and Shankly often reflected later that if he had succeeded in taking Charlton from Elland Road to Anfield he would have removed the bedrock of Revie's subsequent revival of United.

In August 1960 he made several significant changes, buying Gordon Milne from Preston for £12,000 and giving the transfer-listed Gerry

The Kop in full cry, exalted and exhorted by Shankly.

BILL SHANKLY

"The first time I met him I had come down to watch a reserve team match at Old Trafford. I pulled my car into the car park and I was about to switch the engine off and get out when suddenly somebody was sitting next to me. I turned round and it was Bill Shankly. And straightaway he went: 'Bobby, Bobby! Everton – have you found out what they've done? They've bought this player that can't play! And they still think they're going to beat Liverpool.' And he just went into this tirade about Everton. He also had a go at Jock Stein about the match Celtic had played against Liverpool in the Cup Winners' Cup. He accused Jock Stein of polishing the pitch. I've never, ever heard anyone so fanatical on the game."
(Bobby Charlton)

"He was always boasting his own club. He would say: 'Matt, we played Sheffield Wednesday – by God, they played well! Oh, they're a great team, just great.' And I'd say: 'Bill, how did your lads finish then?' Then he'd tell you: 'Oh, we won 5-1.' It was always this – they're great and oh, we won. He was some man for lifting people up."
(Sir Matt Busby)

"He signed Alec Lindsay, who was a left back, from Bury and the lad had two years in the reserves at Anfield until, of course, the day came for his debut. Shanks said to him: 'Now look, Alec, when you get the ball I want you to beat a couple of men and smash it into the back of the net just the same way as you did at Bury Football Club.' Alec Lindsay says: 'But boss that wasn't me, it was Bobby Kerr.' So Shanks turns to Bob Paisley and says: 'Christ, Bob, we've signed the wrong player!' "
(Tommy Docherty)

"He wanted to buy a certain player for what was a fortune at the time but the lad wanted to go to another club. The guy did the right thing by phoning Shanks to tell him: 'Sorry, Mr Shankly, but I've decided to join someone else.' Shanks said: 'Well, you never could play anyway,' and put the phone down on him. And that was absolutely typical of Bill. The fellow was a genius when he might have gone

Byrne his chance in the first team, moving Ronnie Moran from left to right back to accommodate him. There were other buys like Kevin Lewis and Tommy Leishman but the season ended in disappointment for the Reds' supporters when the team missed promotion from the Second Division by finishing third behind Alf Ramsey's Ipswich and Sheffield United. The following season was to be much more satisfying for the disaffected followers.

Shankly was scrutinising the sports pages of the *Sunday Post* when his attention was seized by a headline which told him that Ian St John wanted to leave Motherwell. He pounced instantly, getting his man ahead of Newcastle United for a fee of £37,500. It was Liverpool's record transfer fee and part of it was repaid the following week when he played against Everton in the Liverpool Senior Cup. Everton won 4-3 but St John's hat-trick provided the Liverpool goals. Next, Shankly went after the mighty Dundee United centre half Ron Yeats and secured him for £30,000, a bargain as subsequent events were to prove. When Yeats – six feet two inches and 200 lbs – was paraded at Anfield on his arrival Shankly made the assembled sports writers and photographers walk around the player and when he referred to Yeats as the Red Colossus, the name stuck.

The two Scottish signings were of vast importance to the revival of Liverpool, not only strengthening the team massively but creating the beginnings of an excitement about the club and its supporters which Shankly strove relentlessly to heighten. The team made a barnstorming start and when Liverpool won promotion to the First Division on 21 April 1962 the terracings resounded to the chanting from the Kop which had become a distinctive feature of matches at Anfield. The force of Shankly's personality was manifest in the team's army of supporters, who were to become almost as potent as their heroes as Liverpool's new momentum gathered power.

Shankly continued to recast the side while it adjusted to the more rigorous demands of competition in the top league and when Jimmy Furnell hit a patch of uncertain form he was replaced in goal by Tommy Lawrence. Then, with his usual alertness he noticed that Willie Stevenson, the former Rangers half back, who had emigrated to Australia earlier in the year, was back in the country. Stevenson was duly signed and increased the Scottish contingent at Anfield to four. It was now common for Liverpool players to be capped and with seven or eight internationalists regularly in the side, including Tommy Lawrence, who vindicated Shankly's judgment with three appearances for Scotland, the team began to appear increasingly formidable. The apparently miraculous powers of restoration possessed by the restless, striving man from Glenbuck were consummated when the team seized the championship less than two years after promotion from the Second Division.

At this point Shankly's achievements took on the aura of a phenomenon. Television conveyed the immense enthusiasm, the extravagant fanaticism of the Liverpool support and made it a familiar part of a revitalised Britain so that for a spell Anfield distilled and reflected the mood of a country in the grip of change and youthful excitement. Tuneful energy poured out of the city and the supporters on the Kop perfectly distilled the atmosphere of the times when they adopted the Gerry and the Pacemakers anthem, *You'll Never Walk Alone*, and made it their theme, to be imitated throughout Britain, the plain man's plain song.

It was to be heard at Wembley the following season. The title had been removed to Old Trafford by Manchester United, who had squeezed past Leeds United on goal average, and it was Leeds who desperately desired to soothe their disappointment with a victory over Liverpool in the FA Cup final. While the Scousers battered the national stadium with their racket the game itself developed into a head to head battle between the two best defences in the First Division. Five minutes into the match Leeds' Bobby Collins collided with Gerry Byrne and broke the Liverpool player's collar bone, a double misfortune because no substitutes were then allowed. However, Byrne earned himself a permanent place in Shankly's heart by asking to be allowed to play on after treatment. His capacity to endure pain was severely tested in a contest which produced no goals by the end of normal time but he fashioned the breakthrough three minutes into the extra time period when he crossed for Roger Hunt to score the opening goal.

The red banners cascaded over the terracings only to be replaced by the white of Leeds when Billy Bremner shot the equaliser from a Charlton header. It was left to Ian St John to give Liverpool the Cup for the first time in 72 years when he advanced to meet a sweeping cross from Callaghan. The diminutive Scottish striker had to swivel in mid-air to reach the ball as it arrived at an awkward height but he met it with a forceful header which swept gloriously into the net in the finest moment of St John's career.

Just as a Cup victory in 1963 signalled a golden era for Manchester United so, in Shankly's view, the Wembley defeat of Leeds United heralded the future dominance of Liverpool. Shankly relieved Busby of the championship in 1966, the same season that the Reds reached the final of the European Cup Winners' Cup to meet Borussia Dortmund on a soaking night at Hampden Park. It could have been the occasion for a Scottish manager to win a European trophy on Scottish soil for the first time, but although Liverpool scored two of the game's three goals, Yeats put one of them past his own goalkeeper.

Liverpool continued to learn the European ropes and in 1967 they were handed a thrashing by the emergent Ajax Amsterdam, beaten 5-1 in a match played in a fog so thick that Shankly was able to walk, unnoticed by the referee or linesmen, on to the pitch while play was in progress to deliver instructions to Willie Stevenson and Geoff Strong. Despite the margin of the defeat, Shankly told his players they could still get through at Anfield. His former Preston colleague Tom Finney would not have been surprised to hear his prognosis. When Finney played his first game at Deepdale he was greatly encouraged by Shankly's urgings. "Keep fighting! We can do it yet," the Scot shouted at him with two minutes left to play. Preston were losing by four goals at the time.

Liverpool kept fighting, earning the gratitude of a deprived city by walking on long after the Beatles had walked out, and after he had overseen a period of transition Shankly guided the team to the double of the League championship and a European trophy when Borussia Moenchengladbach were defeated 3-2 on aggregate in a two-leg final for the UEFA Cup in May 1973.

There was one more honour left for Shankly, when Liverpool won the FA Cup in 1974, beating Newcastle United 3-0, but those who watched him in the aftermath of the victory realised that something had gone out of him. Shankly believed he was drained by the relentless demands of football and decided that he should retire. When he told his wife Nessie, she replied: "Are you sure you want to do that?"

Nessie knew him better than he knew himself. He stunned Liverpool,

to Anfield and next day he couldn't play at all."
(*Bobby Robson*)

"I was 18 when he signed me and I had grass growing out of my ears. We stopped at traffic lights in the road between Preston and Liverpool when a car smashes into us from behind. Shanks storms out and gives the driver: 'Hey, whit ye daein?' Then we drive on and a police car with the siren going jams us into the kerb. The policeman walks over to the front of the car and tells Shanks that he has no back light and Shanks tells him that some idiot had smashed it down the road and he couldn't very well sit at the traffic lights all night, could he? The policeman says: 'Well, you can't drive without a rear light.'

"Shanks leans out and says: 'How d'ye mean I cannae drive? I've got England's next captain alongside me.' I'm looking round to see if he'd sneaked Bobby Moore in somewhere and the policeman asks him: 'What are you on about?' Shanks says: 'I've just signed England's next captain. He's called Emlyn Hughes and it may sound Welsh but he's English and I'm driving him to Liverpool because that's his new home.' The policeman looks at me – 18 years of age – and puts his book away because obviously thinks Shanks is a lunatic. But as it happens he was right because I was fortunate enough to go on and play for England. With him you were always the best in the world even if you didn't know it yourself."
(*Emlyn Hughes*)

BILL SHANKLY

"My wife is not interested in football whatsoever, not the least bit interested, but after a game she would come down and maybe a few of the lads and their wives would go for a meal. One night we were playing in the European Cup at Old Trafford and Bill Shankly came over to talk to me and then my wife arrived and I introduced her. Suddenly I saw Jock Stein in the corner and I had to talk to him so I excused myself for a moment. It turned out to be ten minutes before I got back and Bill says: 'Great wife you've got, Pat – she knows the game inside out.' I thought, I don't believe this, and when he went away I said: 'Pam, what did you say to Bill Shankly?' She said: 'Two words – yes and no.' I told her: 'Well, you must have said them at the right time because he's telling everybody you're an expert on football now.'"

(Pat Crerand)

club and city, by announcing his decision to quit the game in July 1974 and he stuck to his intention despite considerable inducements by the Anfield board and impassioned pleas from supporters, some of whom were actually distraught at the thought of his going. He was adamant that after 40 years in the game he needed to retire but in reality he probably only required a thorough rest, an extended holiday perhaps. He left satisfied that he had ensured his succession through Bob Paisley, as indeed he had, but inevitably he began to sense his old deep hunger to be involved in the game, only to discover that he was superfluous to Liverpool's needs. Lack of tact on both sides created a needless schism between man and club, although the supporters never lost a particle of their reverence and affection for him.

His family, as always, was supportive but Shankly was rootless and lonely outside his domestic confines, and although he offered his help free to any club looking for guidance, there was only one team he truly wanted to steer to new heights. In a sense he did so with Liverpool. In nine years under Bob Paisley 13 trophies were displayed at the Anfield boardroom; three European Cups, six championships, three Milk Cups and the UEFA Cup. Paisley supervised a period of unprecedented success which surpassed Shankly's accumulation of titles but it does not diminish his successor's achievement to say that without Shankly it would not have been possible to achieve – perhaps even imagine – such a remarkable and prolonged ascendancy in both the domestic and European arenas. On one level he was a truly remarkable football manager and on another he was a shaman, capable of exalting the ordinary aspirations of ordinary people, capable of making dreams realisable and reality dreamlike.

A desire to expand the mundane circumstances of everyday life united him with the people of Liverpool. They idolised him because he encouraged them to venerate themselves and, strangely for a man of such Calvinist temperament, he also released what ultimately appeared as a tendency to self-pity in the Mediterranean fashion, so that the scenes of extravagant public grief which followed the Hillsborough disaster were regarded with perplexity by those who had experienced the catastrophes of Munich, Ibrox or Bradford, none of which saw football grounds turned into shrines as Anfield was in May 1989.

He regretted that he had never guided Liverpool to a European Cup but when the team had its name inscribed on the trophy after beating the unfortunate Borussia Moenchengladbach in Rome in 1977 there were many who felt he had played a tangible part in the triumph, a perception shared by Emlyn Hughes when he said: "When we won the European Cup I was fortunate enough to be captain of the club and as I walked up the steps to collect the trophy I was thinking that it was really Shanks who won the cup because Shanks made Liverpool a club. He made them a team, he gave the fans the chance to say, 'Hey, that's my team. That's what I want.' I count myself so fortunate to have met Shanks, and to have 13 years of my life under him is a magnificent thing."

When he died on 29 September 1981, *The Times* said of him:

His strength of character, based always on the techniques and reading of the game and backed by the roar of the Kop, forged a sledgehammer rather than a rapier. Some rush in into the limelight, some back into it. Shankly tramped into it and showed little surprise when he was treated like a god.

The most eloquent tribute, however, was paid by Ian St John, one of six former Liverpool players chosen to carry his coffin. In his eulogy, St John said: "Shanks was capable of exaggerating any situation to get the best out of his players – it is impossible to exaggerate his loss."

★ ★ ★

On 9 September 1985, the day before Scotland met Wales at Ninian Park to decide which team would maintain a chance of reaching the World Cup finals in Mexico the following summer, Jock Stein betrayed what appeared to be an entirely uncharacteristic fear of the possibility of defeat. Speaking in an interview for the BBC Radio 2 evening sports bulletin he said: "This is the last game of the qualifying season as far as we're concerned and I think that you could say that it is the most important because the prize is big for a win, but the other thing – you're just frightened to think of it."

Jock Stein was not a man who frightened easily and it appeared that he was contradicting himself when he concluded the interview with the assertion that, all things being equal, Scotland would get the result needed to carry the country on towards Mexico but, as was so often the case with this complex and intense personality, there was a subtext to his words, which revealed the nature of "the other thing" which so alarmed him. It emerged the following afternoon in the final answer of another BBC interview which turned out to be the last he would ever give. Asked what it would mean to him if the game failed to go Scotland's way, he replied:

Jock Stein as an Albion Rovers player.

> The biggest thing that wouldn't work for me would be if it was a game that brought a bit of bad behaviour into the crowd and brought football again under the microscope of people who are trying to stop the game, because we've got Prime Ministers and Sports Ministers and other Ministers who are all trying to tell us how we should administer the game. They know nothing about the game and maybe they don't know so much about politics either, but they're trying to run football and most of them don't go to a football match.
>
> If they had their way they would kill football and it's only good games of football such as we might have tonight that will keep the sport alive. Another bad game, another bad scene, another bad time would offer certain people the opportunity to hit the game of football – and that's not good.

A few hours later Scotland got the result which carried them to a play-off with Australia for the last remaining place in the Mexican finals when they drew 1-1 in a match of almost unbearable tension and, as their manager had hoped, there were no unseemly incidents in a capacity crowd of 39,500, mostly composed of Scots despite the Welsh FA's inevitably futile attempts to restrain the northward flow of precious tickets. But Scottish football suffered an immeasurable loss at the very moment of triumph when Jock Stein stumbled as he walked towards the tunnel at the final whistle, the victim of a massive heart attack which quickly proved fatal, and when word of his death rippled out to the tartan-clad supporters celebrating in the Cardiff bars the reaction was touchingly poignant. Drink was taken but the mood was sober, often reverent. To observe the introspective demeanour of supporters, who had earlier in the evening demonstrated their claim to be the most raucously committed in football, was to be vouchsafed something of Stein's impressive ability to communicate his

Stein in the mid-1950s as Celtic reserve coach.

Recalled from obscurity in Wales, Stein's playing career revived unexpectedly.

Jock and Jean Stein with the Scottish Cup, 1954.

measured values to a people with a wayward tendency to distort their own perspectives on the world.

In the aftermath of his death a great deal was written and spoken about his indifferent health during the summer of 1985 and it was apparent to all who were familiar with him that in the days before the Welsh game he was out of condition and obviously more tense than on such occasions in the past. This is not to reflect with hindsight; there had been comment at the team hotel in Bristol that the manager was unusually pallid and the subject was raised with him at least twice, but he brushed it aside as inconsequential.

In conversation, however, he frequently returned to the fear which had haunted him for three months, but it was not an apprehension of defeat which troubled him. In fact, he was preoccupied with the consequences of the riot at the European Cup final in Brussels in which 39 Juventus supporters were crushed to death as Liverpool fans surged into them on the terracings before the match.

Tolerance of disorder in British football crowds had evaporated at a stroke and although the expulsion of English clubs from European competition had not extended to Scotland – or to Wales, for that matter – Stein was acutely aware that the slightest infraction was likely to have malign consequences for the game north of the border. Hence his instruction to his assistant, Alex Ferguson, to send the Scottish players to applaud their supporters at the final whistle and his insistence that the Scots should be seen to behave with dignity – he placed vehement emphasis on the word – on and off the field, no matter how the Ninian Park contest resolved itself.

There were no untoward incidents involving either the jubilant Scots or the disheartened Welsh, who also had a claim on his affections. The day before he died he had been approached by a Welsh radio reporter who asked if Stein would care to give an interview about his days in Llanelly (as the town was formerly known) and although demands upon his attention were particularly fierce and time was scarce, he made himself available willingly to recollect the days in Wales when he first became a full-time footballer.

Prior to his move to Llanelly in the summer of 1950 Stein's life was typical of the Lanarkshire tableau. He was born on 5 October 1922 in Burnbank, a mining district of Hamilton, and as the son of a miner he was practically predestined to make his way through school to the age of 14 and then take his turn in the pithead queue. His mother Jane was not keen for him to subordinate himself to such a confined destiny and perhaps to humour her he worked first in a local carpet factory, but in the space of a few months he had taken a job underground.

Mrs Stein's reluctance to see her only son take his place at the coal-face was understandable. Fires, explosions and gassing incidents were commonplace and her husband George had been exposed to concentrations of gas which badly affected his health. There had been death in the house too often when one of the three Stein girls died at the age of 15 and the misfortune was compounded when George Stein suffered a stroke which meant that his son became the family's principal earner while he was still a teenager. Football was the usual solace of the industrial working man and when the youthful Stein gravitated towards the game he was practically bound to spend time with Blantyre Victoria, where his father had been on the club committee.

As a tall player without a notable turn of speed his niche was in central defence and before long, in 1942, he was offered a trial with

The first triumph – Jock Stein congratulates his Dunfermline players after their win in the 1961 Scottish Cup final replay.

Albion Rovers. The opposition turned out to be Celtic and the Parkhead team ran up an easy 3-0 lead while Stein found himself marooned by the speed of the game, but in the second half he came to grips with his job and the Rovers fought back to leave the field with a very satisfactory 4-4 draw. He played in another two trials which ended in emphatic defeats, 4-1 to Hibernian and 7-2 to Falkirk, so that at the end of his three-match test period he had operated in the centre of a defence which had conceded an average of five goals a game. But the Coatbridge manager Webber Lees was nevertheless prepared to offer him a contract. Stein displayed the indifference to blandishments which was to characterise his later career and hung back in the hope that he might attract a more rewarding proposal from some other quarter but he had the wit to see that none was likely and within a couple of weeks he signed for Albion Rovers.

Unlike Shankly, he was not consumed by the idea that in football lay his destiny and he was often to remark that its most seductive virtue was the fact that it offered him a chance to earn extra money. He had a guaranteed job in the pits which exempted him from conscription into the Forces and his temperament was such that he very likely regarded himself as greatly fortunate to have achieved such a combination of security and cash in hand to help support his family. He played steadily rather than spectacularly for seven years during which time he emerged as the players' spokesman whenever a grievance had to be resolved with Webber Lees and in the natural course of events he was made team captain, regarded by management, colleagues and support alike as a real player for the jersey, a cornerstone of a team whose fortunes were generally on the bleak side.

Albion Rovers were then, as now, unembarrassed by riches and Stein was not happy about his remuneration by the time the club returned to the Second Division for the 1949-50 season. There was bickering between player and management, who turned down an offer from Kilmarnock which he would have preferred to accept, and at the end of the season he accepted a contract from Llanelly to play non-League football in Wales, a move which immediately made him better off but which threatened to strand him up a blind alley. For this reason he left his wife and child behind in their newly acquired council house in Hamilton.

Stein was not a man who was ever to transplant himself easily and his first full-scale excursion out of Lanarkshire established a disinclination to shift far from his roots. He was held in good regard by the football supporters in the Welsh town but the separation from his wife Jean and daughter Ray was not practical and although they joined him in Llanelly the family was seriously alarmed when they heard that the house in Hamilton, which they had kept on as insurance for the future, had been broken into for a second time.

What happened next has been related many times but it retains an unlikely romance. It was as though the slow progress of Stein's life, which had at last taken him from the pits and granted him a full-time career in football, had come to a halt and could not lead anywhere but backwards to an existence divided between shifts at the coal-face and on a lower division Scottish ground. Instead, implausible fate took a hand. On the Sunday morning after he received news of the second burglary he walked briskly towards the Llanelly Town stadium to tell his manager that he could no longer stay in Wales, but *en route* he was surprised to see Jack Goldsborough, the Llanelly team boss, striding in turn towards him. Goldsborough's news was so unexpected that Stein found it first difficult to digest and then almost impossible to convey to his wife.

In the midst of his despair the gate to his future had swung open miraculously and Celtic beckoned him through. There had been nothing to suggest that the Parkhead club was likely to seek him out in Wales when they had apparently been oblivious to his existence in Scotland, but they needed a dependable centre half to double up as a squad player and an experienced presence in the reserves. The Celtic reserve team trainer thought of Stein, who also had the virtue of being an inexpensive commodity, and in late 1951 they paid Llanelly £1,200 for his services. Thrift was never to lead the club to a more rewarding investment. Part of the surprise which the signing occasioned outside the Stein household was due to the fact that, aside from being a comparative unknown, he was an unknown Protestant from an area riven with sectarian sensitivities. When he played for Blantyre Vics he wore the blue of Rangers and not the other Old Firm strip sported by the rival side, Blantyre Celtic.

However, like Hughie Gallacher before him (and with infinitely greater success), Stein had bridged the religious divide when he married Jean McAuley, a Roman Catholic girl, albeit a lapsed one. His own religious background was no barrier to a place in the first team. Celtic were quickly glad of the cover he provided when the regular centre-halves, Mallan and Boden, were injured and he was asked to play against St Mirren. He performed more than adequately and apart from a short subsequent absence of a month, made the centre-half position his own until he quit playing. Even more remarkably he was quickly in a position of considerable responsibility when he was nominated by Sean Fallon, the team captain, to be his vice-captain. Fallon broke his arm not long afterwards and Stein assumed command on the field, an elevation which was not greeted with wholehearted enthusiasm by the more established Parkhead residents, particularly certain of the international-class players.

His sturdiness of character carried him over that hurdle and in his long run in the first team he accumulated the disparate knowledge he

A calming presence as Scotland manager: Stein prior to the World Cup finals in 1982.

would employ in his managerial career. He learned the use of authority along with a tactical appreciation of the game, an essential for a man with no reserves of speed. And he discovered that playing with such a high profile club as Celtic permitted him to become known to a sizeable audience off the park. During his captaincy Celtic won the Coronation Cup in 1953 and beat Arsenal, Manchester United and Hibernian to take the trophy against general expectations. For those who could read the runes and knew how to fill out a bookie's line (two departments in which Stein was capable) there was a handsome return to be made the following season when Celtic won the Scottish League and Cup double.

In 1956 his playing days came to an end, truncated by a damaged ankle, but he was invited to stay on to coach the reserves and the contrast between the decline of the first team and the unforeseen professionalism of the second string excited comment in the Parkhead boardroom. It was not enough to establish him as the logical successor to the amiable Jimmy McGrory, a legendary Celtic centre-forward but an ineffective manager, too easily dominated by the club's well-intentioned but domineering chairman, Sir Robert Kelly. Celtic were happy enough to sign Protestant players but power in the club at that time was a Catholic fiefdom in Stein's view, then and later.

He went instead to Dunfermline where the club was lurching towards relegation from the First Division and needed to win its remaining six League games to escape. The first match in March 1960 was against Celtic. It was as though fate had orchestrated man and club in a jig which was to link and separate them repetitively but at the beginning of this new round of the dance, Celtic were almost spun off the floor. Ten seconds into his debut game as a manager he was in charge of a winning team when Dunfermline took the lead and although the Parkhead players recovered their poise enough to score twice they were beaten 3-2 in an exuberant contest which revitalised the East End Park team so spectacularly that they went on to victories in the next five games. It was the first time that Dunfermline had ever won six consecutive First Division matches.

Stein made signings within the constraints of his budget during the close season which followed but he was wise enough to realise that the team was not built for the long haul of a championship challenge and he was reasonably happy to keep them decently clear of the demotion zone in the 1960–61 season. He knew that in such a situation his best hope of success lay in a sprint event, a knock-out competition. In the Scottish Cup, Dunfermline beat Berwick Rangers and Stranraer before being drawn against Aberdeen, Cup finalists only two years previously. Their status was no protection against Stein's guile and to general surprise Aberdeen were handed a 6-3 beating on their own midden. In the following round Dunfermline had the luck to entertain Alloa Athletic of the Second Division at East End Park in a tie which attracted a remarkably substantial crowd and they were gratified by a 4-0 win which took the club to the first Scottish Cup semi-final of its history, a tense affair involving a goalless match and a replay settled by a St Mirren own goal.

In his first full season as as club manager Stein had guided Dunfermline to the club's first Scottish Cup final. Destiny, of course, presented Celtic as the opposition before a crowd of 113,328 at Hampden Park. The Fifers were punching short in the first few minutes when Williamson was injured and although he gamely returned, his role was hardly greater than a passenger and the team was back to ten men in the closing stages of a scoreless draw.

Wisdom and form suggested that Dunfermline had blown their chance; Stein knew they had the beating of his former club. In the replay his players took a battering for most of a rain-drenched first half, however, but after enduring a barrage of Celtic attacks for 67 minutes they broke clear for Peebles to cross and Thomson to head beyond Haffey. With two minutes left to play, the Celtic goalkeeper, who was prone to flights of concentration, dropped a harmless ball into the path of Dickson who merely had to trundle it over the line. Afterwards, when the team bus crossed the River Forth on the last stage of its journey home, it was cheered and saluted as it passed through the villages on its route and it pleased Stein that many of them were mining communities.

Dunfermline did not win any further honours during his time at East End Park but he established the Fifers as a serious force in Scottish football for the best part of the decade and the victory over Celtic at Hampden guaranteed a place in the following season's Cup Winners' Cup followed by a run in the same tournament in 1968-69. In 1968 he was entitled to meditate on how well he had laid the foundation for success when Dunfermline won the Scottish Cup for the second time, starting their campaign with a 2-0 victory over Celtic, the holders, of whom Stein was manager.

He had moved from Dunfermline to Easter Road in April 1964 and revived a listless side to win the innovative Summer Cup. The Old Firm had not deigned to take part in a tournament which failed to become a fixture but it did give Stein another chance to demonstrate his inspirational faculties, and as the season passed its midway point the odds against Hibs winning the championship had greatly reduced. They were to end their campaign four points adrift of the title which was decided on goal average when Kilmarnock edged the flag out of Hearts' reach on the final day of the season. Stein's influence on the league was remarkable because Dunfermline finished third in a table which saw neither Old Firm partner in the top four places, a circumstance which has not recurred since 1965. There is a very plausible argument to suggest that Hibs would have won the flag that season if Stein had stayed on at Easter Road. On 10 March, however, he had gone back to Glasgow, to Parkhead, where he would utterly transform the Scottish football landscape.

When Stein returned, the Celtic chairman Robert Kelly said: "He left Celtic because like everyone else he had to learn his trade but there was always the understanding that he would return." It was not an understanding shared by Jock Stein, who had asked Kelly's advice when Hibs approached him at Dunfermline, and it is hard to believe that the manager had not been offering the subliminal message that perhaps Celtic were as much in need of his services as the Edinburgh club. By the spring of 1965 it was evident that his presence at Parkhead was required urgently. With the exception of 1954 when they won the double under Stein's captaincy Celtic had been a mid-table outfit since the war and they were to finish a mediocre eighth in the 1965 championship.

He arrived at Parkhead with the suspicion that attempts were being made to constrict his field of fire. Sean Fallon, former Celtic player and a devoted club man, had already been appointed coach and Kelly had suggested that a joint management arrangement might be suitable. Stein informed his chairman that it would not and set about shuffling his playing pack until he had achieved a formation which reached the Scottish Cup final where Dunfermline inevitably provided the opposition. For the match at Hampden he decided to withdraw Bobby Murdoch deeper into midfield, prompting Kelly to voice scepticism about the player's ability to perform at half-back. Stein was obliged to put one in the post for the older man. "Watch on Saturday and you'll see if he's a half-back or not", he replied, and when Kelly watched Murdoch he saw a man rejuvenated in a side which took the trophy with a 3-2 win in an exuberant final. Celtic were back in the winner's enclosure and it would take more than a decade to remove them.

The extraordinary and unsurpassed achievements of the next nine years have been minutely recorded in numerous football histories but the sheer quantity of honours won under his regime remains dazzling; ten championships, nine of them consecutive, eight Scottish Cup wins from eleven appearances, six victories from a phenomenal sequence of thirteen League Cup finals and, of course, the seminal European Cup victory and a runners-up place in the same tournament three years later.

There were critics who held that Stein's record was diminished because Celtic were performing on a small domestic stage and only the naïve can deny that Glasgow's Old Firm are always likely to enjoy a prolonged ascendancy when they can command an audience of half the population of Scotland within 20 miles' radius of the city. However, as has been pointed out elsewhere in these pages, Scottish clubs reached their peak of achievement in European football during the second half of the 1960s so Celtic were not operating against quiescent opposition and in the five full seasons which followed Stein's arrival at Parkhead the League and Cup were divided between four teams while seven clubs shared the equivalent trophies in England.

More seriously, in some sections of the English press there were grossly patronising estimates of Stein as a man whose talents could not be perceived as great because he had chosen to work in the confines of the Scottish game rather than exercise his talents on the southern public. Any parochialism on display betrayed the accusers rather than Stein, who nourished a very considerable sense of his own place in the chronicles of football – a sensitivity which was extended to any remark he regarded as a slight on Scotland. Shortly before his death he was greatly irritated by a telephone conversation with a certain well-known radio commentator who called him to get his reaction to the fact that Liverpool had reached the European Cup final at the same time as Everton qualified for the final of the Cup Winners' Cup. The broadcaster, speaking from London, informed Stein that it was a wondrous achievement because no city had previously supplied clubs for the two finals in the same season. Stein's indignation simmered for days until it erupted in this tirade, which occurred during a recorded conversation.

> I said that he was mistaken, that it wasn't so great because it had happened before. This man said that Liverpool was definitely the first city to do it. I said: "No, it happened in this country, it happened in Scotland. Rangers lost in the Cup Winners' Cup final the year we won the European Cup."
>
> It's how you see it. It angers you. I was watching [President] Reagan talking to journalists on television the other day and he said: "You know we have great relationships with England and Germany now." I think it's incredible that when we bring them up on these things – particularly the English – they all say we're small-minded but they would never be

classed as tied to Scotland. When we won the semi-final of the European Cup I remember Kenneth Wolstenholme saying: "We've made it!" We became British that night. I don't mind that because I like to see the British game being successful but I'd prefer to see the Scottish game successful.

What Celtic did in 1967 was worth an awful lot because it brought something new to the game and created new targets. British clubs got to the European Cup final after that because they knew it was possible. We didn't think it was possible until we began to get nearer and then we started to think that anything could happen. But it was us who opened the door.

In later life he occasionally confessed to regretting that he had not tried his hand in England when the opportunity came his way, as it did on more than one occasion. Wolves were interested in attracting him to Molyneux while he was with Hibs, a consideration which spurred Robert Kelly into offering him the job of manager at Parkhead, while Coventry City saw him as the ideal replacement for Jimmy Hill, but the closest he came to leaving Celtic for a southern club was in the aftermath of the European Cup final defeat of 1970 when he was approached by Manchester United and invited to take charge of the Old Trafford team.

Pat Crerand acted as intermediary but the negotiations were carried out with Sir Matt Busby against the unlikely backdrop of a motorway service station in the north of England, a venue which reflected Busby's taste for spy thrillers of the Le Carré variety. The two men talked for the better part of an hour and it was certainly Busby's impression that they had agreed terms, but on returning to Scotland Stein encountered firm resistance from his wife Jean, and being a man whose domestic arrangements were invariably a priority he declined the offer, to Busby's considerable chagrin, although in truth the Celtic manager had reservations about the freedom he would have to appoint his own assistants to replace certain of the United incumbents.

It is tantalising to speculate on what might have taken place at Old Trafford under a Stein regime and it is impossible to conceive that he would have supervised anything comparable to the massive sense of anticlimax which pervaded United during the 1970s, with the exception of Tommy Docherty's lively but short-lived period in office. United made another approach four years later which again came to nothing as did a pair of less well-publicised attempts to lure him to, of all places, Ibrox. The author of these offers was Kenny Hope, a Rangers director who twice met Stein at Hamilton racecourse to sound him about the chance of taking over the other Old Firm partner, but although Stein was flattered by the approaches and gave them a degree of consideration, he informed Hope that it would be an impossible move given his own deep convictions about the value of loyalty, frequently repeated to his Celtic players.

For most of those who knew Stein well, the critical event of his career occurred in July 1975 when he was involved in a traumatic car crash while returning to Scotland from Manchester Airport along with Jean Stein, Bob and Greta Shankly and the Glasgow bookmaker Tony Queen, all of whom had been on holiday in Minorca together. Near Lockerbie the party's Mercedes, with Stein at the wheel, was involved in a head-on collision with another car driving the wrong way down a stretch of dual carriageway. Stein and Queen were badly injured, a factor which did not prevent the Celtic manager being breathalysed while he lay at the roadside awaiting medical help, and his life lay in the balance. Even when it was apparent that he had begun to recover in hospital in Dumfries there were grave doubts about his ability to return to the stressful arena of football management and in 1975-76, without his guidance, Celtic failed to win an honour. He returned during the close season to supervise a revival of fortunes, but it was clear that something had been knocked out of him by such a close brush with death and he indicated that he was aware of as much himself when he suggested to his directors that perhaps it was time to let a younger man take the physical strain of coaching from his shoulders. From Stein's own recollections some years later it is clear that he took it for granted that the post of general manager would be available for him.

He was shocked and hurt when the board announced in May 1978 that his successor as manager would be his former captain, Billy McNeill, then in charge at Aberdeen. For Stein, who had recommended McNeill, there was the offer of the position of commercial manager. It was a doubly inappropriate suggestion because in the first place Stein was well known to be uneasy with financial matters and, more importantly, he was quite simply the most knowledgeable figure in Scottish football and, arguably, the British game. The Leeds United chairman Manny Cussins valued his experience to the extent that he was able to persuade him to fill the vacant managerial seat at Elland Road but Leeds United were to have the benefit of his presence for the briefest of sojourns, a mere 44 days. He returned to Scotland to take over as manager of Scotland, the job which should have been his years previously, and which was now on offer after Ally McLeod's resignation in the wake

Jock Stein with Alex Ferguson.

Twilight of the gods? A crowd congregates at Hampden Park on a favourable evening for football, but with development costs soaring, it increasingly seemed that another golden age for the stadium was unlikely.

Above Hampden Park on a big match day in 1990, but the memorable World Cup evenings of massed crowds on the terracings had become a memory because of FIFA safety regulations. *Below* At Ibrox, Britain's most advanced stadium, plans were revealed to build another tier in the Main Stand to accommodate a further 7,000 spectators, who booked their places through a debenture scheme. This was announced at the same time as Queen's Park's plan to develop Hampden Park and sell part of the site to a supermarket chain, was vetoed by the Secretary of State for Scotland.

Above Wallace Mercer arrives at a press conference to reveal his plan for the takeover of Hibernian, whose fans instantly renamed him Wallace Merger. *Below* Walking tall in Italy. Like the Irish detachment, the Scots won the hearts and minds of an Italian population apprehensive about hooliganism. In the event, no Scots were arrested during the finals, extending a happy record.

Above Bollan congratulates Downie on scoring against Saudi Arabia, while McGoldrick arrives in support. With the score tied at 2-2 after extra time however, Saudi Arabia won on penalty kicks. *Below* Exemplary Scots earned applause in Italy.

Above A heartening crowd of 53,000 turned out to watch Scotland play Saudi Arabia in the final of the World Youth tournament staged in Scotland in 1989. Before the final, the Scottish crowd repaid the compliment. *Below* Proverbs 22, verse 6.

For goalkeeper Jim Leighton, victory against Sweden was an event to savour after having been dropped for the FA Cup final a month previously.

With nine minutes remaining against Brazil and the score tied at 0–0, Leighton lost control of Alemao's shot.

Above Careca beat Gillespie to the loose ball to squeeze it across the empty goal and Muller tapped in at the back post. *Below* Tartan Army cadet, already seasoned by the look of it.

Souness, the Ibrox catalyst.

of the Argentina fiasco.

Stein brought an immensely reassuring presence to the Scotland camp after the manic shambles in South America and when the Scots approached their qualifying group for the 1982 finals in Spain he called the percentage correctly, presiding over a win against Sweden in Stockholm which proved to be the result which launched the side on a successful progress through a group which also contained Portugal, Northern Ireland and Israel. In the finals Scotland were knocked out in the first round, having beaten New Zealand, drawn with the Soviet Union and lost to Brazil, but although Stein was displeased with such an early exit he was fully aware that he had subdued the Scottish gift for self-laceration on and off the field, without neutering the ingrained passion of supporters and players alike.

He remained in charge for the next World Cup campaign which saw the Scots beat Iceland 3–0 and Spain 3–1 (in one of the most outstanding matches ever seen at Hampden) in the opening games, so that they could absorb a 1–0 defeat in the return with Spain in Seville. Wales were next on the list but they arrived at Hampden inflamed by a grievance nourished by their manager Mike England, who repeatedly spoke of the financial loss sustained by the Welsh FA because of the abolition of the Home Championship series, which England had contrived with Scotland's connivance. Mark Hughes scored the single goal of an abrasive game and Wales inflicted Scotland's first World Cup defeat at home since 1965.

From that moment Stein lived under evident strain. When he reached home on the night of the Welsh match he was poorly and had to take medicine prescribed to relieve his heart condition. His next match should have been against England at Wembley and he was angered when the Government ordered the fixture to be switched to Hampden because of fears of trouble from Scottish supporters in London. Although Scotland won 1–0 he was preoccupied with the World Cup qualifying match scheduled for Reykjavik three days later. Again the Scots came away with a 1–0 victory but only after Jim Leighton had saved a penalty kick and Jim Bett had scored in the final five minutes.

The Heysel disaster occurred on the following evening and as the summer passed he became increasingly agitated at the possibility of trouble when Scotland visited Ninian Park for the return match with Wales. It was not that he anticipated disorder so much as the fact that there were others who did and who, in his opinion, would seize the opportunity it afforded to divert attention from the quarantine imposed upon the English clubs. As it happened, the two British countries conducted themselves with propriety on the terracings and in their contest and Scotland achieved the 1–1 draw which carried them on towards Mexico but the strain at last overpowered Stein and he collapsed as he rose from the bench at the final whistle to move up the players' tunnel. He had suffered a massive heart attack but he was conscious for a few minutes in the Ninian Park treatment room. It seemed momentarily that he might have passed the worst when he murmured, "That feels better, Doc," to Stuart Hillis, the Scotland team doctor, but within seconds he was gone.

On the last morning of his life Stein wore his track suit to join a Scottish squad warm-up and spent some time with his assistant Alex Ferguson taking penalty kicks to test Jim Leighton. A TV film crew was recording his efforts and he was aware that he could not strike the ball from the twelve yard spot with the power he would

Silent crowds throng the route at
Jock Stein's funeral in Glasgow.

have liked. He rolled it forward and exclaimed: "Ladies' tee, Ladies' tee!", apparently to nobody in particular but in reality for the benefit of the camera. When he realised that, in fact, the cameraman was changing his film, he repeated the performance and added another encore to make certain his act had been captured, all with the habitual ingenuousness he displayed whenever he was manipulating the media, one of his specialised skills.

He could be boyishly charming and frighteningly enraged. His repertoire spanned the soft word and the bullying threat as well as the kind of sly joke at a listener's expense which was often delivered with a delayed action fuse attached. He was restless but also contemplative and for all his understanding of the publicity machine there was a profound privacy about him which sometimes suggested a degree of loneliness. On the subject of football he was invariably compelling. "Ach, we're here to talk sense," was a favourite retort if he considered he had been asked a foolish question and foolish interrogators did not usually linger in his presence. The fault he would most readily concede in himself was that he erred on the side of loyalty, persevering with players of no great capacity if they showed willingness to perform to their limits and beyond.

A few weeks before his death he told the author of this book that he could not imagine what he would do after he retired. "No life beyond football – no life at all." Perhaps he had some premonition that at Ninian Park his words would be transformed into literal truth but at any event those who knew him well often pause to reflect that without him football has much less life about it and that life itself is short of a vital presence.

It was not, after all, simply because of his bulk that Jock Stein was invariably known as the Big Man.

Home, the conquering heroes: the European Cup at Parkhead.

CHAPTER FOUR

Old Firms, New Deals

THE DECADE after 1970 was the darkest period of the history of football in Scotland and for ten years the game was afflicted by a series of disturbing setbacks until it seemed that it had lost ground which could never be recovered. The Ibrox Disaster, serious crowd disorders in Barcelona, Birmingham and at Hampden Park, and the débâcle of the World Cup expedition to Argentina in 1978 combined to send League attendances into a demoralising downward spiral which saw the total of spectators in the top division fall substantially below the two million mark at the beginning of the 1980s. Yet not only was the decline arrested, it was reversed so completely that in 1988 the Scottish League was able to declare attendance figures which exceeded any recorded in the previous 25 years, despite the drastic lowering of ground capacities which had occurred in the intervening period.

It is arguable, although by no means certain, that the game in Scotland had become so debilitated in the 1970s that a revival of some kind was bound to occur but the scale of the recovery offered a powerful contrast to the experience throughout most of the rest of Europe where the sport had entered a period of stagnation. The most vivid comparison of all was with England where football staggered under the weight of a ghastly constellation of tragedies in Brussels, Bradford and Sheffield combined with persistent and sinister outbreaks of organised violence which caused English teams to be placed under house arrest and denied access to European competition. How was it that clubs in Scotland arrived at a vigorous prosperity at the very moment when their English counterparts were stigmatised as an infamous presence in international sport?

At least part of the answer is that when traumas occurred in the Scottish game, they were met with a decisive response. After the 1971 disaster, Ibrox was reconstructed as the finest club stadium in Britain. The decline in crowds was remedied by a reorganisation of the Scottish League to form an élite Premier Division. Finally, the riot at the 1980 Scottish Cup final between Rangers and Celtic was followed by the hasty introduction of the Criminal Justice (Scotland) Act which made it illegal to be in possession of alcohol within a sports arena, or even to attend a sporting event under the influence of drink, a draconian measure which struck at the most common cause of Scottish spectator violence.

The question of timing is also critical because the difficulties which beset Scottish football become apparent several years before they erupted in England and, in fact, storm warnings had begun to appear in the 1960s although few observers had the prescience to interpret them correctly. On Stairway 13 at Ibrox, for example, there were two deaths and 44 injuries in a crush in 1961, 11 injured in 1967 and 30 casualties, including two seriously injured, in yet another accident at the same spot in 1969. Such incidents were inevitable, as anyone who remembers the fearsome Ibrox staircases will testify. At the end of every match spectators would make a rush down the precipitous steps in their efforts to get home ahead of the crowd and Stairway

The wreckage of Stairway 13 which claimed 66 lives at Ibrox.

13 was invariably the worst affected because it was the nearest exit to Copland Road subway station.

On 2 January 1971 the annual New Year confrontation between Rangers and Celtic took place at Ibrox at a low point in the home team's fortunes. Rangers began the match without any hope of depriving Celtic of their championship crown and had even been beaten 3-1 by Falkirk the day before, Andy Roxburgh scoring one of the goals in an exuberant Bairns victory. The title was not bound for Ibrox; the only concern of the Rangers faithful was that it should not go to Parkhead. They regularly punctuated the afternoon with choruses of *The Northern Lights*, a recognition that only Aberdeen, neck and neck with Celtic, could prevent the flag being retained in the East End of Glasgow for a sixth consecutive season.

Apart from the songs, the afternoon was not animated and the packed terracings at each end were veiled by a mist which drifted off the Clyde throughout the match, obscuring the supporters' view of each other. As the contest reached its final minute, Jimmy Johnstone beat Peter McCloy in the home goal to give Celtic an unforeseen lead and Rangers supporters standing near the exits turned to leave, only to be summoned back by the immense roar from their own end as the contest produced an astonishing twist, an equaliser by Colin Stein with only 15 seconds left to play. Those supporters trying to regain the Rangers end were met by a jubilant surge of their fellows leaving the arena; on Stairway 13 someone fell and a lethal swirl of collapsing bodies began to pile across the steps ending with 66 killed and 145 injured.

Ironically, the day had otherwise been unusually peaceful with only two arrests for drunkenness inside the ground from a crowd of 80,000 but it was the worst accident in the history of British football and the subsequent official inquiry was harsh in its criticism of the Rangers directors' failure to learn from previous incidents on the fatal staircase. At first the club made comparatively slight changes to the ground, including anti-crush measures on Stairway 13, but two years after the accident the covered north enclosure was turned into a stand by the installation of 9,000 bench seats, to the disgruntlement of the hard-core support which had commandeered the area during its terracing days.

With the enforcement of new safety rules for football stadia in 1975 Ibrox, which had accommodated 118,567 spectators for the Rangers-Celtic New Year game in 1939, had its capacity reduced to 65,000 and this was the signal for a dramatic transformation of the stadium. The initial estimated cost of £6 million was quickly exceeded at a time of rising inflation and the final bill came to £10 million. But the club was not in danger of veering into the kind of serious financial difficulty which almost ruined Chelsea, who attempted a grandiose reconstruction of Stamford Bridge during the same period. Unlike Chelsea, there was no chance of Rangers being relegated to the lower divisions and they also had the cushion of an annual profit of around £1 million from Rangers Pools, the most lucrative club lottery organisation in Britain.

In addition, there was the benefit of Rangers' close association with the John Lawrence construction group of companies, but despite these natural advantages it would not have been possible for the new Ibrox to have emerged in the mid-1980s, when the cost would have risen to £30 million, a sum beyond even Rangers' means. What the club got for its prudent outlay was a spectacular sporting arena, modelled on

Spectators improvise stretchers
from torn fencing at the first
Ibrox disaster of 1902.

the Dortmund stadium where Scotland had played during the 1974 World Cup finals, with the east and west terracings replaced by a pair of goalpost frame stands seating a total of 15,000 spectators. In place of the north enclosure there appeared the Govan Stand with a capacity of 10,300 and the only link with the old Ibrox was the South Stand, a listed building which was retained for the sake of its atmosphere. When the redevelopment was completed in 1981, Ibrox had a capacity of 45,000, including accommodation for the 9,000 traditionalists who preferred to stand in the untouched south enclosure.

The remodelled arena conclusively gave the lie to those who insisted that the unique flavour of British football crowds, their spontaneous and frequently entertaining chants and songs, would be dissipated in more sophisticated venues. The present generation of Rangers supporters are accommodated in a stadium which would adorn any city in the United States, but the surroundings have not inclined them towards delicacy. After Hearts had visited Ibrox for a League fixture, the Edinburgh manager Alex MacDonald remarked, "That isn't just a stadium – it's a weapon", and the intimidating character of the Rangers support in battle order is accentuated by the imposing sweep and colour of the stands which, taken together with the bedlam of the fans, can have a laxative effect on unaccustomed teams such as Gornik of Poland, whose players were physically sick in the dressing-room as they prepared for a European Cup tie in October 1987.

Although Rangers were responsible for what was easily the most spectacular stadium redevelopment in Britain, they were not the only Scottish club to undertake a thorough overhaul of their facilities. Aberdeen had begun to modernise Pittodrie after a destructive fire swept through much of the main stand in 1971, fortunately avoiding the board room where the Scottish Cup was on display. Bench seats were installed on the terracings although they proved unpopular on the uncovered south side, where spectators were apt to feel the worst rigours of a northern climate made more severe by the proximity of the North Sea only a few hundred yards away, and eventually tip-up seats and a cantilever roof made conditions more bearable.

Aberdeen were in a position to fund their redevelopment with the profits from a period of success unparalleled in the club's history, under the consecutive guidance of Ally McLeod, Billy McNeill and Alex Ferguson, and the directors were alive to the fact that a city enjoying the fruits of the North Sea oil exploration boom had produced a generation of spectators who expected more sophisticated facilities than were customary at Scottish grounds. They were also pragmatic enough to accept a reduction in capacity from 45,000 to 22,600, preferring a stadium full to capacity several times a year to one which reached its limits only when Rangers or Celtic were in town.

Of course, most clubs were unable to mine profitable seams of success or fanaticism in order to finance refurbishment of their premises but two striking examples from the lower divisions showed what could be done with a mixture of ambition and imagination. Senior football came late to Clydebank, where League fixtures were first played in 1965 but nourishment of slim resources saw the team reach the Premier Division in 1977, when a new stand was built out of the money Clydebank received for selling Davie Cooper to Rangers. At the same time the board decided to install bench seats throughout the terracings so that New Kilbowie, with a revised capacity of 9,500, became the second all-seated stadium in the country, a move which excused Clydebank from registration under the Safety of Sports Grounds Act governing grounds holding more than 10,000 spectators. Again, there were no protests from the team's followers, although Clydebank's managing director Jackie Steedman remarked subsequently that bench seating did not restrict the more traditional type of customer whose response was simply to stand on the seats provided.

Laudable as Clydebank's modernisation has been, it was surpassed in 1989 by the achievement of St Johnstone, who managed to equip themselves with a custom-built stadium at no cost to the club. This remarkable and unlikely feat came about after a property developer approached the St Johnstone board and offered to dispose of their outdated stadium at Muirton Park in the centre of Perth by selling it to be converted into a shopping centre. With commendable foresight, the directors decided to proceed with the scheme but without the services of a middle-man and eventually struck a deal with the Asda supermarket chain who were given Muirton in return for building a state of the art ground on the edge of Perth. At the beginning of the 1989-90 season, St Johnstone played their first home match at MacDiarmid Park, named after the farmer who donated the ground upon which it stands.

A replica of Ibrox on a smaller scale, with an all-seated capacity of 10,000, the new stadium was designed with particular emphasis on safety features. It was opened 17 years after Lord Wheatley concluded his Report of the Inquiry into Crowd Safety at Sports Grounds, prompted by the Ibrox accident, with the words: "One thing is certain. The public demand for something to be done has been growing over the years. I am sure I am reflecting public opinion when I say that something must be done now."

MacDiarmid Park was, like Ibrox, Pittodrie and Kilbowie, a fulfilment of the desire for radical change expressed by the Wheatley Report. St Johnstone took almost two decades to respond to his injunction to modernise but the timeliness of their eventual effort was illuminated with awful clarity on 15 April 1989 when their new stadium was in the final stages of construction. On that afternoon 96 spectators died in a crush during the Liverpool-Nottingham Forest FA Cup tie in Sheffield and Hillsborough relieved Ibrox of its undesired reputation as the scene of Britain's worst football tragedy.

*　　*　　*

If the decay of outmoded stadia could be identified as the most perilous threat to the native game, football in Scotland was also placed in jeopardy by the periodic eruptions of supporters, some of whom should have carried a Government health warning on match days. Crowd disorder became endemic in Europe throughout the 1970s but as Ernie Walker, the retiring secretary of the SFA, observed, "We had nothing to learn from anyone about football hooliganism. It was practically our gift to the world."

Whoever suggested that Scottish history could be summed up as "one long brawl" very nearly anticipated the chronicle of club football in Scotland for the best part of a century, at least from the combative events which tended to shape the outsider's perspective. On the field it usually seemed that contenders from beyond the Glasgow city boundary were not so much engaged on giant-killing

SEAN CONNERY

Sean Connery, actor, was born in Edinburgh in 1936. He made his name playing James Bond but might well have played professional football instead. He remains a keen follower of Scotland's fortunes and is often to be seen at international and club games involving Scottish sides.

"Going to school or going to work, one always kicked a ball. In the holidays in Scotland – well, they called them holidays but it meant the moment you finished delivering milk – we used to go to the park in Edinburgh called the Meadows, although we knew it as the Meedies. And you would play until the light went down. I didn't know anybody who didn't play when I was a kid.

"I went on to play amateur for Fet-Lor and I signed professional forms with Bonnyrigg Rose at a time when junior football was big. I was a very keen Celtic fan, too. The kind of player who stands out in my memory would be almost unacceptable today, guys like Charlie Tully of Celtic and Torry Gillick, the very dynamic centre forward for Rangers. We used to call them tanner ba' players, sand dancers. You'd see them take the ball down to the corner flag then into the penalty area and back out again and maybe stand with their foot on the ball while they were at it.

"When I was a boy we were all lifted over the turnstiles to get into grounds because none of us had the money to pay, and anyway, the clubs knew it was a way of keeping up interest amongst the kids. And I must say I saw a few punch-ups but it was all internal, to do with football – one fan fighting another fan from another club – which I think was quite healthy in its own way because it was nothing to do with switchblades or anything like

exploits as a permanent struggle to overthrow the Goliath twins in the form of Rangers and Celtic. If such a generalisation falls short of a rigorous account of the Scottish scene between 1890 and 1980 it is hard to recognise any alternative mythology which might do better service, especially since the followers of both clubs were the first to undertake a serious exploration of the concept of the football supporter as licensed brigand. For roughly 15 years after the mid-1960s, large numbers of their adherents travelled to away fixtures with an appetite for rampage which would have gratified the Vikings, as the inhabitants of a number of English cities were to discover in the course of several Anglo-Scottish fixtures, some of which were grotesquely categorised as friendlies.

Divided against themselves, Glasgow fans were intimidating enough, but on the single occasion when they found a common cause they must have been awesome to contemplate. The Hampden Riot of 1909 is an episode which periodically resurfaces in Scottish football narratives because it is the only incidence of the Scottish Cup being withheld, after the finalists sensibly refused to meet for a third time following two drawn attempts to settle the destination of the trophy.

It was the second unresolved contest which created mayhem when the spectators were misled by a rumour that there would be extra time and when this proved false they turned in wrath upon the constabulary and ground officials. Hundreds were injured, some seriously, but the detail which arrests the modern eye concerns the burning of the Hampden payboxes. It is evidence of the indignation of the thwarted customers that they were prepared to multiply arson by pouring whisky on the flames, even if it was a low-grade hooch colloquially known as "Kill the Carter". Not even for Rangers or Celtic was it worth the chance of winning the Scottish Cup to play once more in front of 60,000 Glaswegians roused enough to employ whisky as an incendiary for something other than their throats.

The scenes at Hampden were described by the *Glasgow Herald* as "downright malevolent, cowardly and brutal" but the relationship between the clubs was not then anything like so polarised as it would later become. Celtic were identifiably and proudly the team of the large numbers of Roman Catholic immigrants who had arrived in the West of Scotland in cycles which coincided with the Irish potato famines of the 19th century, and the club's capacity to annexe football honours had been evident almost from the day it was founded amidst the teeming slums of Glasgow's East End. A model for the expression of Roman Catholic solidarity in sport already existed in Edinburgh where Hibernian, founded in 1875, had won the Scottish Cup in 1887 when they beat Dumbarton 2-1 in the final, but in Glasgow the Irish population was much greater and Celtic became the paramount immigrant club, to some resentment from their counterparts in the capital.

Any team drawn from the native Protestant population of the west which could challenge Celtic's ascendancy on a consistent basis was guaranteed a substantial support and Queen's Park momentarily seemed to be the logical choice but their refusal to become a professional club rendered them ineffective and it was Rangers who proved to have the stamina required to meet the challenge. It was also Rangers who had willingly provided the opposition when Celtic played their first proper match and the pair met so frequently in their pursuit of honours that they came to be known as the Old Firm. If there were comparatively early signs of sectarian prejudice amongst the supporters of both teams they were nothing compared with the antipathy which ultimately typified their encounters.

Unlike Hibernian, whose first constitution specified that players had to be practising Roman Catholics (the condition was dropped in 1893), Celtic were not inclined to absolute insularity and early club records, thought to have been destroyed but recovered in 1988, show that when an attempt was made to exclude Protestant players in the 1890s it was rejected after little discussion. It is important to note, incidentally, that this took place at a time when Celtic could easily have filled their ranks with Roman Catholics, despite later suggestions that the habit of signing Protestants was an expediency forced upon the club because, as the Glasgow argot has it, "there wisnae enough good Tims" to guarantee the habit of success. It is interesting to note that the Celtic team which beat Rangers 1-0 in the 1989 Scottish Cup final contained only one Protestant player, Derek Whyte.

Rangers, meanwhile, were willing to harbour Roman Catholics such as Willie Kivlichan, a Galashiels medical man who was transferred to Celtic shortly before the Hampden Riot Cup final and who filled in on the right wing for Alex Bennett, who moved in the opposite direction from Parkhead to Ibrox, not in a transfer deal between the clubs but as a free agent. If the clubs were separated along a religious and cultural divide which inevitably heightened awareness of their differences, the boundaries were not so rigid as is often assumed. The stiffening of prejudice took place with the intensification of politics in Ireland, first when the Ulster Unionists threatened armed revolt in the event of a successful Irish Home Rule Bill and subsequently when the nationalist uprising took place in Dublin in 1916 in the context of a particularly grim period for Britain during the First World War.

The coming of the Harland & Wolff shipbuilding company with its powerful associations with Belfast has been held responsible for an injection of fierce sectarian feeling into Govan and no doubt there was a slackening of any ecumenical impulse which might have existed around Ibrox at the time, but the truth appears to be that emotions for and against Irish nationalism simply concentrated themselves as the War of Independence in Ireland became bloody and wearisome, and from about 1920 the ill-disposition of each support for the other became a sour and rancorous feature of Glasgow football as well as daily life in many parts of the West of Scotland, to remain so for half a century or more.

Tragedy occasionally broke the religious mould, as when the brilliant young Celtic goalkeeper John Thomson (a Protestant) died after a head injury sustained when he dived at the feet of Sam English during an Old Firm match at Ibrox on 5 September 1931. The Rangers supporters jeered at his prostrate form until silenced by the team captain Davie Meiklejohn, who indicated to them that the goalkeeper had suffered an unusually serious injury, while English was the target for subsequent abuse from the Celtic following, but neither set of partisans were then aware of the gravity of Thomson's condition. When the teams next met at Parkhead in the New Year game the mood was sombre and the mutual baiting was extremely subdued.

Such displays of decency were never prolonged, but far from deterring spectators the sometimes ferocious rivalry between the clubs saw them accumulate a steadily stronger following which inevitably increased both their revenue and their chance of winning honours, and with each success they became more monolithic until it was beyond

that. It was usually just overheated argument.

"I took my two boys to a Celtic-Rangers match and they'd never seen anything like it in their life. The atmosphere was electrifying and they couldn't believe that when a goal was scored one end of the park would go demented, dancing and singing, while the other end of the park was absolutely, utterly silent. That sense of excitement is very important in football.

"I've played striker for Scotland a few times – in my fantasies. I beat them all, especially England, because I was there at that terrible game, the 9-3 defeat at Wembley. I cannot even remember the three. I knew all about the nine, though."

John Thomson's fatal collision
with Sam English.

the reach of any other club to sustain a prolonged challenge to their dominance. The habit of winning was not matched by a parallel growth of dignity in the face of occasional adversity; the phrase "bottles were thrown" is not uncommon in match reports from the thirties and hostilities were not interrupted by the Second World War. In 1940 the semi-final of the mistitled Glasgow Charity Cup ended in a 5–1 victory for Rangers after a bad-tempered match which provoked the SFA into suspending five players, and in September 1941 at Ibrox Jimmy Delaney and Johnny Crum of Celtic were stretchered off the park while their assailants went unpunished. Clydeside had ample menace from the Luftwaffe but the supporters insisted on their own right to aerial intimidation. Bottles were thrown.

There was similar molestation in the semi-final of the Victory Cup in June 1946 when Celtic's Willie Gallagher was injured and left the field, while Jimmy Sirrel, another casualty, stayed on but to almost no effect. With 20 minutes left Rangers, who led 1-0, were awarded a penalty which was much disputed by the Celtic players until George Paterson and Jimmy Mallan were sent off. This was the signal for a launch of bottles in force, providing a display which most observers judged to be the most spectacular in years. Paterson and Mallan were handed three months' suspension apiece and there was a four-week ban on Matt Lynch, who had been booked after the end of the match, despite written testimony from Rangers' Jimmy Duncanson to the effect that the Parkhead player was innocent.

Celtic felt that they were the victims of prejudice by parties within the Scottish Football Association and in this they were almost certainly correct. Some SFA members had been offended by the action of the Irish Prime Minister, Eamonn de Valera, in offering condolences to the German Ambassador in Dublin on the occasion of Hitler's death, and the increasing habit of waving the Irish tricolour by the Celtic support did their team's cause no good with the game's ruling body.

The Irish flag was to become the focus of an unutterably stupid argument in 1952 when the SFA put pressure on Celtic to remove the tricolour which flew amongst other flags above the Jungle section of the terracing. Celtic refused to take the flag down and were supported in their resistance by Rangers until the matter was allowed to drop in official circles, but the episode perfectly illustrated the nature of a civic division which was incomprehensible to most outsiders, particularly those in England, where religion is more a question of private apathy rather than an excuse for public confrontation. The surreal nature of the issue is best suggested by the fact that the tricolour is invariably referred to as consisting of green, white and gold when, in fact, it is made up of green for Catholic Ireland, orange for the Protestant persuasion, and white for peace between the two, a sentiment which evaporates when the flag is waved at Old Firm games. In such fashion the tribal conflict extended into the 1960s where it seemed increasingly anachronistic and disagreeable.

In accordance with the principle that lack of success on the field fuelled trouble off it, Celtic supporters were the more disruptive in the first half of the decade with their most notorious contribution being a pitch invasion of Ibrox in March 1962 in an attempt to halt the progress of a Scottish semi-final tie in which St Mirren led 3-0. Both sides had to be escorted from the park, although they completed the match with Celtic scoring a consolation goal. This at least was a household disturbance but the increasing incidence of European football meant that trouble was periodically exported, almost always to England, and incidents exposed to a much greater public as a result of television coverage.

In 1966 Celtic visited Liverpool for the second leg of a Cup Winners' Cup semi-final tie and their supporters produced a barrage of bottles at the Anfield Road end when a Bobby Lennox goal which would have levelled the contest on aggregate was disallowed for offside in the final minute. In October 1970 there was severe crowd disorder at half-time in a second round European Cup tie in Dublin when Waterford trailed Celtic 4-0 and in September 1978 fighting broke out on the terracings at Burnley when the home team dismissed Celtic from the short-lived Anglo-Scottish Cup. The depredations of Celtic's following were, however, mild compared to the antics of Rangers' lunatic element who seriously disgraced themselves with a full-scale riot during the second leg of a Fairs Cup semi-final tie against Newcastle at St James' Park, which the Glasgow side lost 2-0.

In *The Newcastle United Story* the author, John Gibson, wrote:

> There is no more pleasant supporter than Jock in victory, no more wild a man in defeat. A few drams too many and the sight of the English raising their flag to herald the fall of the Scots is all too much. They came over the barricades in waves after United's second goal had posted the Rangers death notices. Beer bottles rained down from the night sky as the tartan madmen swept the frightened players into the sanctuary of the tunnel, where they stayed for 17 minutes while police fought to restore sanity. The irony of ironies was that two Scotsmen, Scott and Sinclair, scored the goals which proved all too much for their fellow countrymen to take.

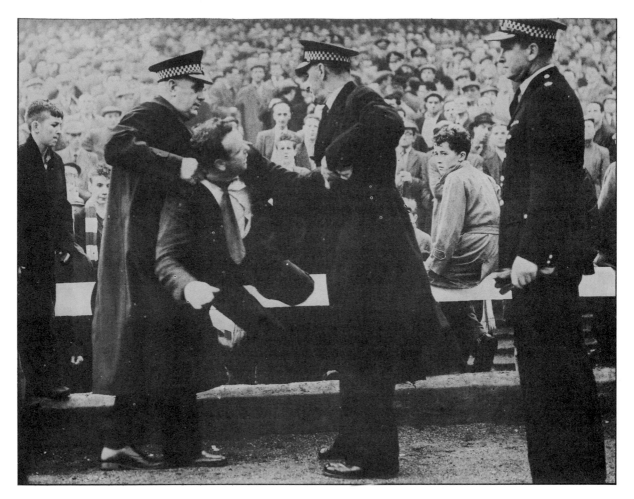

Old Firm matches became a byword for crowd disorder.

The St James's Park riot occurred at a time when the European football authorities viewed crowd trouble as an occasional hazard. They were less phlegmatic when Rangers beat Moscow Dynamo 3-2 in the 1972 Cup Winners' Cup final in Barcelona, an occasion which ended in a pitched battle between the Scots and the Spanish Guarda Civil. Ironically, there had been little provocation during the match, and the police had barely moved to prevent incursions on to the field after each of Rangers' goals, but after the Soviet team revived with two late scores the Rangers fans, desperate to celebrate the acquisition of the club's first European trophy and in the mistaken belief that the referee had signalled full-time, invaded the pitch only to find that the gendarmerie had belatedly decided to wade in with batons drawn. This was meat and drink to the Glaswegians who inflicted significant casualties in the police ranks, to the obvious pleasure of the anti-Franco Catalan locals, but the consequences for the Ibrox club were serious.

Having been presented with the trophy during a perfunctory ceremony in a stadium back room and refused a consequent lap of honour, the Rangers players were denied the chance to defend their prize when UEFA banned the team from European competition for two years, a prohibition which was later halved after skilful representation by the Ibrox manager Willie Waddell. Four years later, however, there was yet another repellent display of aggression in England and a supposedly friendly match between Aston Villa and Rangers was abandoned after 53 minutes with the Glasgow team losing, when vicious brawls broke out on the terracings and the trouble surged on into the city centre. The so-called Battle of Birmingham finally brought it home to the Rangers management that their support had come to be regarded as a serious liability and an embarrassment to Scottish football. Willie Waddell, now general manager, attempted to defuse widespread condemnations of the club's sectarianism by announcing that Roman Catholic players would be acceptable at Ibrox if they had the necessary skills.

No such individuals had apparently been discovered by 10 May 1980 when Rangers met Celtic in a Scottish Cup final for the twelfth time. In the match programme, a question and answer item with the SFA secretary Ernie Walker, included the following extract:

> Q – There's obviously no ready made remedy to the ever increasing crowd indiscipline throughout Britain – do you have a personal theory which would help to eliminate the menace?
> A – Football cannot cure the problem, but it must do everything possible to contain it. Better spectating facilities including more seats would help and things in this direction will start to improve very soon now at Hampden.

By the end of the afternoon it was evident that something significantly more drastic than increased seating would be required to cope with football violence. An unexceptional final was settled by a Danny McGrain shot deflected off George McCluskey to beat the Rangers goalkeeper Peter McCloy but the contest was eclipsed by its aftermath when the jubilant Celtic players carried off the trophy towards their delighted supporters. Remarkably, most of the police on duty had gone outside the ground to shepherd the Rangers fans off the premises only to discover that a large section of the Ibrox contingent had taken advantage of their absence to pour off the terracings in the direction of the celebrations at the Celtic end, with malice in view. It took a mounted police charge across the pitch and the order to draw

Barcelona – Spanish police confront Rangers supporters, with predictable consequences.

The Hampden Riot in 1980 caused batons to be drawn in Glasgow for the first time since the General Strike of 1926. W.P.C. Elaine Mudie and her horse, Ballantrae, charged to separate the brawling factions and Parliament moved to outlaw the hooligans.

batons, not heard in Glasgow since the General Strike of 1926, to subdue the disorder. The chaotic scenes within the stadium were seen throughout the world, provoking deeply felt shame within Scotland at such a rebuke to the country's image. The SFA fined the clubs £20,000 each although Celtic complained that police negligence was to blame and that their supporters had merely been celebrating in the first place, but as far as the public was concerned these were the niceties of a bar-room brawl and most Scots who had no allegiance to the Old Firm wished a plague on both houses.

Reaction was such that the matter was debated in Parliament and the result was the introduction of the Criminal Justice (Scotland) Act 1980, which banned alcohol from being bought or sold at football grounds and from trains and coaches carrying supporters to matches. In addition, any spectator attempting to enter a ground while under the influence of drink was liable to be arrested and it became illegal to carry a container which could be used as a missile. The new law was zealously applied and fans complained that they were forced to surrender cartons of fruit juice, the police reply being that there was no guarantee that the juice was low octane. There were tales of supporters happily sucking oranges which had been injected with vodka.

The effect of the legislation was immediate. The chances of being brained by a bottle while watching a football match, even a Glasgow derby, became much more remote and both the police and the football authorities declared that they were satisfied that a major advance had been made. Unfortunately, the lesson was not applied elsewhere. In 1984 an Official Working Group was commissioned by the Department of the Environment to investigate football hooliganism and their conclusion appeared in a report with the title "Football Spectator Violence", the opening sentence of which was almost bound to inflame tempers north of the border (and in Wales and Northern Ireland). With considerable insensitivity, the authors wrote: "Following incidents of violence involving British supporters before, during and after the England soccer team's matches in Luxembourg and France . . ." The report eventually addressed the

Scottish legislation after 26 pages and declared that "there is strong anecdotal evidence that it has resulted in a marked decline in soccer violence in Scotland." Nevertheless, it concluded that drinking patterns in Scotland and the north-east of England were different from the rest of England and Wales and that the Scottish law should not be imposed on southern supporters. It was certainly true that at football matches the dominant Scottish drinking pattern consisted of alcohol down the throat and back up again rapidly but this liquid version of bulimia was severely constrained by the 1980 Act and the strain on tempers and footwear at games improved dramatically as a result. In addition, supporters were less likely to become belligerent if they were fairly sober and unarmed with handy material to lob into the atmosphere, and although the so-called Casual groups were able to disguise their intent by employing the opposite approach, dressing smartly and concealing Stanley knives, they were now more easily identified in a crowd, as the experience of 'C' Division of the Lothian police force in Edinburgh was to demonstrate at Tynecastle.

Bottles were thrown . . .

In a strange contradiction of the working party's own conclusions their report included a copy of the recommendations of the fourth Conference of European Sports Ministers in 1984 which suggested that it would be wise "to restrict, if not ban, the sale of alcoholic drinks, including beer and, if the sale of such beverages is permitted, to ensure that they are not available in potentially dangerous containers". The Sports Ministers also insisted on the need for decisive segregation of rival supporters.

The space of four days in May 1985 illustrated the difference between well-meant talk and effective action. On 25 May the annual fixture between England and Scotland which should have been played at Wembley took place at Hampden Park, reputedly on the orders of Mrs Thatcher, because of unruly scenes in London on the previous Scottish visit in 1983. Predictably the switch aggrieved some in Scotland and it was pointed out that the arrest rate at Wembley in 1983 was merely equivalent to that at several Football League fixtures played in London during the same season. But most Scots accepted that if the Tartan Army had a tendency to turn boorish anywhere, it would be in London. A handful of supporters protested the decision by watching the game on a portable TV on the steps of Wembley Park but in Glasgow the match went off peaceably enough.

There was, however, a new development at Hampden; for the first time in memory there was a substantial English presence on the terracings and amongst the southern contingent was a large group bearing Nazi insignia and making the Fascist salute throughout the proceedings. They were rigidly segregated from the home support throughout the game and by corralling them between the lines of policemen to and from the ground trouble was contained, but it was apparent that in less controlled circumstances a serious disturbance would have been the inevitable outcome. Four days later in Brussels, precisely such a breakdown in crowd control led to 39 Italian supporters being crushed to death when a section of the Liverpool following surged towards them on the terracings of the decrepit Heysel Stadium.

As a consequence of the Heysel disaster English clubs were banned from taking part in European club competitions for an indefinite period. The penalty was harsh on such clubs as Everton, who had won the Cup Winners' Cup without disruption in Rotterdam ten days before Heysel. But, as in the aftermath of the Hampden riot, public opinion was not in the humour to show compassion to football and its destructive fringe. Unlike many uninformed commentators, including several Westminster MPs and cabinet ministers, UEFA made a distinction between the British football jurisdiction, and Scottish teams (along with the Welsh and Northern Irish) were allowed to continue to play in Europe. This judgment reinforced the perception in Scotland that the native game had been cleaned up to a reasonable degree and was of immense importance in confirming the revival of the game north of the border.

★   ★   ★

Better ground conditions and more civilised behaviour by spectators could not have inspired the football renaissance in Scotland if the game itself was unattractive and by the mid-1970s it was evident that most Scottish League fixtures had ceased to captivate an audience which was basically well disposed towards the sport. This rapid dissipation of interest was all the more alarming because only a short time before, in 1967, the Scottish game had achieved a zenith which it has yet to equal.

The climactic moment was, of course, the golden evening of 25 May in Lisbon when Celtic produced a euphoric display of attacking football to become the first British side to win the European Cup and so overthrow the myth of Latin invulnerability created by the dominance of Real Madrid and their Portuguese and Italian successors in the champions' tournament. Composed entirely of Scots, Celtic were known in their own domain as a truly formidable force but their achievement in winning the Scottish domestic treble that season was so lightly regarded elsewhere that Bill Shankly was the only British manager to make a trip to Portugal for the encounter with Inter Milan, but he at least recognised that under the acute guidance of Jock Stein the Parkhead side had achieved an alchemy of will and technical brilliance which at its best was irresistible.

From time to time subsequent commentators (not all of them Italian) have suggested that Celtic's triumph was in the nature of a freak result. One authoritative British football encyclopedia attributes the Lisbon victory to a combination of "vitality and good luck", the Scots' debt to fortune apparently consisting of the absence through injury of Inter's distinguished left-sided midfield organiser Luis Suarez. The suggestion that the loss of Suarez, influential as he was, swung the contest in Celtic's favour is an ignorant distortion. Inter's performance in the 1967 final was their third in four years and seven of their team – Sarti, Burgnich, Facchetti, Guarneri, Picchi, Mazzola and Corso – had two European Cup winners' medals each as a result, while Mazzola, whose early penalty kick left Celtic trailing, had scored twice against Real Madrid in Vienna in 1964.

Celtic's initial achievement in Lisbon was to win the hearts and minds of the local supporters by Stein's carefully calculated promises that his team would play adventurous football to please those neutral lovers of the game who might be in attendance. The famous scene in the players' tunnel before the match in which the Celtic players raucously belted out a selection of team choruses to the astonishment of their more worldly and urbane opponents is a perfect illustration of the philosophies which collided in the Portuguese sun. The Italian manager Helenio Herrera had refined the ultra-defensive *catenaccio* system which employed a sweeper behind four defenders in a man to man marking pattern reinforced by a midfield which waited, spider-like, for the opportunity

Chalmers scores the winner against Inter Milan.

to pounce upon overstretched opponents on the break.

A single goal advantage for Inter was the usual signal for the team to fall back on prepared positions to engage in a battle of attrition which was remote from the concept of football as a flowing, aggressive sport. Celtic under Stein's direction presented the antithesis of Herrera's assumption and they were prepared to chase goals on the premise that more would be scored than conceded. The team was organised in an enormously flexible 4-2-4 disposition with Murdoch and Auld the links in midfield, Johnstone and Lennox deployed to add speed and width on the flanks and McNeill's aerial power supplemented by the forays of the full backs Craig and Gemmell in periodic excursions upfield in support of the forwards. Celtic in full attacking order were both awesome and exhilarating and a huge live television audience throughout Europe was to be enthralled by their sweeping assaults on the Inter goal.

The game unfolded almost as precisely as an advance reading of the script suggested it would. Craig's tackle from behind on Cappellini offered the Italian champions the chance of a lead in only seven minutes and Mazzola seized it with aplomb, drilling his penalty kick efficiently past Simpson, to cue Inter's retreat into their fortress. Celtic attacked like men demented and Auld and Gemmell both struck the crossbar while Sarti defended his goal with breathtaking agility to repel the Scottish waves. By half-time it was evident that the game had developed into a trial of hearts. Celtic's were younger and in the event more resolute. In the 62nd minute their siege machine penetrated a momentary gap in the Italian screen when Craig rolled a square ball towards Gemmell who unleashed a venomous drive from 25 yards which at last confounded Sarti to bring the teams level. Virtually relentless, Celtic pounded at their opponents until five minutes from full time Murdoch's diagonal shot was redirected by Chalmers into the net and the Glasgow side were champions of Europe. By their thrilling and impressive feat they rewrote the agenda for European football. Prior to 1967 the Champions' Cup had been the exclusive realm of Latin sides – Real Madrid, Benfica and the two Milan teams. For 18 years after Celtic's triumph the trophy left northern Europe only once.

What Celtic had achieved was audacious enough but within a week Glasgow had the opportunity to become the first city to capture the two principal European trophies at the same time when Rangers met

ARNOLD BROWN

Arnold Brown, formerly a chartered accountant and now a successful alternative comedian, was born into a Glasgow Jewish family – "two racial stereotypes for the price of one!" – and found as a schoolboy that he did not fit comfortably into the traditional religious divisions of the city, as reflected in its principal football team.

"One day my father called me into the front room and said: 'Arnold, it's about time you knew the facts of life.' So he told me where bigotry came from, how Rangers and Celtic started the Battle of the Boyne, who won and what the half-time score was, and the meaning of King Billy. Then he took me to my first Rangers-Celtic match. I remember very clearly that before we went in he said, 'Son, I'll tell you what the score is before the game starts. Don't provoke anybody, don't cheer, don't even say a word.'

"We went in to the stadium, well away from the Rangers and Celtic people, to the neutral section protected by the United Nations, and it was an education for a young boy from a sheltered home. I saw some wonderful tricks that day – the uppercut to the chin, the broken beer bottle flung into the crowd, the head butt – and that was only the police in action.

"It was no picnic being Jewish in Glasgow without a team to call your own. Eventually most of the Jewish supporters decided they would follow Third Lanark. Unfortunately, Third Lanark turned out to be the only Scottish club to go out of business since the war and I often thought retrospectively that God punished Third Lanark because Saturday is the Jewish Sabbath and we should have been at the synagogue instead of Cathkin Park.

"When Scotland played Israel

Bayern Munich in the final of the Cup Winners' Cup. Rangers, who so often seemed to be an ill-starred club during this period, were obliged to travel to Nuremberg for a match which was virtually a home tie for Bayern Munich, whose supporters were not likely to be deterred by the prospect of a 100-mile trip up the autobahn. The Ibrox team appproached the match burdened rather than uplifted by the knowledge that the pioneering success of their fiercest rivals had redoubled the pressure from their own supporters to achieve something like parity. Sadly, the appetite for attacking flair which had been sharpened in Lisbon could not have been gratified by the Rangers team which played on 31 May 1967.

Four months earlier they had been dismissed from the Scottish Cup in sensational circumstances when the rank outsiders of Berwick Rangers handed them their first opening round Scottish Cup defeat in 30 years, and the management saw fit to make the forwards George McLean and Jim Forrest scapegoats for the humiliation at Shielfield Park. With his attacking options depressingly narrow the Rangers manager Scot Symon, already under a cloud because of Berwick, fielded three half backs between the wingers Johnston and Henderson, and the Scots' prospects dimmed further when it quickly became apparent that Henderson, on whom so much depended, was not on song against the Bayern full back Kupferschmidt.

Even so, Rangers were offered an outstanding chance to win the tie in the 33rd minute when the guileful Dave Smith contrived an opening for Roger Hynd on the six-yard line, but the big man failed to get enough purchase on his shot and the West German goalkeeper Sepp Maier was able to deflect it. With Bayern also unable to lift their game to any noticeable degree the match drifted towards a desultory draw and the provision for a half hour of extra time was invoked. It seemed woefully appropriate that the deciding goal, after 19 minutes of added time, should be scored by a half back when Franz Roth beat Martin in the Rangers goal.

If the occasion naturally seemed melancholy to the Rangers players and supporters it was nevertheless an astonishing feat for any city to have provided finalists for the two principal European competitions, an achievement unmatched in Britain until 1985 when Liverpool and Everton repeated the circumstances. But if the Old Firm represented the apex of Scottish excellence abroad in 1967 they were reinforced by spectacular contributions from less likely sources. Kilmarnock constructed a powerful run in the Fairs Cities Cup, the forerunner of the present UEFA Cup, and they came remarkably close to giving Scotland a finalist in the third European competition, being dismissed from the tournament by Leeds United in a memorable semi-final tie in which the first leg at Elland Road produced the extraordinary scoreline of Leeds United 4 Kilmarnock 2 after only 38 minutes of play. In the 142 minutes which remained neither team could add to the aggregate, although at Rugby Park Leeds' Welsh international goalkeeper Gary Sprake was required to make two outstanding saves to deny Brian McIlroy the goals which would have swung the contest towards Kilmarnock.

Dundee United had qualified to play in Europe for the first time and were promptly written off when the second-round draw for the Fairs Cup paired them with the trophy holders Barcelona, but in a dramatic upset Bill Hainey and Finn Seaman, with a penalty kick, scored to give United a 2-1 victory in the Nou Camp stadium, while the Tannadice team were even more convincing in the return leg in

Dundee, where goals by Hainey and Ian Mitchell took their aggregate advantage to 4-1, a phenomenal performance over two legs which was not diminished by their dismissal in the next round at the hands of Juventus, although even then the Scots recorded a 1-0 home victory. Dunfermline also represented Scotland in the Fairs Cup and although they went out in the second round they were beaten by the narrowest of margins, winning 4-2 in Fife and losing 2-0 in Yugoslavia to go out on the away goals rule to the eventual winners of the trophy, Dynamo Zagreb.

For the next few years the Scottish presence in Europe remained prominent and Celtic returned to the European Cup final in 1970 after an epic two-leg victory over Leeds United in the semi-finals, but when the Parkhead club travelled to Milan to meet Feyenoord of Holland the Scots repeated the error of Inter in 1967 and underrated their opponents. It took a goal three minutes from the end of injury time to see them beaten 2-1 and it is impossible to believe that Jock Stein would have permitted a similar frailty of will if Celtic had held out to achieve a replay. But it would be equally churlish to suggest that the Dutch side were not entirely worthy winners. Nevertheless, two European Cup finals in three years was further evidence of the entitlement of Stein and Celtic to be considered as equals in the highest ranks of club football.

By a peculiar recasting of the principal actors of 1967, Celtic again faced Inter Milan in the European Cup while Rangers encountered Bayern Munich in the Cup Winners' Cup in the semi-finals of the 1972 tournaments with both second leg matches being played in Glasgow on the same evening, a conjunction which would now be impossible under UEFA rules. As usual, football-minded Glaswegians appeared in multitudes for the occasion, supplemented by throngs of supporters from the rest of Scotland to produce a crowd of 75,000 at Parkhead and an assembly of 80,000 at Ibrox with a live television audience estimated at over 100 million watching throughout Europe.

The script of 1967 was reversed when Rangers disposed of a Bayern side which contained no fewer than seven internationalists, six of whom played in West Germany's impressive 3-1 European Championship victory over England at Wembley five days after their visit to Ibrox. Rangers could have gone through on a goalless draw at home, when they returned from the first leg in Munich with a 1-1 draw but they produced a convincing 2-0 victory in a match which would have graced the final of the tournament. Celtic meanwhile had kicked off half an hour after the start of the Ibrox match so that European viewers could take in the later action from Parkhead, and the television audience was treated to a bonus half hour when neither the Scots nor Inter Milan could resolve their struggle by the end of normal time. A dour contest was eventually settled by a penalty kick decider which saw the unfortunate Dixie Deans rifle his attempt over the crossbar and Inter proceeded to the final in Rotterdam where Ajax Amsterdam extended the Dutch dominion in Europe with a 2-0 win.

While Celtic failed to reach their third Champions' Cup final, Rangers made it to the last stage of the Cup Winners' Cup competition for the third time, their 1967 defeat by Bayern having been preceded by a 4-1 reverse against Fiorentina in the very first final, a two-leg affair in 1961. Moscow Dynamo presented the ultimate obstacle to Rangers' ambition to step out of the deep shadow of Celtic's Lisbon success and for 50 minutes in the Camp Nou stadium the Scots celebrated what threatened to be a total rout of the Soviet side. Midway through

at Hampden Park in a World Cup match it created a terrible dilemma. I had to ask the rabbi which team I should support and should I stand up for the two national anthems or shout abuse during both of them like everybody else.

"And I remember two friends of mine who decided to go to a big Rangers-Celtic Cup final which was not only played on the Sabbath but on the most holy day of the Jewish calendar, the Day of Atonement. We all bought the paper next day to read the report and there was a big picture on the front page of the two of them cheering like mad. They had to leave town very quickly, before they were stoned."

the first half Colin Stein converted a cross from Willie Johnston and Rangers' margin was doubled six minutes before the interval when Johnston, one of the smallest individuals on view, rose to meet a high ball delivered by Dave Smith with a whiplash header. Four minutes after half-time the irrepressible Johnston was supplied with another high ball by Stein for his second and Rangers' third goal of the evening. The disparity between the teams was duplicated in the stands where a forlorn band of 400 Soviet supporters found themselves nullified amid the cacophony of an expeditionary force of 16,000 Scottish travellers, many of whom displayed an alarming tendency to expand their excursion to include the field of play so that each Rangers goal signalled a delay in the proceedings to the understandable exasperation of the Dynamo players and officials.

Having first confirmed their reputation as unreliable competitors away from home the Russians revived without warning to score through Eschtrekov with half an hour left to play and once more, three minutes from time, when Makavikov beat McCloy in a finale which did nothing to diminish the notorious incidence of heart failure in the West of Scotland where the game was being monitored on radio because television coverage was restricted to deferred highlights. The unsavoury scenes which erupted when the Rangers fans swamped the pitch in the belief that the referee had ended the contest when, in fact, there were 60 seconds to go, deprived the Ibrox players of their long anticipated chance to parade a European trophy in a lap of honour, a particularly poignant anticlimax for the team captain John Greig, who had come to epitomise a wholesome determination to respond to the challenge set by the relentless accumulation of honours by Celtic under Stein.

The sins of the supporters were further visited on the players when UEFA forbade Rangers to defend their prize as a punishment for the disorder in Spain but if events at the Camp Nou had been unsavoury they nevertheless concluded a period of remarkable success for Scottish sides against Continental opposition and in just over a decade four clubs – Celtic, Rangers, Kilmarnock and Dundee – had between them appeared in an extraordinary total of five European finals and six semi-finals.

★   ★   ★

Even such an effective record abroad was not enough to disguise the malaise at home. On the single evening, 19 April 1972, when the Old Firm attracted 155,000 spectators to see them take on Bayern Munich and Inter Milan, the combined attendance at Ibrox and Parkhead was more than any of 12 Scottish First Division sides could attract at home during the entire course of the season's League programme and it was evident that football was likely to experience the rapid erosion of its base in an age when the game's traditional audience – the industrial working class – was enjoying unprecedented affluence and a vastly greater choice of leisure activities than had ever previously been available. Scottish football was aware of its ebbing strength long before the antidote was discovered and there were several vigorous but unavailing attempts to staunch the flow of custom from the terracings.

Early in 1973 Rangers hired a hall in Glasgow and invited every other club in the League to discuss their solution to the decline in spectator interest and, in his position as general manager at Ibrox, Willie

Waddell suggested a series of radical changes in the game's system of rewards, including proposals for cash incentives for goalscorers and the withdrawal of points from teams who shared goalless draws. The suggestions were impractical but they had the merit of inaugurating a serious reappraisal of the structure of Scottish football, a debate which produced an overhaul of the Scottish League two years later. In place of the established arrangement of two divisions with two teams being promoted and relegated from one to the other each season, a streamlined Premier Division of ten teams was created with the First and Second Divisions composed of 14 clubs each, and the Edinburgh side Ferranti Thistle, under their new name of Meadowbank Thistle, was admitted to the League to even up the numbers.

Almost half of the teams in the old First Division were deprived at a stroke of their lucrative income from meetings with the top four or five clubs, who remedied the shortfall in their own fixtures by playing each other four times in each league season and the Premier Division clubs – with the exception of Rangers, whose gates fell slightly – were gratified by a marked increase in attendance figures. Some rose impressively, Motherwell, for example, recording an increase of 174 per cent but the total figures for the League in the year after reorganisation declined slightly, which suggested that the gap between the rich and poor would grow wider as the Premier clubs took an increasing percentage of the cash available in the Scottish game. This was a tendency which became even more marked when it was decided in 1981 that clubs would keep all of the gate money from their home games.

Anyone with a rudimentary grasp of accountancy could have guessed the financial implications of the League reshuffle but it would have taken a clairvoyant to foresee the transformation of football in Scotland that was set in train at the same time. The first year of the Premier Division was like any other Scottish season, only more so. Rangers had been the last champions of the old League and they were the first winners of the new and by way of emphasis of Glasgow's domination of the game, they also won the Scottish Cup and League Cup. Rangers were deprived of their title by Celtic in 1977 but achieved a second domestic treble under Jock Wallace the following year only to surrender the championship to Parkhead once more in 1979.

But although it appeared that the *ancien régime* would proceed undisturbed into the new era, the impact of the Premier Division was felt most potently at the other end of the table. In the final season of the former First Division, Dundee United, Aberdeen and Dundee finished fourth, fifth and sixth respectively, well adrift of Rangers but comfortably distant from the relegation area. A year later, struggling to avoid demotion, the three were locked together on the same number of points but Dundee, who had scored the same number of goals as Aberdeen and more, in fact, than Dundee United, were relegated because of their defensive deficiencies. With a failure rate of 20 per cent the Premier Division had given birth to new imperatives and there was no longer an undemanding zone in mid-table where lack of serious ambition could be accommodated.

For Dundee the drop to a lower League was not followed by the swift return anticipated by their supporters and it took the team three years to be restored to the élite, followed by relegation within a year. Dundee rejoined the top ten in 1981 and began to retrieve their position but the damage to the club's financial base and morale had been substantial and the painful process of regeneration was made harder

CHRIS ANDERSON

Shortly before his untimely death from motor neurone disease in 1987, Chris Anderson, the vice-chairman of Aberdeen, recollected how the club had set about revitalising itself to meet the challenges of the Premier Division and so moved into the most successful era of its history.

"Most of the city clubs in Scotland occupied the fat middle of the old First Division and Hibs, Hearts, Dundee, Dundee United and Aberdeen were all there. It didn't matter whether you were top of the league because you weren't going to be bottom but the Premier Division changed all that and we were very nearly relegated for the first time in our history which was the trigger for us to clear the decks and start afresh. We looked at everything, the players, the manager, the stadium, and the fact that Aberdeen was the offshore oil capital of Europe.

"We drew up a profile of our ideal manager and that turned out to be Ally McLeod who breathed new life into the club and the players and, indeed, the whole city. It was a magical time for us because everyone was dancing on air and he instilled confidence in the players and proved that we could be successful so that by the time he was elevated to become Scottish team manager we thought we had established a sound base, so we looked for somebody with a good track record as a player, with command and authority and vision and that man was Billy McNeill, who was only with us for a short time before he moved on to Celtic.

"The pundits said we were crazy to appoint Alex Ferguson but again we had analysed it clinically and coldly and we needed someone with a wide and abundant

to bear by the knowledge that Dundee United had secured ascendancy over their city rivals.

Dundee's plight was depressing enough but there was widespread alarm when Hearts' unpreparedness for the rigours of Premier Division competition was exposed. In 1977 the Tynecastle club was relegated for the first time in its history. Willie Ormond, who had recently resigned as Scotland manager, was put in charge of the team and he guided Hearts back to the top league at Dundee's expense but the playing pool required a major injection of fresh blood for which finance was not made available and Tynecastle was again a First Division venue the following season.

Hearts had returned to the top of the division when the board decided that a mid-term change of guidance was appropriate and Ormond, who as a former Hibs player had been regarded with suspicion by a section of the Maroons' support, was sacked and replaced by Bobby Moncur, but although Hearts were promoted once more they rarely displayed signs of defying the pull of gravity and the inevitable demotion occurred yet again within a season. During this period football in Edinburgh began to resemble a Whitehall farce with Hibs relegated while Hearts moved up in 1980, and the clubs passing each other in opposite directions through the same revolving door a year later.

The travails at Tynecastle had become so enervating that Hearts' support, potentially the third-biggest in Scotland, had shrunk to the point of atrophy while the financial degeneration was a bailiff's joy. In 1981, aware that they could be heading for a listing in *Stubbs' Gazette*, Hearts' directors persuaded the shareholders to agree to a constitutional change which made 350,000 shares available, effectively placing the club on the open market. Kenny Waugh, a city bookmaker and publican, attempted a takeover but he was beaten to the punch by the youthful Edinburgh property developer Wallace Mercer, a man of quixotic temperament. Moncur resigned as manager soon after the boardroom manipulations and was replaced by Tony Ford, whose credentials were not apparent to the Tynecastle supporters or to many others for that matter. Willie Pettigrew and Derek Addison were signed from Dundee United for £155,000, a sum which Hearts did not actually possess, and the team as a whole was providing the kind of discount football which guaranteed an extension of their stay in the First Division. Tony Ford was speedily propelled out on to Gorgie Road clutching his P45, and Alex MacDonald, who had been signed from Rangers to add his extensive experience to the playing strength, displayed such welcome astuteness as a coach that he was elevated to the manager's seat in February 1982, the moment at which it can be said that professionalism at last returned to Tynecastle as a resident.

★   ★   ★

While the deterioration of Hearts presented a melancholy vision of the penalties of Premier Division failure for a proud club, Aberdeen and Dundee United transformed themselves into models for a Scottish football hierarchy which did not automatically accord precedence to Rangers and Celtic. Both clubs had been galvanised by their reprieve from First Division membership at the close of the first season after reorganisation and each took advantage of circumstances which offered them a platform for a sustained assault on the game's prizes. Even if they had been relegated it is impossible to believe that

Aberdeen would have been as traumatised by the experience as Hearts or Dundee. A shining example of good husbandry, the club was run by a board of only three directors, all of whom had at some time in their careers played professional football.

They decided to overhaul the club at a particularly favourable moment in the fortunes of the north-east. The industrial heartland of central Scotland which had provided most of the country's footballers in the past was suffering from a dramatic erosion of its manufacturing base in contrast to Aberdeen where the traditional activities of fishing and farming had been supplemented by the discovery of oil in the North Sea. The lights of the floating rig townships shone across the coastal waters of a region which found itself awash with cash and an unprecedented energy while at Pittodrie the directors recognised that the club had to be steered through a similar period of transition and regeneration.

Accordingly, when Jimmy Bonthrone resigned as manager in 1975 the board looked for a successor whose style would reflect and harness the vitality of his surroundings and their gaze was magnetically drawn to the opposite end of the country, where Ayr United under Ally McLeod had finished higher than Aberdeen at the end of the first

knowledge of the game, who had coaching and technical abilities so, warts and all, Alex Ferguson was our target. We were pretty confident that even if it took a little time, Fergie would do the job for us and so he did.

"On top of those appointments we tried out ideas like our Dons Line information service which took 300 calls in the first hour and 2,500 on the first day. We wanted rapport with the supporters and for them to be close to the club, other than seeing the game on Saturday. Some of our changes were resisted by others in the game, predictably, because for all that Scotland has rebelliousness and gallousness and tremendous energy, there has always been a great hard core of conservatism which is unreceptive to good or revolutionary ideas, but although some people laughed at us in the beginning, a lot of our ideas came to be accepted as the norm. However, we did it ourselves because we knew there would be no real help inside Scotland with the ideas which we wanted to introduce."

Ferguson, in charge of heightened ambition at Pittodrie.

Premier Division championship campaign. McLeod's achievement at Ayr was even more impressive in the context of the slim resources available to him. Ayr was primarily an agricultural market town as Aberdeen had been, but with a considerably smaller population, and United's gates were hardly more than half those at Pittodrie. In McLeod, however, the club had uncovered a flamboyant character who regarded excitement as an energy resource to be exploited and refined to the discomfiture – on several occasions – of opponents as substantial as Rangers and Celtic.

McLeod had no prejudice against supplementing his inspirational powers by offering his players handsome bonuses for victories over the Old Firm but nobody could deny that the manager's personality had an alchemic effect on the team and its support, transmuting tradesmen into exhibitionists, and even if the impact was half illusion there was a definite force of will around Somerset Park which made it a peculiarly awkward venue for the kind of opponents who would not in normal circumstances have entertained too much self-doubt. When he left United for Aberdeen, the town of Ayr appeared to have suffered a deeply felt bereavement. Petitions were signed pleading with him to stay. When he resigned as national team manager three years later, the rest of Scotland was in the throes of similar depression, though for very different reasons, and there were those who wished he had paid more attention to the petition.

At Pittodrie, however, he expanded his career as a charismatic motivator and his faith in his own ability was never anchored by consideration of a disproportionate lack of experience. When he negotiated his salary with the Aberdeen chairman Dick Donald he offered to take a wage on the understanding that it would be doubled if the team won a trophy within 18 months under his guidance. Donald, a member of a family of showbusiness entrepreneurs who owned the prosperous His Majesty's Theatre in Aberdeen, agreed instantly and his grasp of the economics of vaudeville turned out to be percipient because McLeod was appointed Scotland manager after a year and a half, by which time the League Cup had been brought to the Pittodrie boardroom.

When McLeod left for Park Gardens he was replaced by Billy McNeill, the former Celtic captain who had begun teething managerially with Clyde and although it could be said that Aberdeen failed to win anything during his spell in the north-east, he carried the club to second place in the championship, two points behind Rangers. Aberdeen also appeared in the Scottish Cup final in 1978, to be denied the honour again by Rangers in a 2-1 victory, but those alert to the subcurrents of the game in Scotland perceived that McNeill had greatly consolidated progress at Pittodrie where a team which might have achieved a double conceded precedence only to a club which had achieved the domestic treble. Within weeks of the Cup final McNeill had moved on to Parkhead as successor to Jock Stein and for the third time in as many years Aberdeen were obliged to fill their manager's seat.

Their next candidate was to preside over one of the most startling chapters in the history of any Scottish club but at the time a straw poll of observers would probably have yielded a majority who thought that Aberdeen had bought themselves a packet of trouble in the shape of Alex Ferguson. A former Rangers centre forward who won nothing during his playing career, Ferguson had revived the fortunes of St Mirren, even touring the streets of Paisley in a car equipped with a

loudhailer to exhort the locals to come and see his team, but his period at Love Street ended in unseemly circumstances when he was sacked. Aberdeen selected their new manager knowing that he intended to appeal to an industrial tribunal about his treatment by a rival club.

In his first year at Pittodrie Ferguson was distracted both by the acrimonious circumstances of his departure from Love Street and by the prolonged terminal illness of his father, and he made frequent and fatiguing trips to and from Glasgow. The team slipped down the table to fourth place but in 1980 the Aberdeen directors were rewarded with the symbiosis they had cultivated for years when the Old Firm's monopoly on the championship was broken for the first time in 14 seasons. Having drawn on the sturdy and dependable temper of the north-east of Scotland to create the firm basis of a challenging club they had looked to the west of the country to provide the inspirational, even fiery leadership, that would be required to sustain a head to head challenge with the Glasgow monoliths, and under Ferguson Aberdeen achieved the critical shift from passivity to assertiveness which at last disrupted the established pattern of Scottish club football.

Alex Ferguson matched Ally McLeod with a League Cup win and added three championships and four Scottish Cup victories. By way of emphasis of the new priorities, the trophy was won twice against Rangers and once against Celtic, both of whom regarded a Hampden final as the next best thing to a home tie. Three of the Scottish Cup successes were consecutive, a feat only Rangers had previously achieved this century. As far as the northern supporters were concerned, however, nothing in the litany of accumulated honours could rival the acquisition of the European Cup Winners' Cup in 11 May 1983 in Gothenburg, an occasion memorable for its oddly dreamlike atmosphere. Although Real Madrid, still an illustrious name in European football, were the other finalists the attendance was extremely low, probably because the game was screened live in Sweden and because an electrical storm which had threatened to break for two hours before the match finally erupted in impressive fashion at the very moment when neutrals had to decide whether to head for the stadium or remain in their armchairs. Of the 17,804 present something like 15,000 had made the short journey across the North Sea from Scotland, including a large contingent of fishermen from the north-east ports, who had arranged to sell their catch in Gothenburg. After Black had opened the scoring, only for Juanito to equalise with a penalty kick, Aberdeen showed how much they had learned about resilience and resolve when Hewitt scored the winning goal with a glorious header in extra time.

★   ★   ★

Within three days of Aberdeen's triumph in Gothenburg (all the more gratifying for the complete absence of spectator trouble in the city or at the match) Dundee United spectacularly emphasised the fact that provincialism was an alterable state of mind rather than a certainty of geography when they also burst through the cordon drawn around the League championship by Rangers and Celtic to take the title to Tannadice for the first time in the club's history. As at Pittodrie, the effect of a near escape from relegation had concentrated minds and talents at Tannadice wonderfully and, again resembling Aberdeen, United responded by putting distance between themselves and the demotion zone, so much so that in the subsequent decade their worst position was fifth with a 24-point margin separating them from Kilmarnock who went down in 1981 along with Hearts.

Aberdeen had a city to themselves but United were obliged to compete within a similar population for a share of the available audience with Dundee, who had in any case traditionally been the dominant club on Tayside. By one of the ironies which abound in the history of the clubs who are Britain's closest neighbours, the United directors looked to Dens Park to find the man who was to transfigure their club's fortunes and in November 1971 Jim McLean walked a hundred yards along Tannadice Street to begin one of the most durable managerial tenures in the modern game. He could have stayed with Dundee whose own manager, John Prentice, had just resigned but the Dens Park board overlooked their own coach and preferred to appoint the former Rangers boss Davie White.

From the moment of his appointment McLean insisted that his new club would have to discover and nourish its own talent rather than compete, with slender resources, on a transfer market which naturally favoured richer teams. In countrywide expeditions designed to trawl for promising juvenile players and sift for those who might graduate into the professional game, perhaps with international honours, McLean had the inestimable advantage of what appeared to be a psychic ability to discern the profile of the complete footballer disguised within the gangly frame of a half-formed adolescent.

For more than a decade and a half McLean's most repetitive adage portrayed Tannadice as a corner shop compared to the supermarkets of Ibrox and Parkhead but the image best illustrated the volume of support at the respective grounds; there was always caviar rather than corned beef on display at Tannadice even if the total attendance in any

Paul Hegarty, The Dundee United captain, as full time signals Dundee United's defeat in the 1987 UEFA Cup final.

The Dundee United management celebrate the club's first ever championship in May 1983, but it took time for Jim McLean (right) to realise he could afford to smile.

season rarely exceeded half of the number who flocked to either of the Glasgow clubs. By the middle of the 1980s squads for Scotland's World Cup matches frequently contained half a dozen United graduates while the Scottish team which was defeated on penalty kicks in the final of the FIFA Youth World Cup in June 1989 used five Tannadice apprentices. As McLean habitually produced talent after precocious talent in a line stretching from Andy Gray through Dave Narey and Maurice Malpas to Richard Gough and Kevin Gallacher, it was easy to believe that when the Tannadice lights burned into the night there was an experiment in genetic engineering in progress to clone some new prodigy in a tangerine jersey. In fact, the perpetual revelation of precocious gifts was the result of a diligent and endless scrutiny of eager boys attracted to local coaching sessions by notices pinned to trees in parks from Dingwall to Gretna.

The first trophy ever to be installed in the Tannadice boardroom arrived in 1980 when the so-called New Firm of Dundee United and Aberdeen contested a 0-0 draw at Hampden followed by a 3-0 victory for McLean's team in a replay at Dens Park, of all venues, and United retained the trophy by another 3-0 margin the following year when again the final was played at Dens Park, a circumstance which greatly grieved the supporters of the beaten team, who happened to be Dundee. As though United were possessed by a bizarre compulsion to register their triumphs on the opposite side of the street the game which decided the 1983 Scottish championship was also won in a derby at Dens Park on the final day of the season when the race ran to a quite improbable finale. United led by a single point at the beginning of a melodramatic afternoon which saw their nearest rivals Celtic visit Ibrox and Aberdeen at home to Hibs. If Dundee had scored one more goal against their neighbours the Premier Division title chase would have ended in a dead heat because Celtic's 4-2 defeat of Rangers would have placed them level with United on points with both teams having identical scoring records. In such a circumstance Aberdeen could have carried the flag north with an 8-0 victory against Hibs; they won 5-0. In the event, United's 2-1 win at Dens confirmed a remarkable metamorphosis under their lugubrious manager.

McLean was less well rewarded at other climactic moments, Scottish Cup finals at Hampden Park in particular. Five times United travelled to Glasgow to contest the trophy and five times they lost, on three occasions to Celtic, once to Rangers and once to St Mirren in 1987, the latter defeat marking the first of a dolorous four days for the Tayside team as they went on to a 1-1 draw with Gothenburg in the second leg of the UEFA Cup final, a result which saw them lose the tie on a 2-1 aggregate. It was a cruelly unrewarding end to what had been a momentous season for the club, who had accounted for such European notables as Barcelona and Borussia Moenchengladbach on their way to the UEFA finals. The United players were clearly drained by the demands of a programme which had seen many of them play over 80 games. Appearances in Scotland's World Cup finals campaign in Mexico the previous summer cost them an effective close season break. Nevertheless, defeat against Gothenburg afforded the opportunity to witness an extraordinary display of sportsmanship by the Tayside supporters. Denied a European trophy on their own ground by a Gothenburg goal which was the direct result of a questionable decision on the part of a Rumanian referee who ignored what appeared to be a foul on Paul Sturrock, the United following transcended their

Downcast Dundee United fans absorb defeat by Gothenburg at Tannadice. Nevertheless, they cheered both sides on a lap of honour and were rewarded when UEFA bestowed a Fair Play award upon them, with £25,000 which was spent on stadium improvements.

disappointment to acclaim both teams as they took a lap of honour after the final whistle, even throwing their scarves and favours for the Swedish players to wave as they paraded the cup.

This singular demonstration of goodwill was seen by a television audience in 19 countries and it so impressed the European football authorities that they bestowed an inaugural fair play award on the United fans in the shape of a £25,000 prize which McLean declared would be spent on improving ground facilities. In the aftermath of the Heysel tragedy two years earlier it was both deeply poignant and greatly heartening that an unfashionable club forced to endure a double disappointment at the apex of the team's fortunes could provide such an affirmation of the values which inspired the Victorian pioneers of the simplest game.

*   *   *

The encouraging revival of full-blooded football life outside Glasgow was also demonstrated by a belated and wholly unexpected flourish at Tynecastle. With Alex MacDonald in charge of the team, assisted by his former Ibrox playing partner Sandy Jardine, Hearts stabilised after their third return to the Premier Division in 1983 and established themselves handily in mid-table for the next two seasons but there was nothing to suggest that in 1985-86 they were about to offer an utterly compelling challenge which would sustain the championship race until the last seconds of the final afternoon of the League programme. After an indifferent start to the season which included a depressing 6-2 defeat by St Mirren, Hearts' opportunity arrived at the beginning of December when the teams above them in the table – Aberdeen, Celtic and Dundee United – were permitted to postpone their League fixtures because of the absence of club players required for Scotland's arduous trip to Australia for the second leg of the match to decide the final place in the Mexican World Cup finals the following summer.

Hearts had no such demands on their strength and were able to play Clydebank and Dundee, taking three points from four to move level with Aberdeen at the top of the Premier Division. When Dundee United defeated Aberdeen on 21 December, Hearts reached the top of the League where they remained until 3 May 1986, buoyed by a happy combination of comparative freedom from injuries and suspensions and a formidable consistency which was underpinned by a home record without defeat. Such was Hearts' self-confidence that they also swept to the Scottish Cup final so that the team had set up the opportunity of an extraordinary double within the space of seven days at the end of the season.

Hearts could, in fact, have put the title beyond Celtic's reach with any kind of emphatic win against Clydebank in the final Tynecastle match of the campaign, but the Edinburgh players reacted nervously to the implications of possible defeat and settled for a cautious 1-0 victory which, as events were to prove, effectively cost them the championship. Celtic, with a game in hand against Motherwell, duly hauled themselves to within two points during the following midweek but their chance of snatching the flag from Hearts' grasp depended upon a defeat for the Tynecastle side at Dundee on the final Saturday while they themselves secured at least a four-goal margin over St Mirren at Love Street.

A cavalcade of maroon-favoured vehicles made their way towards Tayside on 3 May, including detachments from England, the Republic

By reverting to the characteristic British
game, the object of mockery by the critics,
the Scots launched themselves at Sweden
to score in only ten minutes when McCall
prodded McPherson's back-header across
the line.

Above A second goal from Johnston's penalty kick put Scotland 2-0 ahead against Sweden but a late goal by Stromberg kept the result in doubt and it was relief as much as triumph which brought the Scottish substitutes off their seats at the end. *Below* Viking with helmet contemplates the riddle of a tartan sombrero in Genoa.

Above Cayasso scores for Costa Rica in Scotland's opening World Cup finals match in Italy to trigger a week of despondency. *Below* Andy Roxburgh.

Above The 1990 Scottish Cup final was played to a finish after one game with an unprecedented penalty-kick decider after a goal-less draw. Here, Aberdeen's Dutch goalkeeper Theo Snelders saves from Anton Rogan of Celtic . . . and permits himself a spasm of ecstasy. Brian Irvine scored with the following kick to beat Packy Bonner and carry the trophy north.

Alex McLeish of Aberdeen and Celtic's Packy Bonner encounter each other in the 1990 Scottish Cup final, a goal-less draw at the end of 90 minutes.

Above Billy McNeill exhorts Celtic as extra time beckons in the Scottish Cup final against Aberdeen.
Below Andy Roxburgh and fans, Oslo 1988.

Above Maurice Johnston and girlfriend Karen Bell as the player pledges renewed allegiance to Celtic, April 1989. *Below* Johnston with another suitor, 10 July 1989. His jilting of Celtic had been contentious. His arrival at Ibrox astounded the Scottish football world and made headlines as far away as Australia.

McCormick cartoon.

of Ireland and West Germany, and there was hardly an individual amongst the 10,000 Hearts fans whose grasp of the afternoon's permutations would not have done justice to a tallyman. The outcome which would most simply resolve who got the championship was a win or draw for Hearts but as the travelling support prepared for revels they were not to know that a virus had rampaged through the team, debilitating Kenny Black, Brian Whittaker, John Colquhoun and Neil Berry and causing the elegant Craig Levein to be kept in his bed while the championship decider was fought out at Dens Park, which had begun to develop a reputation for operatic finales to rival La Scala.

For most of the match Hearts were not unduly troubled by a Dundee side playing without menace but the psychological climate became turbulent when news spread through the ground that Celtic were in the business of annihilating St Mirren at Love Street. Two goals each from Brian McClair and Maurice Johnston and another scored by Paul McStay put Celtic 5-0 ahead after 54 minutes. This news added to the suffocating tension at Dens Park where Black had replaced Whittaker at the start of the second half, an exchange of one invalid for another, but with seven minutes to go and half of the Edinburgh team visibly struggling, the game was still goalless and Celtic remained impotent. The title veered from east to west in the time it took for Connor of Dundee to deliver a corner kick from the right, knocked on by Brown to the unmarked Albert Kidd who had only to switch it past Smith, entirely exposed in the visitors' goal. The will of their supporters was palpable but Hearts had no reserves of strength or inspiration to call upon and Kidd was able to twist the knife with a second goal two minutes from full-time.

The scenes on the terracings and in the stands resembled a public acknowledgment of bereavement; children in tears, men swathing their faces in maroon scarves to hide their distraught features like Muslim women with their chadors, an elderly couple wordlessly clutching each other in mutual consolation.

The news of Hearts' distress had been conveyed instantly to Love Street where a detonation of noise from the crowd told the Celtic players that the Edinburgh team had fallen behind. Their supporters celebrated extravagantly when the final whistle signalled the 34th championship to be credited to Parkhead in 98 years. The Hearts following, meanwhile, was entitled to suppose that their side's demise had been orchestrated by Torquemada on advice from the Marquis de Sade. Twenty-one years earlier Hearts had also found themselves within a game of the title when they played Kilmarnock at Tynecastle in the concluding match of the 1964-65 season only to be beaten 2-0 and lose the flag on the goal average rule which applied at that time and which came to a result by dividing the goals for by the goals against. The Edinburgh club proposed to the Scottish League that if goals were to decide a championship then the method should be a simple subtraction of goals conceded from those scored, a motion which was promptly accepted. If goal differences had prevailed in 1965, Hearts would have been Scottish champions and they would have been winners in 1986 if the goal average rule had not been changed.

As for the damage done to them at Dens Park, Hearts had not conceded a goal from a corner kick in any of the 35 Premier Division matches which preceded their encounter with Dundee, nor had Albert Kidd scored in any other League game that season but if the Tynecastle supporters were inclined, naturally enough, to dwell on the seven minutes which they believed separated their team from what would

A disbelieving Alex MacDonald, the Hearts manager, as the title was torn from his grasp.

certainly have been a remarkable achievement, they might consider that in fact the margin was even tighter than they had first supposed. In the opening match of the 1985-86 season Hearts had gone a goal ahead against Celtic at Tynecastle when John Colquhoun scored in the first half, a lead which was sustained until 80 seconds from time when Paul McStay equalised with a shot which deflected past Henry Smith off a defender. At the time the loss of a point so late in the game disappointed but did not depress the Hearts players but, of course, they were not regarded as realistic title contenders. Celtic, who like Rangers, live in the permanent expectation that they will dispute the destination of every domestic honour, knew that the concluding moments of a contest can be as critical as any other.

Hearts were obliged to digest the same lesson in harrowing circumstances and in a foreseeable aftermath to their trauma at Dens Park they were comprehensively beaten 3-0 by Aberdeen in the Scottish Cup final a week later. Although their double loss was responsible for a massive sense of anticlimax in Edinburgh, the Aberdeen manager Alex Ferguson was both gracious and accurate when he declared that even if no honours had gone to Tynecastle, the season belonged to Hearts. And so it did because, aside from the team's contribution to a highly memorable year, their supporters had revealed a developed sense of dignity when they lingered long after full time at both Dens and Hampden to demand that they be allowed to acclaim their beaten team.

Like Dundee United fans in their salutes to Gothenburg, the Hearts following heightened the sense that football in Scotland had earned the right to a more wholesome enthusiasm and the thousands who aligned themselves to the Maroons made an even more precisely assessed contribution to the welfare of the Scottish game. By their performances on the field Hearts had resuscitated an enormous latent interest in their activities so that total attendances in the League side again swelled to impressive levels which attracted admiration and curiosity throughout Europe.

★　　★　　★

Hearts supporters at Dens Park, their emotions wrenched by a cruel twist to their championship ambitions.

In the excitement of Hearts' unpredictable surge the reversal in fortunes of yet one more east coast team was not greeted with the attention it would otherwise have deserved. There was not a Second Division club which wanted to see Dunfermline promoted from the bottom league for the simple reason that, inspired by the frequently dishevelled but enormously enthusiastic figure of Jim Leishman, the Fife club marched around the least-favoured venues in the country with a support which was as sizeable as it was devoted. The prayers of club treasurers in places like Stenhousemuir and Coatbridge were denied when Dunfermline moved up a league and arrived with a band of retainers which was already more numerous than anything else on show in the First Division and when, within the space of another season, the Pars' upward momentum launched them into the Premier Division they could number crowds that were bigger than some clubs in the élite and several in the English First Division.

Leishman's unorthodox style of management – inspirational parables and joke competitions were typical of his pre-match routines – was reinforced by the coaching expertise of his assistants, Gregor Abel and his successor Iain Munro, and in their first season in the Premier Division they beat Celtic in the League and knocked Rangers out of the Scottish Cup. However, they found it beyond their resources to consolidate a position in the top ten and were relegated within a single term although they subsequently bounced back after one season in the First Division. Dunfermline's experience illustrated an obvious design flaw in the Premier Division which was emphasised by the decision to admit only one promoted team each year after the 1987-88 season, namely, that the division between rich and poor in Scotland was increasingly hard to bridge. By and large, though, Dunfermline's support remained steady during the team's return to the First Division and all the signs indicated that Fife would continue to add its quota of devotees to the swelling numbers who passed through Scottish turnstiles each week.

While the east coast yielded a new generation of teams remodelled to meet the demanding criteria of the new football order in Scotland, it was left to Celtic to maintain the challenge from Glasgow with a steady acquisition of championships, their sixth in 13 years of the Premier Division being captured in 1988, the club's centenary year. By contrast, Rangers entered on an extraordinarily barren spell of League campaigns which saw them become no more than a mid-table outfit in everything except support, and even that bedrock of previous Ibrox superiority showed alarming signs of disenchantment. The total of home crowds for the 1981-82 League season even fell below the 300,000 mark, an average of 16,400, and as season succeeded season with no sign of Rangers winning the single honour which mattered to the club's huge but dormant following, the team's indifferent performance became a phenomenon. Newspaper headlines habitually referred to Rangers as a sleeping giant but the club was in a coma as far as its supporters were concerned. There was evidence of an attempt to come to terms with the imperatives of a changed world in late 1983 after the resignation of John Greig as manager.

He had been appointed to the position in May 1978 after the sudden departure of Jock Wallace, who resigned after a dispute over his salary only days after taking the club to its second treble in three years. Greig stepped straight up from the team's ranks when in other circumstances he might have expected to continue playing for another year or two before cutting his managerial teeth at the likes of Falkirk and Hearts prior to a return to the club with which he was irrevocably associated. Billy McNeill, who had captained Celtic at the same time as Greig had been Rangers' skipper, had followed just such a preparatory course with Clyde and Aberdeen before he too was called back to Parkhead to succeed Jock Stein in the same month that his playing rival took up the reins at Ibrox.

In their first season as Old Firm managers it looked as if Greig would pilot his side to yet another clean sweep, the fourth of his career as a player and manager, but although the League Cup and Scottish Cup ended up in the Ibrox trophy room, it was Celtic who denied Rangers the championship in an epic Old Firm match at Parkhead on 21 May 1979. Celtic had to win to seize the prize while Rangers only required a draw and a single point from either of their remaining matches against Partick Thistle and Hibernian. The Parkhead game was a rearranged fixture and Rangers had already beaten Celtic that month with a 1-0 victory at Hampden, which was used because of reconstruction work at Ibrox.

For most of the course of the pair's final encounter of the season Rangers were again in command, leading 1-0 at half-time by an Alex MacDonald goal and with an extra man when Johnny Doyle was sent off ten minutes after the interval. Exactly midway through the second half the contest entered a Wagnerian phase when Roy Aitken equalised, the prelude to a remorseless application of will on Celtic's part which produced another goal when McLuskey netted with 15 minutes remaining, only for Russell to bring the sides level two minutes afterwards. With both sets of supporters in a state of mania the protagonists hurled themselves at each other frantically and even the ball seemed to have acquired a kind of demented energy with seven minutes left when it spun from McLuskey's boot off the palms of McCloy in the Rangers goal and finished with a ricochet from the hapless Jackson into his own net. Still the bombardment continued, although now principally around McCloy who was beaten once more in the final minute by a venomous shot from McLeod.

Greig's first act at full-time was to move to the Celtic bench and shake hands with Billy McNeill. He had come within minutes of a grand slam but he was never to get any closer and his record of two League Cup victories and two successful Scottish Cup finals in five seasons, which would have gratified virtually any other support in the country, could not quell the voracious appetite for the championship which alone could satisfy the Ibrox legions. When Greig resigned, distressed by incessant pressure from the media and public which had begun to affect his family, the Rangers directors and supporters were unanimous in their choice of successor; Alex Ferguson, former Rangers player and architect of Aberdeen's transformation into a significant football power, was the man who would launch Rangers back to the top of the League.

Their hopes were confounded. Ferguson discussed the possibility with the then Rangers chairman John Paton but chose to stay at Pittodrie, a decision partly based on his realisation that the Ibrox board was in a state of flux. Bemused and rejected, Rangers then turned to Tannadice for another likely saviour, but Jim McLean too (after a weekend swaying from one option to the other) preferred to stay with a supposedly peripheral club rather than take charge of the most powerful institution in Scottish football. For the Rangers board, these rebuffs were made particularly painful by the fact that they had publicly stated that they would not have restricted either man in their

Wallace salutes his second spell in charge of Rangers, but he could not revive a languishing club.

signing policies; Roman Catholic players could earn their wages in the bastion of Scottish Protestantism if they so desired. This is what they had repeatedly been told would indicate the club's willingness to help demolish the relics of 17th-century politics and defuse the sectarian aggression of a militant core of their support yet it was insufficient to persuade Ferguson or McLean to forego control of the new generation of champions.

Thwarted in their attempt to commandeer the resources of the present, Rangers looked backwards for inspiration, to the man who had equalled Jock Stein's achievement of two clean sweeps of domestic honours, and so Jock Wallace arrived from Motherwell for a second spell of command at Ibrox, with the Fir Park club receiving £125,000 in compensation for the loss of his services. Although presumably he could now have insisted on the same liberty to freely recruit men of any persuasion it can be safely assumed that the number of prayers of intercession dedicated to his success fell some way short of landslide proportions.

For a spell, Wallace's methods produced the desired results and after his inaugural fixture against Aberdeen at Pittodrie the team went 22 matches without defeat.

Ian Ferguson and Cammy Fraser arrived from Dundee and the Skol League Cup was retained with a satisfying victory over Celtic in which Ally McCoist scored a hat-trick, but at the end of the season Rangers were 15 points behind Ferguson's Aberdeen and the margin between the sides increased to 21 points a year later. In September 1984 even Wallace appeared to stand on the brink of apostasy in the eyes of Ibrox fundamentalists when Rangers travelled to Dublin for a first round UEFA Cup tie only to be beaten 3-2 by the Irish part-timers of Bohemians, who came within six minutes of winning on aggregate in the second leg at Ibrox before Paterson and Redford scored late goals to see the Scots through.

Rangers rose to a more stirring performance when they were dismissed from the tournament by Inter Milan in the next round on a 4-3 aggregate but the significant outcome of the second leg at Ibrox was the fact that the club's Northern Irish captain John McLelland flew to London to sign for Watford, the previous season's beaten FA Cup finalists and a friendly enough outfit, but otherwise no more than a middle of the table London club. They had nevertheless been able to offer McLelland substantially higher wages than Rangers were willing to pay despite the fact that the Irishman made it clear he was willing to come to an accommodation which would keep him in Scotland.

There was to be only one more trophy during Jock Wallace's tenure, the Skol League Cup again, and the Scottish Cup proved to be as infertile as the League when Rangers were knocked out by Dundee in consecutive seasons before Hearts beat them in the first round of the tournament in 1986. Far from narrowing the gulf between themselves and Aberdeen, Celtic or Dundee United, or even Hearts, it was evident that Rangers were floundering a decade behind the leaders of the Premier Division pack with little likelihood of revival. There was a substantial display of disgruntlement at the club's AGM, always a lively affair, on 11 October 1985. Shareholders harassed the directors and even turned on the comedian Andy Cameron, whose credentials as a publicly avowed Rangers supporter were immaculate, when he informed the directors: "It's obvious to us you'll never sign a Catholic – why don't you come out and say it?" The comic was hissed when he added "I don't care if you never sign a Catholic player or sign ten. What matters is that Rangers have the best team." Cameron was disabused of the notion that his ecumenical tendency was shared by the bulk of his fellows when he was buttonholed outside and advised by a defender of the faith from Bargeddie that he should "support Celtic and play in Hibernian halls". But a reformation was at hand as a result of a boardroom reshuffle which eventually saw effective power at Ibrox placed in the hands of David Holmes, a director of the John Lawrence building company which controlled the club, a man anxious to see Rangers expand to its limits as a business enterprise, who grasped that it would take a revolutionary stroke to free the club from its depressing predicament.

Having concluded that new guidance was required in the manager's office Holmes ignored previous Ibrox conventions and identified Graeme Souness as the transforming agent. Souness had moved on from his illustrious interlude with Liverpool to play with Sampdoria of Genoa but on at least three occasions the previous year he had been heard to mention that he would be gratified by the opportunity to join Rangers as player-manager. The notion was not inspired by the elevation of Kenny Dalglish to just such a post with Liverpool; Souness's first intimations of immortality preceded the appointment of Dalglish at Anfield by two months.

His accession was announced on 7 April 1986 and although he was captain of Scotland it was instantly noted that he had never played for a Scottish club, a fact which increased the exotic ambience which suddenly enveloped Rangers who had with one mighty leap of the imagination liberated their immense reservoir of dormant support, so much so that when they met Celtic in the Glasgow Cup final at Ibrox there was a capacity crowd to witness and celebrate a 3-2 win in extra time. The Ibrox legions attached immense significance to the fact that Celtic were newly crowned champions after the barnstorming finale which had frustrated Hearts, and for all his sophistication Souness supplemented his instruction in the peculiarities of Glasgow's internecine collision which had begun on the final day of the League season when Rangers confirmed a place in the following season's UEFA Cup by excluding Dundee on goal difference. They should have been uplifted by the thought of another challenge in

European football but the Rangers players had been despondent in the dressing-room. Their achievement was overshadowed by the news that Hearts had been surpassed by the Parkhead challenge.

But the Rangers players were soon emboldened by the style of the new régime, those of them, that is, who survived the purges which were applied to the playing strength. Fifteen players left and nine new men arrived during Souness's first season as the club's dazzled supporters came to realise that Rangers' financial clout, perhaps the most powerful in Britain, was to be applied as it had never been before. The Ibrox spending carousel turned the Scottish football world upside down and was the occasion for incredulity and sometimes resentment from English clubs who were used to regarding Scotland as a source of talent to be plundered at will from a Mickey Mouse league. The first season's transfer costs were not especially high, particularly when fees for outgoing players were deducted, and a major infusion of highly professional talent was secured for an outlay of only £1,725,000.

There was a less obvious cost to be counted as Souness bought and sold almost obsessively. The Rangers wage bill escalated sharply as the century-old flow of players north to south across the border was spectacularly reversed. East Anglia was an early target with Chris Woods being removed from Norwich and Terry Butcher enticed from Ipswich, the latter deal being to the surprise and irritation of Tottenham Hotspur who had not imagined that the massive England defender would prefer a career in Scotland to the lure of London. Their complacency cost them his signature. Spurs were soon glad enough to accept £450,000 in Scottish banknotes for the granite-hard Graham Roberts although their manager David Pleat made the peculiar comment: "He kicked people in England and now I suppose he'll go up and kick people in Scotland." The London club was definitely not amused the following season when Souness further diluted the playing strength at White Hart Lane by purchasing Richard Gough, whom Dundee United had refused to sell to Rangers a year previously. Spurs were anxious to convey to their supporters the notion that their team captain had only been allowed to go because Rangers had doubled the £750,000 he had cost them from Dundee United, which was an exaggeration to the tune of £400,000. The spree continued under new management when Rangers were bought by the youthful Scottish industrial entrepreneur David Murray in the autumn of 1988 and by the end of Souness's third full season in charge the arrival of Trevor Steven from Everton carried his spending beyond the £10 million mark although the sale of departing players brought an income of around £4 million.

Rangers had become the supernova of British football but their expansionist policy was anything but risk-free. When David Murray purchased the controlling interest from Lawrence Marlborough he acquired a business whose assets might have totalled £20 million (what is the value of a football stadium, other than in its development potential?) but he also fell heir to a capital debt of around £8 million with an annual interest charge of over £1 million which cancelled out the contribution from the Rangers Pools organisation. Murray promised that Souness, who had been made a director after buying a £600,000 share in the club, would continue to have cash made available to buy top quality players as the need arose and the new owner directed his formidable business energies to the task of dismantling the debt.

The excitement and publicity generated since the advent of Souness was such that the team's sponsors, the Scottish & Newcastle brewing concern, declared themselves delighted with the returns on their initial investment. In the summer of 1989 Rangers were able to announce sponsorship deals worth a total of £9 million, with £4 million contributed by the Admiral sportswear company. When the new contract was announced, Rangers' recently appointed chief executive Alan Montgomery declared that two-thirds of the club's income would be derived from sources other than gate money. Even that was to be increased when plans for an upgrading of the stadium's capacity were revealed, involving the construction of a second tier of 7,000 seats in the south stand to accommodate a total of 52,000 spectators. The supplementary space was to be sold by a scheme common enough in the United States but comparatively novel in Britain whereby investors would pay up to £1600 to secure the right to a seat for 35 years on top of which they would buy an annual season-ticket, although, if they were unable to attend Ibrox for any length of time, the club would offer to sell their ticket and split the proceeds between Rangers and the seat-holder. If such sweeping financial changes put Rangers in a different league from the rest of Scottish football, the directors were candid about their desire to be included in any arrangement which might bring about a European League of superclubs.

The return on Rangers' investment which mattered most to the supporters had to be on the field and Souness speedily rewarded them with a Skol League Cup victory in October 1986, made sweeter by the defeat of Celtic in the final, but the big dividend arrived at Pittodrie on 2 May 1987 when a Terry Butcher header was enough to secure a 1-1 draw to take the championship to Ibrox for the first time in nine years. The following season it looked as though Rangers would have to install arrival and departure lounges at Ibrox to cope with the turnover in personnel when £3,775,000 was spent to bring a full team of 11 players – four Englishmen, five Scots, a Dane and an Israeli – to Glasgow. Not all were around for the duration, Mark Falco being purchased from Watford in July 1987 and sold to Queen's Park Rangers in December, while Jan Bartram was signed from Silkeborg in January 1988 and returned to Denmark in July, having provided much incidental amusement during his brief domicile in Glasgow.

The Danish internationalist had been enticed by Souness's promises that Rangers were in the process of constructing a team in the European mould but Bartram discovered that the Premier Division was not a haven for football played at the pace of carpet bowls and he confided his disgruntlement to journalists at a Denmark team gathering, mentioning *en passant* that his manager, who was not averse to Rangers applying themselves in the physical department, was "a bastard". This comment flew back to Ibrox ahead of Bartram, who was invited to explain himself in a private session with Souness on his return and the Dane eventually emerged to explain to an avid press corps that something had been gained in translation and that he had, in fact, referred to his boss as "a rascal". Two months later Bartram bared his heart to the Danish press once more, this time declaring that he would not return to Glasgow where he would certainly be lynched by the Rangers fans who were by his account a proper bunch of rascals. Souness was not the loser by such a hasty turnaround of personnel; he bought Mark Falco for £270,000 and sold him for £350,000, while Bartram came at £180,000 and went at £315,000.

Of course, when David Holmes first introduced Graeme Souness to the media as a Rangers manager the question of the club's signing policy arose promptly and Holmes as speedily replied that there were

Alex Smith, sacked by St Mirren less than a year after guiding the Paisley team to a rare Scottish Cup triumph.

no longer any religious barriers at Ibrox. Previous assurances of this kind had turned out to have all the validity of an Aborigine land treaty so scepticism was inevitable but Souness was married to a Roman Catholic and when he was interested in signing the Glasgow-born R.C. Ray Houghton from Oxford United some of the hard-core supporters were alarmed enough to display a banner which read "Keep Ibrox Protestant" as the team came out to warm up before a League match. Souness remonstrated angrily with its bearers in full view of the rest of the crowd, an epochal action for a Rangers manager. This flurry of controversy was, it transpired, a forewarning of the tornado which would engulf Ibrox in the summer of 1989.

More generally, the pace set by Rangers in the transfer market created a new standard by which Scottish clubs were judged. Although he declared in April 1989 that his ideal would be a European Cup-winning team composed entirely of Scottish players, only ten of the 27 signings made by the end of the same season were Scots and a mere five came from other clubs in Scotland at a cost of £1,530,000 which meant that a net total of around £4.5 million had flowed out of the country from the Ibrox bank account. The more the Ibrox wheel of fortune whirled around the more it created pressure on other managements to raid their savings accounts.

Aberdeen had entered an inevitable period of reconstruction which was made more difficult by the departure of Alex Ferguson (who had acquired an O.B.E. along the way) on 6 November 1986, after eight breathless years at Pittodrie. He was succeeded by Ian Porterfield, formerly of Rotherham and Sheffield United, and Aberdeen followed Rangers' example by seeking playing recruits south of the border, where they signed Peter Nicholas from Luton Town and Gary Hacket from Shrewsbury, but neither player was able to settle and both left after a short spell in the north. In an attempt to revitalise the somewhat sterile Aberdeen attack Porterfield restored Charlie Nicholas to Scotland but the striker, formerly so cavalier while with Celtic, had run to seed later in his interlude with Arsenal and could not immediately harness his old flamboyance. Another attacker, the disaffected Joe Miller, was eventually allowed to depart for Celtic but long before he went he was preceded by Porterfield himself.

Porterfield's replacement was Alex Smith who, like Alex Ferguson before him, had been sacked by St Mirren after one more perverse episode in the history of a club with an apparent penchant for getting rid of its more successful managers. Smith had moved to Love Street after a lengthy tenure with Stirling Albion when Alex Miller quit Paisley in November 1986 to take over Hibernian. Six months later Smith had guided St Mirren to their first trophy in 29 years when they emerged unexpectedly from the pack to beat Dundee United 1-0 at Hampden Park. It should have been a platform for the team to assault the upper reaches of the Premier Division but disintegration was in the air the following season when there were so many injuries in the playing pool it looked as though St Mirren would have to start travelling to away fixtures by ambulance. There were perpetual arguments about bonus payments and the atmosphere was not improved when Frank McGarvey walked out on the club after a dressing-room flare-up with the assistant manager, Jimmy Bone, while his fellow striker Ian Ferguson was jeered by the Paisley supporters when he made it clear that if his contract belonged to St Mirren his heart belonged to Rangers, who secured his services for £850,000 in

February 1988 after St Mirren had failed to defend the Scottish Cup from a challenge by part-time Clydebank. Jimmy Bone was dismissed and, within a few weeks, so was Alex Smith but for both men the bullet proved to be a bonus because Bone moved up the League to Dundee United and Smith went to Pittodrie.

At Aberdeen he continued the trend for Scottish managers to look to sources outside the country for players and Smith discovered a rewarding seam in Holland when he imported Paul Mason and Willem Van der Ark along with Theo Snelders, an athletic goalkeeper who achieved the unlikely feat of replacing Jim Leighton in the Pittodrie followers' affections after the Scot had moved to Manchester United. The brio which had characterised the headiest days of Alex Ferguson's rule continued to elude the team but under Smith and Jocky Scott Aberdeen revived to finish Premier Division runners-up to Rangers, on whom they inflicted a stinging 3-0 defeat in the final League match of the season.

Others made similar attempts to add an unaccustomed exotic flavour to the Scottish game and Hibs earned credit when they persuaded Steve Archibald to move to Edinburgh at the end of his contract with Barcelona. "I had several offers but Hibs were the club who made me feel wanted," said Archibald, although he ultimately asked to be put on the transfer list because his family were unsettled in their new home. Hibs also pleased their supporters by retaining the services of the talented young midfielder John Collins at a time when several teams in England were keen to bid for him and a share issue to raise capital in 1988 proved successful. Not everyone had the resources to compete in a market where demand put a premium on the supply of players but Motherwell explored an alternative path by offering contracts to teenagers under the Government's Youth Opportunities scheme which produced a pleasing reward when Tom Boyd won three under-21 caps for Scotland and inspired suggestions that the Fir Park manager Tommy McLean had inherited the same eye for juvenile potential as his brother Jim at Tannadice. Boyd made his full début for Scotland against Romania in September 1990.

The force of history meant that Celtic bore the principal share of the burden of preventing a revitalised Rangers from monopolising the Scottish honours but at first the Parkhead club seemed mesmerised by the metamorphosis which had been worked at Govan. At the end of 1986 Celtic held a nine-point League advantage over their rivals but even that margin evaporated like snow under a flame-thrower as Rangers advanced towards their coveted first title and the Celtic manager David Hay paid the inevitable price, leaving his desk keys to Billy McNeill who had been in exile in England for four years after demanding – and being refused – a contract with the club after an initial spell of five years in charge at Parkhead. McNeill had been broadened by his experiences at Aston Villa and Manchester City but he was faced with an unenviable welcome when he returned to Glasgow to encounter a queue of players anxious to head in the opposite direction. Murdo McLeod's departure for Borussia Dortmund deprived the team of a powerful ball-winner in midfield but the Celtic support was deeply depressed by the loss of an entire forward line in Brian McClair (to Manchester United), Maurice Johnston (Nantes) and Alan McInally (Aston Villa) and the partnership of McClair and Johnston in particular seemed irreplaceable.

McNeill reconstructed his attack with Motherwell's Andy Walker and Frank McAvennie from West Ham, and he bought the Aberdeen pair of Joe Miller and Billy Stark along with the pacy Sheffield Wednesday full back Chris Morris, all for a total of £1,950,000. It was a very long way short of the kind of cheques which were being countersigned by Rangers directors but it was nevertheless a sizeable cash outlay which ameliorated the Celtic support's long-held suspicion that the club was quicker to sell good players than to pay for their replacements. More crucially, there was a quick return on the field. It was to Celtic's advantage that Rangers hit a period of severe turbulence in their defence of the championship. Indiscipline, injuries and the sheer number of new men at Ibrox combined to disrupt continuity of team selection and Rangers struggled to achieve consistency.

Conversely, Celtic's morale had been stiffened by McNeill's signings and by the profound desire to mark the club's centenary year by frustrating their fiercest rivals, a wish which was spectacularly consummated when the League flag was won against Dundee at Parkhead in front of 63,000 spectators whose enthusiasm was only exceeded by the bedlam at Hampden Park on 14 May 1988 when Dundee United provided the opposition in the Scottish Cup final. With 15 minutes left to play United led by a Kevin Gallacher goal in the first half but Celtic once again demonstrated their phenomenal ability to overcome adversity with resolution when McAvennie equalised and then went on to score an improbable winner in the dying seconds to conclude the club's first century with a dramatically satisfying flourish.

★ ★ ★

Celtic supporters were not so much jubilant as ecstatic at their team's centenary success mainly because they believed it demonstrated that the ominous build-up of expensive players at Ibrox had not been sufficient to defend the championship which Souness had decreed to be his permanent priority, but there were mutterings amongst the Parkhead following when Celtic failed to consolidate their squad during the summer of 1988, apart from the acquisition of the Leicester City goalkeeper Ian Andrews who was needed as cover for the injured Pat Bonner.

Billy McNeill and players celebrate Celtic's stirring victory in the 1988 Scottish Cup final, a fitting climax to the club's first century of existence.

It was a racing certainty that the pendulum would swing back towards Rangers. Most of the costly recruits had been properly assimilated by the beginning of the 1988-89 season and it was quickly evident that field discipline at Ibrox had taken a turn for the virtuous and that there would be fewer disruptions to the team through suspensions. What nobody could have anticipated was the stunning reversal of fortune which occurred at Ibrox in the first Old Firm game of the season of 25 August.

Although Celtic took an immediate lead in the match they were outclassed and outfought by a Rangers side in irresistible form who swept to a 5-1 lead with the help of breathtakingly inept defensive play by the visitors and a farcical goalkeeping blunder by Ian Andrews which suffocated Celtic's frail hopes of a revival within moments of the start of the second half. When Rangers scored their fifth goal with more than a quarter of the contest still to play Souness was entitled to suppose that his spending strategy had been spectacularly vindicated but alternative criteria were operating in the stands where the Rangers support hungered for another two or three goals to exorcise the recollection of Celtic's 7-1 victory in the Old Firm League Cup final of 1957, a result which was freeze-dried in the Glasgow folk memory. If Souness and his English contingent were not aware of the magical significance of a 31-year-old scoreline, the Celtic players were only too conscious of the humiliation which threatened to overtake them. After the match Tommy Burns, a man whose commitment to the green and white hoops appeared to have been cast at the Parkhead Forge, said: "It was as awful an experience as I have ever had against Rangers. In the second half I just prayed and prayed that they wouldn't get to seven . . ."

Seven it was not to be, but five was still an extraordinary total in a Glasgow derby and the biggest League margin between the sides since 3 January 1966 when Celtic ran up the same score at Parkhead to signal the start of their ascendancy under Jock Stein. After the 5-1 battering at Ibrox Celtic stumbled through the first quarter of the season but although they recovered sufficiently to win the next Old Firm encounter 3-1 on their own ground (and they could easily have scored twice as many goals) the comfort was illusory and Rangers piled on the misery with a 4-1 victory in the New Year game, following up

Enter Graeme Souness.

with their first win at Parkhead in nine years in the ultimate League collision of the season.

The pair had additional business with each other in the final of the Scottish Cup which Rangers needed to complete a domestic treble but in the event Celtic showed greater tactical awareness and spirit than their unexpectedly sluggish opponents to win by the only goal of a dour and unmemorable match at Hampden. There was extra cause for jubilation around the East End of Glasgow when it was announced that Maurice Johnston had been signed from the French club Nantes for a record fee of £1.2 million and the Celtic faithful celebrated a holiday in their hearts at the news of the player's decision to return to Scotland for a second spell at Parkhead.

The team badly lacked glamour and those who found themselves drawn to Celtic because of the club's attractive commitment to attacking play were concerned by the repeated loss of top grade strikers. As Kenny Dalglish had been lured south by Liverpool, so Charlie Nicholas migrated to Arsenal, Brian McClair went off to Manchester United followed by Johnston, who had come to Celtic after complaining of homesickness at Watford in 1984, a condition he overcame by 1987 when he felt able to set up home in France. Billy McNeill had responded to the loss of the McClair-Johnston partnership by bringing Frank McAvennie north from West Ham for £680,000, although it was typical of Celtic's luck in the publicity stakes that he was signed on the same day that Rangers paraded Richard Gough as a £1.1 million capture from Tottenham. The blond striker had made himself the supporters' darling with his unforgettable match-winning goals in the 1988 Cup final but he spent most of the following season badgering the exasperated McNeill to allow him to move back to West Ham. When he was eventually permitted to leave in April 1989 his departure strengthened the feeling on the terracings that, compared to Rangers, Celtic were in danger of becoming a penny-ante outfit.

They were certainly not stuck for cash when McAvennie resumed his career at Upton Park, Celtic having relieved West Ham of £1.25 million for his services and the decision to spend it on Maurice

Maurice Johnston inflicts damage on Rangers for Celtic.

Johnston without doubt revived a dispirited side in time for the Cup final but even before Celtic collected the trophy their transfer coup had begun to look distinctly shaky and on 26 May the player publicly declared that the deal was off, citing contractual difficulties which turned out to be a backdated tax bill of £350,000 which would become liable to payment if he returned to Britain.

Thoroughly alarmed by this turn of events, Celtic appealed to FIFA and were told that the documents in their possession established that Johnston was definitely contracted to them and the governing body of world football also informed Nantes that he would have to be registered to play in Scotland by 1 July. A dispute which was already muddied by accusations and counter-claims turned rancorous when Johnston won a court order on 29 June to prevent Celtic from continuing to insist to FIFA that he was a Parkhead property. By taking the matter to law he guaranteed that the rupture would be complete; Celtic immediately retorted that they wanted out of the deal and the club chairman Jack McGinn added in a remark which would soon be invested with spectacular irony that Johnston could now play wherever he liked. It was literally beyond the conception of everyone at Celtic that of all the football clubs in all the world, he would choose Rangers.

The Glasgow rumour factory, which had been working on overtime since Souness arrived in the city, quickly suggested Johnston for Ibrox but the common opinion was that from Rangers' point of view the player was a double liability, being not only a Roman Catholic but a former Celtic player whose renewed pledge of loyalty to the other club had been uttered in the most public of circumstances two months before. Yet these were precisely the features which made Johnston alluring to a personality like Graeme Souness, whose taste for the bold stroke was reinforced by a relish for the apparently perverse manoeuvre.

This was the man, after all, who had exploded the inadequate pay structure which prevailed under previous administrations, who had reversed the century-old flow of transfers from Scotland to England

'Yes, my son, hoping Mo Johnston breaks a leg is indeed a sin – say one Hail Mary.' (Ian White, *Scotsman*)

Maurice Johnston scores against Celtic, November 1989.

Sun spread as Mo joins Rangers.

David Murray brought a fresh surge of dynamism to Rangers when he bought the club in 1988.

Maurice Johnston's antics in July 1990 kept Irish eyes smiling as seen in this cartoon in the *Sunday Tribune*, Dublin. (Gerry Crowley)

BET HE DIDN'T EXPECT TO DO PENANCE AT RANGERS

and who had insisted, quietly but with impressive emphasis, that he would not be constricted by a sectarian tradition he regarded with distaste. Shortly before Johnston absorbed his attention, Souness had remarked that only two or three dozen British players were good enough to enhance his squad. A forward who had established a new World Cup scoring record for Scotland with eight goals in the space of a single season was bound to be included in the élite. Such a decision could not be taken by Souness in isolation but he found a willing confederate in David Murray, who had bought the club seven months previously.

The news broke on the morning of 10 July, preceded by a brilliantly executed exclusive story in the *Sun* newspaper but such was the incredulity that only when the signing was confirmed at lunchtime did the impact begin to reverberate. Agency reporters were instantly out to secure the most quotable citizens but measurement of the general reaction was a job for Richter rather than Reuter. Outsiders, unfamiliar with the tribal priorities of the West of Scotland, who happened to be around Glasgow at the time, found that the public response beggared their comprehension. People stopped in the streets to ask each other if they had heard the news, if it could be believed, if such a thing could be *allowed*. The *Evening Times* responded to the mood of stupefaction with a special edition rushed to the pavement vendors along with full-faced poster-sized portraits of Johnston which were quickly defaced by offended partisans of both persuasions. Next morning the Scottish daily papers (as well as Scottish editions of English dailies) devoted themselves to the story to the point where the coverage in some tabloids exceeded the space they had thought proper to expend on the devastation caused by the bomb which had exploded a Pan Am 747 airliner above Lockerbie six months earlier.

The story ran for days with a demented energy. It transpired that Nantes had been slow to repay the £400,000 which Celtic had handed over as a first instalment on the player's original and abortive agreement to move to Glasgow, so that in FIFA's eyes Johnston was a Celtic player at the very moment he was introduced to the press as a Rangers forward and that he had remained so for a further three days until the Parkhead club was finally reimbursed. A woman in Dumbarton was granted the better part of a page in Scotland's biggest-selling newspaper when she claimed that death threats had been directed at her dog, which she had named Mo in honour of Johnston during his time at Celtic. The wretched animal was pictured wearing a green and white scarf and tammy, possibly to stress that fidelity was more durable in a mongrel than in a Glasgow footballer.

The astounding quantity of newsprint expended on the affair suggested a society in the grip of a collective fever, like the unaccountable mania for Rudolph Valentino which erupted in the United States after the matinee star died suddenly in 1926, but while there was a lively enough interest in the signing it would be entirely inaccurate to suggest that most Scots regarded it as anything other than a sideshow. Certainly, the player had incurred the detestation of his former admirers in the Celtic support and on both sides there were malformed characters who professed a hatred for him which was as real as it was repellent but one of the more disturbing aspects of this vehemence was the way it was magnified almost to the point of incitement by some sections of the media. To ask Rangers diehards in Larkhall for their opinion of Johnston was the equivalent of polling the Ku Klux Klan on Jesse Jackson's prospects of making it as President of

Torn loyalties. (David Moffat, *Evening Times*)

the United States. Elsewhere, most Rangers supporters were reconciled to the advent of Catholic players but were doubtful about Johnston's capacity or willingness to stay what might prove to be a turbulent course.

The player was subjected to trial by ordeal within a month of the new season when Rangers played at Parkhead in the first Old Firm derby of the season. Some notion of the traumatising impact the Johnston signing had made upon his former admirers was revealed when Graeme Souness meandered down the tunnel an hour before the kick-off. A small but vociferous congregation of Celtic supporters was quick to offer advice to the commander of their arch rivals.

"Hey Graeme! Watch that skunk – he'll stab you in the back one day," shouted one apoplectic home fan, demonstrating a newly discovered fraternity with the architect of the revival of Rangers. Unsurprisingly, Johnston proved to be jittery during the subsequent contest, missing two clear chances to score against his former team-mates as the game moved towards a 1-1 draw in front of 55,000 baying partisans.

The real moment of truth came ten weeks later when the clubs met at Ibrox on November 4. Like the mediaeval churchmen who diverted themselves by disputing the number of angels who could dance on a pinhead, Rangers supporters had periodically attempted to fathom what might happen to the unimaginable Catholic who might one day be presented with an opportunity to score a winning goal against Celtic.

The answer was revealed in circumstances which suggested that both clubs were at the disposal of the gods of melodrama. With barely a minute of play remaining in an evenly contested match, Rangers broke down the right flank. The ball was cut back across the goalmouth and Johnston, beckoned by no more than a half chance, was in position to clip a low shot past Bonner for the only goal of the game. He sprinted on to receive the acclaim of the delirious home fans behind Bonner's goal, while at the opposite end, pain was etched into the expressions of his former worshippers.

Any question of Johnston's acceptance into the Ibrox pantheon was dispelled when he accepted Player of the Year awards from 14 Rangers supporters clubs, and he was even able to survive a ludicrous episode in the club's preparations for the 1990-91 season in Italy, where he became foolishly drunk and was sent home bearing the scars of a fall from grace, amongst other things.

After a brief period of self-examination he was forgiven by Souness,

Evening Times strip cartoon

who himself had once been told by Jack Charlton, in similar circumstances, that drink would turn him into "a bum". Johnston was permitted another chance and, in view of his contribution to the social history of the West of Scotland, it was probably just that he should be offered the chance to diminish the venial exploit which might easily have eclipsed his singular talents.

In signing Johnston Rangers had been audacious, even outrageous. In one stroke they had secured a prolific scorer and broken a taboo which threatened to be a serious barrier to Rangers' chances of admission to any federation of the principal European clubs. They could not put a stop to the sectarianism amongst their followers but they had begun to distance themselves from its contaminating influence.

To paraphrase Shakespeare, in making the green one blue Souness had earned the right to a degree of respect from those in Scotland who could never be accused of supporting Rangers in any other circumstances.

★   ★   ★

Rangers took their second championship in three years under Graeme Souness in April 1989 and they were only denied a clean sweep of the domestic treble by Celtic's narrow 1-0 victory in the Scottish Cup final. In those three years the championship and the Skol Cup did not leave Glasgow and the Scottish Cup was removed once by St Mirren at the end of an exceptional tournament which saw virtually all the favourites knocked out in the early stages. The old dynamic of the Rangers-Celtic axis appeared to have restored itself, even if the increasing imbalance between the pair suggested that Celtic might not be equipped in the long run to sustain parity without changes in the club's structure, a possibility which the Parkhead chairman Jack McGinn rejected in March 1990. He pointed out that in the previous decade Celtic had won four championships and finished runners-up on four occasions, and had also engraved the club's name on the Scottish Cup four times, and the Scottish League Cup once.

Impressive as such a record undoubtedly was, it could not disguise the fact that Rangers' ascendancy was ominously liable to increase and that Celtic had not emerged as their principal challengers. Celtic ended the 1989-90 season without winning an honour and slumping to fifth place in the championship. The club's response was to spend £2 million on buying Martin Hayes from Arsenal, John Collins from Hibernian and securing the return of Charlie Nicholas, after sojourns at Arsenal and Aberdeen.

It was, in fact, Aberdeen who revived under Alex Smith to offer Rangers significant resistance to their ambitions. The Pittodrie team finished second in the league and won both of the season's cups by beating the two Old Firm sides in Glasgow, Rangers in the Skol Cup final and Celtic in a Scottish Cup final which made history by being settled on penalty kicks without a replay. The decisive moment in the shoot-out came after Aberdeen's goalkeeper Theo Snelders saved an attempt by Anton Rogan and Brian Irvine then beat Pat Bonner to carry the cup north.

Aberdeen supporters were entitled to believe that if their side had not been afflicted by a crippling burst of injuries to key players exactly half way through the season, the league campaign might have been a much closer run affair. The general hope was that Aberdeen's challenge

Panel 1: AT LAST CELTIC HAVE AGREED TO ALLOW CAMERAS INTO THAT FAMOUS INNER SANCTUM THE GREEN ROOM

Panel 2: GREEN DOOR, WHAT'S THAT SECRET YOU'RE KEEPING

Panel 3: THE GREEN BED, THE GREEN MATTRESS AND THE GREENSTUFF!!

would be reinforced by a more powerful response from Parkhead and that Dundee United and Hearts might revive their designs on the title, so that Rangers might be diverted on several fronts.

A sceptical view of Celtic's financial arrangements, as viewed by David Moffat of the *Evening Times*.

★   ★   ★

Elsewhere, there were lively diversions from the business of contemplating Rangers' attempts to emerge as a football super power. The Scottish League received an application from an Irish consortium which asked permission for a club called Dublin City to play in Scotland. The fact that the club had no team, ground or even a strip did not abash the innovative Irishmen, even when their opening attempt was rejected.

Working behind the scenes they came close to buying the second division club Montrose and were only denied a foothold in the league when the Montrose officials asked for a guarantee that the club would continue to function in the town of its birth. It emerged that the Irishmen had proposed to accommodate Montrose at a fresh home in Dublin.

Meanwhile, just as the Scottish League was asked to extend membership to a new club with Irish provenance, it appeared that it might lose another whose ancestry had its roots in Ireland. Hibernian, founded with Irish connections in 1875, had won the championship four times and were the first British club to play in the European Cup in 1955-56, reaching the semi-finals of the competition.

Hibs had been pioneers, too, in introducing floodlights to Scotland, installing undersoil heating and have a sponsor's name emblazoned on their shirts. However, after an unsteady few years in the late 1970s when the team alternated between the Premier and First Divisions, the Easter Road side remained largely in the shadow of Hearts. By 1990, the club had accumulated an alarming number of debts and in May Hibs were ripe for an attempted takeover.

Nobody could have imagined that it would have been mounted by Hearts chairman Wallace Mercer, who bid £6.12 million for the shares which would give him a controlling interest at Easter Road. Mercer's intention, which was greeted with a mixture of incredulity, shock and anger by both sets of supporters, was to incorporate Hibs into Hearts, vacate both city grounds and move the single remaining Edinburgh club to a green field site close to the western motorway link with Glasgow.

Perplexed by public agitation against his attempt to buy Hibs and condemn the club to extinction, Wallace Mercer broods over his options.

Although he presented the proposed deal as a merger, it was clear that he intended only one Premier Division side to operate in Edinburgh from the 1990-91 season. Mercer amplified his desires, saying: "There is considerable merit to Edinburgh and the Lothians of combining together the two principal clubs to try and create one unit which could compete at the highest level with clubs from the West of Scotland, and also have the opportunity of competing at the highest level in European football, should the situation ever arrive of a European League.

"Sadly, I appreciate there is going to be a considerable amount of emotional distress if the matter succeeds but it is up to others to judge if there would be emotional distress if it did not succeed."

It did not succeed and Mercer himself was to suffer emotional distress when the furore created by his proposals caused him to receive death threats from overwrought or plain lunatic partisans. Ultimately he abandoned the attempt, although he made it clear that he had assembled the £12 million or so which would have been required to pay off Hibs' debts, secure control of the club and bring about its extinction after 115 years.

Mercer did persist with his plan to shift Hearts to a custom-built stadium on the edge of the city and on 3 August he asked for planning approval to demolish Tynecastle and use the site for house building. On the same day, Scottish newspapers were alive with speculation about Mo Johnston's future at Ibrox, after Rangers' high profile Catholic signing had been sent home in disgrace from pre-season training in Tuscany, and there were photographs of Jim Leishman leaving East End Park in tears, having refused the Dunfermline directors' offer to bring him on the board, a move which effectively removed him from his previous position as manager.

On August 3, too, Hibs announced that David Duff had been replaced as chairman by Alastair Dow, a West of Scotland businessman. It had been quite a day. The new season was still three weeks away. Such a ferment of headlines and speculation suggested that a vintage season of controversy, celebration and despair – the mixture as before – was in prospect once more.

Sure enough, within a month of the big kick-off, the Hearts manager, Alex MacDonald, had been sacked, to his players' distress, and was replaced by Joe Jordan, while Scotland, with a team lacerated by injuries, defeated powerful Romania in an unexpectedly good beginning to the European Championship-qualifying campaign. St Johnstone had signed a Soviet internationalist and Partick Thistle were looking at two of the Cameroon World Cup squad with a view to buying – although only, of course, if they were better than anyone already on the Firhill staff.

★   ★   ★

What was certainly clear in 1990 was that the game in Scotland had passed through a major period of transition of about 20 years' duration.

The Scots strain of football had always been highly distinctive and its separateness served it well in the 1980s when Scottish clubs and supporters avoided the purdah which had been imposed on their English counterparts and which isolated the innocent and adventurous as wholly as it did the complacent or the sinister. Part of Scotland's good fortune depended on the luck of timing; had the Barcelona riot occurred after the Heysel disaster it is impossible to conceive that Scottish clubs would have been allowed to continue in European competitions without similar sanctions being imposed against them. Although Scots like to suppose that they have an obvious and unique identity many discovered when they travelled abroad as supporters that a large percentage of foreigners could not fathom the reason for Scottish clubs being allowed to take part in European competitions when the English were banned. Of course, Scots are regarded as an individual football entity because of the happy chance of being in on the game's beginnings, a fact which is not widely understood elsewhere in the world, but it particularly perplexes those who think that the terms English and British are interchangeable and who consequently wonder where the Scots come into the picture.

Scots, then, exist precariously in their marginal world of football, a serious incident or accident away from being merged with the English in outside perceptions, a notion permanently guaranteed to provoke indignation north of the border. The major clubs have played an important part in reinforcing the notion of Scotland as a place where matters are ordered differently from England and, perhaps, suggesting that this state of affairs exists away from the field of play too. Aberdeen and Dundee United contributed by reaching the finals of European competitions while Rangers, Celtic, Hearts and Dunfermline have significantly swelled attendance figures in general with the mobilisation of their supports. Rangers inevitably attracted criticism because on occasion they employed as few as three Scots in their team but the club's ability to reverse the traditional flow of talent from north to south also added a measure to Scottish self-confidence, and if the presence of high-grade English players in Scotland surprised sceptics on both sides of the border, it also permitted the emergence of fresh perspectives which were not necessarily welcomed in either country.

Jock Stein, whose views on football tended to come out on the shrewd side, used to insist that Scotland should be capable of nourishing eight clubs capable of sustaining a challenge in Europe, but the job was only half done. It remained a paradox that Aberdeen and Dundee United had been honed by the Premier Division to go all the way in Europe while football in the Scottish League was played at manic speed which seemed inimical to the kind of studied technical game admired in most other countries. On the other hand, Rangers' English winger Mark Walters found a receptive audience in Scotland when he said in April 1989: "If I was with an English club which had won a League and Cup double I would not be ignored for a place in the international squad. But some people in England have a superiority complex about what goes on in Scotland."

And was it merely a coincidence that when the Scottish National Party fuelled one of their cyclical ascents in popularity with the slogan "Scotland in Europe", it happened to coincide with a period in which football offered a vivid example of Scots accepted into the European community while the English were kept at bay because of unacceptable behaviour? The misfortunes of the English clubs did not occasion gloating within the Scottish game so much as practical attempts to extend support through the presence of Scottish officials on the governing committee of European football.

As the 1990s approached, the principal Scottish clubs were entitled to a degree of satisfaction at the way they had negotiated turbulent rites of passage in the most recent phase of their native sport. Rangers and

Celtic had reclaimed much of their former dominance but the Premier Division structure guaranteed that the championship boasted a much sharper competitive edge and more clubs were equipped to explore the new dimensions to be found in European leagues or satellite television, whose operators talked fortunes as though they were cascading out of the latest version of football heaven. In May 1989 the Scottish Football Association and the Scottish League announced a £12.25 million contract with the British Satellite Broadcasting Company to run over four seasons during which BSB would have the screening rights to a total of 20 live matches a season. Bob Hunter, the managing director of the company's Sports Channel, explained BSB's decision to buy into the game when he said: "Scotland is a very important market to BSB in our development and distribution. Scots tend to watch more sport than people in other parts of the United Kingdom and everyone is aware of the passion Scots show towards football. We are making a major investment in Scotland and Scottish football."

What investment Scottish football was likely to make in the changing European scene was less easy to quantify. Silvio Berlusconi, the multi-millionaire president of AC Milan, a man who controlled cable television channels in Italy and France, appointed himself chief spokesman for those who favoured the creation of a European League. Berlusconi proposed a highly selective tournament which would not guarantee places for all of the countries of Europe, far less the bulk of the most famous sides. It was clear, for example, that if Rangers might have a chance of inclusion in such a structure, Celtic were far from certain to join them, just as Real Madrid might be invited at the expense of Atletico Madrid. Such a state of affairs could only lead to the formation of rival leagues and a fragmentation of UEFA's authority over the European game.

A more plausible scenario pictured the three European club tournaments organised on similar lines to the American football conference system, with clubs qualifying for the various competitions in the usual way but being divided into seeded groups of eight to play on a home and away basis, the top two sides in each group moving forward to an all-in knockout contest to be played over a week in one designated country to produce a trophy winner. Since ten midweek nights were set aside each season to accommodate the full course of the European cups, very few additional dates would require to be found. However, since the additional fixtures, no matter how glamorous or lucrative, would increase the burden on clubs in Scotland and England whose national commitments had been overloaded for years, it was evident that the scheme would require domestic restructuring.

One answer to the problem in Scotland envisaged an expansion of the Premier Division to 12 teams playing each other three times a season, with three rounds of the Skol Cup being played on Saturdays to make up the number of fixtures necessary to satisfy the football pools companies which provided another source of guaranteed annual income.

The compatibility of such notions with the old order of domestic affairs would plainly require a mixture of diplomacy and ingenuity in order to succeed but cash in the form of sponsorship, marketing and broadcasting contracts was known to have remarkable powers of lubrication, especially with the advent of satellite television. As Scotland's clubs embarked upon the celebration of their League centenary in 1990 they waited, like Romeo, on some consequences yet hanging in the stars.

PLAYERS BOUGHT BY GRAEME SOUNESS, JUNE 1986 – AUG 1990

Date	Player	From	Fee
June 1986	Colin West	Watford	£200,000
July 1986	Chris Woods	Norwich	£600,000
Aug 1986	Terry Butcher	Ipswich	£725,000
Aug 1986	Jimmy Nicholl	West Brom	£70,000
Nov 1986	Lindsay Hamilton	Stenhousemuir	£25,000
Dec 1986	Graham Roberts	Tottenham	£450,000
Dec 1986	Neil Woods	Doncaster	£100,000
Mar 1987	Jimmy Phillips	Bolton	£75,000
Mar 1987	Davie Kirkwood	East Fife	£30,000
June 1987	Avi Cohen	Maccabi	£100,000
June 1987	John McGregor	Liverpool	FREE
July 1987	Mark Falco	Watford	£270,000
Aug 1987	Trevor Francis	Atalanta	£75,000
Aug 1987	Ian McCall	Dunfermline	£200,000
Oct 1987	Richard Gough	Tottenham	£1,100,000
Nov 1987	Ray Wilkins	Paris SG	£150,000
Dec 1987	Mark Walters	Aston Villa	£500,000
Jan 1988	John Brown	Dundee	£350,000
Jan 1988	Jan Bartram	Silkeborg	£180,000
Feb 1988	Ian Ferguson	St Mirren	£850,000
June 1988	Kevin Drinkell	Norwich	£500,000
July 1988	Gary Stevens	Everton	£1,000,000
Sep 1987	Andy Gray	West Brom	£25,000
Oct 1987	Neale Cooper	Aston Villa	£250,000
Feb 1989	Tom Cowan	Clyde	£100,000
Mar 1989	Mel Sterland	Sheffield Wed	£800,000
July 1989	Trevor Steven	Everton	£1,600,000
July 1989	Maurice Johnston	Nantes	£1,500,000
Aug 1989	Bonni Ginsberg	Maccabi	£200,000
Aug 1989	Davie Dodds	Aberdeen	£100,000
Nov 1989	Chris Vinnicombe	Exeter City	£500,000
Nov 1989	Nigel Spackman	Q.P.R.	£500,000
July 1990	Mark Hateley	Monaco	£500,000
Aug 1990	Peter Huistra	FC Twente	£500,000
Aug 1990	Terry Hurlock	Millwall	£300,000
		TOTAL	£14,425,000

PLAYERS SOLD BY GRAEME SOUNESS, JUNE 1986 – AUG 1990

Date	Player	Club	Fee
June 1986	Derek Johnstone	Partick Thistle	FREE
June 1986	Dave McKinnon	Airdrie	FREE
June 1986	Andy Bruce	Hearts	FREE
June 1986	Andy Davies	Elfsborg	FREE
June 1986	Eric Ferguson	Dunfermline	FREE
Aug 1986	Iain Ferguson	Dundee United	£145,000
Aug 1986	Bobby Williamson	West Brom	£70,000
Oct 1986	John MacDonald	Barnsley	FREE
Dec 1986	Colin Miller	Doncaster	£30,000
Dec 1986	Doug Bell	Hibernian	£30,000
Dec 1986	Craig Paterson	Motherwell	£20,000
Dec 1986	Stuart Beattie	Doncaster	£30,000
Jan 1987	Ted McMinn	Seville	£225,000
May 1987	Robert Russell	Motherwell	FREE
May 1987	Cammy Fraser	Raith Rovers	FREE
July 1987	Dave McPherson	Hearts	£325,000
July 1987	Hugh Burns	Hearts	£75,000
July 1987	Neil Woods	Ipswich	£125,000
Aug 1987	Ally Dawson	Blackburn	£50,000
Sept 1987	Colin West	Sheffield Wed	£150,000
Dec 1987	Mark Falco	Q.P.R.	£350,000
Dec 1987	Robert Fleck	Norwich	£580,000
Mar 1988	Trevor Francis	Q.P.R.	FREE
July 1988	Jan Bartram	Brondby	£315,000
Aug 1988	Graham Roberts	Chelsea	£475,000
Aug 1988	Jimmy Phillips	Oxford United	£150,000
Oct 1988	Dave MacFarlane	Kilmarnock	£100,000
May 1989	Andy Gray	Cheltenham	FREE
June 1989	Avi Cohen	Maccabi	FREE
July 1989	Mel Sterland	Leeds United	£700,000
July 1989	Jimmy Nicholl	Dunfermline	FREE
Aug 1989	Dave Kirkwood	Hearts	£100,000
Aug 1989	Davie Cooper	Motherwell	£50,000
Aug 1989	Nicky Walker	Hearts	£125,000
Oct 1989	Kevin Drinkell	Coventry	£800,000
Nov 1989	Ray Wilkins	Q.P.R.	FREE
Jan 1990	Ian McCall	Bradford	£200,000
Apr 1990	Lindsay Hamilton	St Johnstone	FREE
Apr 1990	Derek Ferguson	Hearts	£750,000
		TOTAL	£5,970,000

(Figures courtesy of *Rangers News*)

PLAYERS BOUGHT BY BILLY McNEILL, JUNE 1987 – AUG 1990

Date	Player	From	Fee
June 1987	Billy Stark	Aberdeen	£80,000
July 1987	Andy Walker	Motherwell	£350,000
July 1987	Chris Morris	Sheffield Wednesday	£125,000
Oct 1987	Frank McAvennie	West Ham	£725,000
Nov 1987	Joe Miller	Aberdeen	£650,000
Nov 1987	Steve Murray	Nottingham Forest	£50,000
July 1988	Ian Andrews	Leicester City	£300,000
Aug 1988	Tommy Coyne	Dundee	£500,000
Feb 1989	Steve McCahill	Dumbarton	£100,000
June 1989	Mike Galloway	Hearts	£550,000
June 1989	Paul Elliott	Pisa	£600,000
July 1989	Dariusz Dziekanowski	Legia Warsaw	£600,000
July 1989	Paul McLaughlin	Queen's Park	FREE
Aug 1989	John Hewitt	Aberdeen	£250,000
Nov 1989	Dariusz Wdowczyk	Legia Warsaw	£400,000
May 1990	Martin Hayes	Arsenal	£650,000
July 1990	Charlie Nicholas	Aberdeen	£450,000
July 1990	John Collins	Hibernian	£900,000
		TOTAL	£7,280,000

PLAYERS SOLD BY BILLY McNEILL, JUNE 1987 – AUG 1990

Date	Player	Club	Fee
June 1987	Brian McClair	Manchester United	£850,000
June 1987	Maurice Johnston	Nantes	£375,000
June 1987	Alan McInally	Aston Villa	£275,000
June 1987	Murdo McLeod	Borussia Dortmund	£250,000
Aug 1987	Mark Smith	Dunfermline	£50,000
Nov 1987	Paul McGugan	Barnsley	£80,000
July 1988	Allen McKnight	West Ham	£275,000
Mar 1989	Frank McAvennie	West Ham	£1,250,000
Apr 1989	Dougie McGuire	Coventry	£40,000
May 1989	Mick McCarthy	Lyon	£500,000
June 1989	Owen Archdeacon	Barnsley	£80,000
July 1989	Tony Shepherd	Carlisle	£60,000
July 1989	Mark McGhee	Newcastle United	£200,000
Dec 1989	Tommy Burns	Kilmarnock	£50,000
Jan 1990	Roy Aitken	Newcastle United	£500,000
Feb 1990	Ian Andrews	Southampton	£250,000
May 1990	Billy Stark	Kilmarnock	£50,000
Aug 1990	Dave Elliott	Partick Thistle	£75,000
		TOTAL	£5,210,000

(Statistics courtesy of the *Celtic View*)

CHAPTER FIVE

The Team

BILL SHANKLY WAS fond of saying that the ideal Scottish team would consist of no more than three Scotsmen, which was his code for implying that the Scottish player is not usually thought of as a temperate influence. The hazards of relating football too closely to the national character are well known but there is a plausible case for suggesting that over the years Scotland teams have exhibited quite a few of the tendencies usually associated with the native personality. There have been occasions when the national side has seemed as amenable to authority as an Afghan hill tribe, unfortunately often when the playing strength was otherwise capable of a sustained campaign.

The Scots have a highly developed capacity, if one may borrow a phrase from Hugh MacDiarmid, for locating themselves where extremes meet, which is why Shankly judged that his countrymen were most effective when insulated by a protective coating of Englishmen. He was able to test the worth of his recipe in regulated conditions at Liverpool but the Scotland team is an unadulterated mixture and for two decades the best efforts of national managers were often spent devising methods of keeping the collective temperature below flashpoint. The exception occurred on the run-up to the 1978 World Cup finals when the SFA put Scotland in the custody of Ally McLeod, the equivalent of handing a juggler a few bottles of nitro glycerine to play with. The consequences were no less excruciating because they were entirely predictable.

Scottish players are asked to haul a ridiculous burden of national aspirations around the world like so many pack mules. It is not necessary to be a separatist to see that a nation which bristles at every imagined slight to its sensitivities but refuses – or fears – to take any significant responsibility for the conduct of its own affairs is always in danger of lurching into absurdity. It was possible for Ian Archer, writing in the *Glasgow Herald* to describe Jock Stein at the time of his near-fatal car crash in 1975 as "arguably the most important man working in the nation at this time", a description which cannot be contradicted with hindsight. Stein was not even Scotland manager at the time. In such a context the game in Scotland might as well be known as Dissociation Football.

The characteristic Scotland team is usually thought to be fuelled by aggression but resentment has been a more powerful driving force, hence the typical pattern of struggling performances against mediocre opposition and stirring displays against sides with much greater resources. Argentina in 1978 provided a perfect example of the Scottish genius for contrariness. Told by McLeod in one of his fabulist moods that they would return to Glasgow with place medals at the very least, the Scots were bemused when Peru played ordinary, competent football and won 3-1. Having given no thought to the possibility that Iran might put up a fight, Scotland scraped a draw (thanks to an Iranian own goal) which was as humiliating as a defeat would have been. Universally written off against a Dutch team rated

The advance guard of the Tartan Army set off on a fresh expedition.

Andy Beattie, Scotland's first manager.

as second favourites to win the trophy, Scotland predictably produced the goal of the tournament in a 3-2 win which was not enough to secure a place in the next round on goal difference. They had lost the war but won a battle with a glorious charge through cannon fire. The ghosts of the Jacobites, those most accomplished of Scottish losers, must have nodded in sympathetic understanding.

Scottish self-confidence is a fragile quality but it was not always so, at least not on the football field where Scotland's superiority was taken for granted in the formative years of the game. For almost exactly 15 years from 8 March 1873 the Scots played 31 internationals and lost only once when they were beaten 5-4 by England in 1879. The winning goal was contentious because in those days Scotland followed the rule that a throw-in must be taken towards the thrower's goal whereas the English allowed it to be played in any direction, a liberty which led to the deciding score. The Scots consoled themselves with the knowledge that England had adopted what was known as the Scottish passing game to improve their performance and they guaranteed satisfaction the following year when Scotland employed a native referee who awarded them three disputed goals in a 5-4 victory, although it has to be said that the home team was cruising 5-2 when they were reduced to ten men through injury.

The Welsh started to participate in internationals in 1876 while the Irish made up what came to be known as the Home International Championship when they took part in the series in 1884. A Canadian touring team turned up in 1888 but the contest which counted was the annual encounter with England and if the team was ever in danger of failing to grasp the primary importance of winning it, there was the perpetual incitement of the supporters to remind them. The theory that Scottish fans only started to invade London after the Wembley Wizards match of 1928 is unjust to the pioneering hordes who were in evidence as early as 1889 when a crowd of 10,000 at The Oval contained a tartan detachment of 1,000 which managed to outshout the home following. It says something for the self-regard of the Scottish football establishment that on the same day as the England match, which ended in a 3-2 victory for the Scots, a second Scotland string was sent to Wrexham and were downhearted when they could only draw 1-1 with Wales, although the fact that their train was held up for five hours at Warrington probably contributed to their torpid performance.

By this time professionalism was legal in England but not in Scotland and the SFA refused to consider paid players for international matches a move which ruled out some 300 seasoned footballers. The cost of this official profligacy was soon evident when England began to win contests between the countries with some regularity. In 1891 the fixture was played at Blackburn where the proportion of Scottish supporters rose to one in three. They were disgusted to see their team beaten by two controversial goals, the first scored by John Goodall who was excoriated both for being well offside and for his treason in playing for England after having enjoyed a superior education in Ayrshire. The second arrived when Wilson established a pattern for future Scottish goalkeepers by dropping the ball into his own goal, or rather through it, because the ball ended up outside the net with the Scots claiming that it had got there without passing through their posts. The referee, Mr Morrow of Ireland, called for a vote which went in favour of the score being allowed, presumably with a dissenting rate of one in three. In the next two matches with England the Scots were

walloped 4-1 and 5-2 and the message penetrated to the selectors that amateurs had no chance against seasoned professionals.

The selectors decided to include hired men in the next Scottish squad to meet the Auld Enemy although they piously insisted on selecting only those professionals whose wages came in Scottish banknotes and rejecting any player who earned his living in England. Scotland instantly won the Home Championship but after a subsequent 3-0 defeat by the English at Goodison Park it was decided that even deserters who preferred to perform in the southern leagues would have to be conscripted into the ranks if the traditional Scottish dominance was to be resumed, although for the better part of a century home supporters were to harbour serious reservations about the commitment of their emigrant footballers.

Nevertheless, the change allowed Scotland to preserve an edge in the series against the much larger neighbour and the 1920s turned out to be particularly gratifying for the Scots, who registered six victories against two defeats and two draws. When the countries reached the milestone of their 50th encounter, on 17 April 1926, Scotland celebrated with a 1-0 win at Old Trafford and *The Times* confirmed the significance of the ritual in the Scottish calendar when it noted "A stranger in Manchester on Saturday night might have fancied himself in Glasgow. Inside the ground, there was the same impression of Scottish enthusiasm and comparative indifference on the part of the English spectators."

The absence of passion on the home side was probably due to the fact that English football had begun to expand its international repertoire and was now regularly engaged in games with foreign opposition such as France, Belgium and Sweden while the Scots resolutely confined their expeditions to those rivals within the United Kingdom, the annual contest with England being considered the supreme test of the Scottish game's health. In 1928 London discovered what it meant to be incorporated as a Glasgow suburb when the fixture was played at Wembley for only the second time. The first occasion four years earlier had not been unduly encouraging because the Scottish share of a 1-1 draw was an own goal by Taylor but the tartan tammies were seen in record numbers despite Scottish misgivings over a side which appeared to be anaemically short of reliable blood, with only three home-based players in the team.

On the face of it, the Scottish selection policy had reversed in the space of three years. At Hampden in 1925 Scotland enjoyed a decisive 2-0 defeat of England without employing an Anglo but ironically the very success of the team guaranteed that its members would be sucked into the southbound drift and a year later no fewer than seven of its players had been transferred to English clubs for a total of £32,050.

Emotions on a downward spiral as Scotland draw 1-1 with Iran. Ally McLeod as seen by those Scottish viewers who possessed the fortitude to watch until the final whistle.

Jimmy McGrory, Celtic and Scotland.

Nevertheless, the team which had been chosen for Wembley in 1928 did not include such gifted individuals as Meiklejohn and McPhail of Rangers or the Celtic pair McStay and McGrory. The absence of the phenomenally free-scoring McGrory was the occasion for disgruntlement amongst his Parkhead admirers when it was learned that his place would be filled by the volatile Hughie Gallacher who had lately served a two-month suspension. However, McGrory had made his debut in a dark blue jersey a month before at Firhill only to be involved in one of the Scots' rare defeats of the period when Ireland won 1-0. A more serious objection to the Scottish selection lay in the size of the forward line which, as everyone with the slightest knowledge of the game is aware, turned out to be the smallest ever fielded by their country. Alex Jackson, at five feet ten inches, was four inches taller than any of his colleagues in the attack but it was the Scots who ended the Wembley match looking down on demoralised opponents.

They were a collection of extravagant talents but none was more professional than the Rangers winger Alan Morton, whose presence on the left wing was a threat from the moment his selection was announced, as the English had come to understand the hard way because with the exception of 1926 he was fielded against them every year from 1920 until 1932 and he appeared to summon an extra relish for his appearance against the white shirts. He was a remorseless force who had taken immense pains to shape himself as the complete player, practising to balance his stronger right foot with such success that he emerged as perhaps the most accomplished left winger to play for Scotland. On the opposite wing, Alex Jackson was a contrasting figure, as swashbuckling and good-humoured off the field as he was in his play. He specialised in drifting inward from his wide beat to meet crosses from the opposite flank with his head, a tactic which earned him a reputation as a scorer as well as a creator of goals and which was ideally suited to complement the depredations of Morton on the left.

Between the two wingers were Alex James, Hughie Gallacher and James Dunn, who had been one of the trio of home-based Scots who had made their way south for the match. Even by the standards of his bantam colleague Dunn seemed fragile but he was not short of application and he possessed a powerful shot and a gift for distribution which found him a ready place in English football within a month of the Wizards match when he moved from Hibernian to Everton for a seven-year stay in Merseyside.

When the team assembled on the eve of the match their rendezvous could hardly be further removed from the kind of monastic seclusion insisted upon by modern coaches. True, they were unlikely to be afflicted with homesickness because when they met in the lounge of the Regent Palace Hotel in Piccadilly it resembled the scene of a Scotland supporters rally. The evening before a match was always the best of times to be Scottish in London. A number of the supporting cast were eventually persuaded to make seats available for the team but the drinking and smoking went on all around and, it has to be said, amongst the official party albeit on a more modest scale. In case the players, especially those based in England, were in need of another sort of stimulant, it was on hand in the form of a piper who treated them to an endless medley of stirring battle anthems.

Eventually, Jimmy McMullan exercised his authority as captain to summon his players upstairs but he was wise enough not to treat such a collection of prodigies to any tactical advice or homilies. "All I've to say is go to your bed, put your head on the pillow – and pray for rain," was his only injunction. Possibly McMullan felt that asking his men to sleep was a long shot because the piper was still in full skirl and remained so until the early hours of the morning but more importantly he understood that their greatest hope of success lay in the chance of a treacherous surface which would offer the Scots the chance to outmanoeuvre the physically stronger but less agile English. The unrelenting downpour which characterised the day of the match realised his hopes and Wembley was slick rather than lush, the very circumstance which rendered bulk a liability.

For a moment as the contest got under way it looked as though Scotland would need more than rain to shift the ground from beneath England. The home team went straight upfield and hit the post but as speedily as they had been alarmed, the Scots advertised their speed on the counterpunch. McMullan, who was to orchestrate much of the ensuing destruction, snapped on to the rebound and calmed his team-mates, as well as the feverish following on the terracings, by walking it out of danger before he slid a pass towards James, who brought Dunn into play. The ball was switched around the Scottish line until it was played out to Morton who kick-started himself past Goodall, the opposing full back, and set off on a marauding route along the line. When the cross looped into the area it ineluctably lingered in the air precisely where Alex Jackson had anticipated it would arrive and his header swept past Hufton to put the Scots into the lead.

On that early foundation the Scots constructed their superiority but its evidence was more slowly apparent. The interval was only two minutes distant when Alex James at last doubled the margin with a left-foot drive. The half-time ceilidh was entirely audible in both dressing-rooms and the English emerged looking resolved to terminate the jigging. For 20 minutes their pride drove them forward but not even the marvellously prolific Dixie Dean could inflict damage on a compact defence which was thoroughly marshalled by McMullan. As the home side's energy began to dissipate, Morton and Jackson were set free to rove menacingly along the flanks once more and in the 65th minute they duplicated their initial strike with casual panache to make it 3-0. James had earlier struck the crossbar but he measured the target correctly when Gallacher presented him with a further opportunity and the Scots' display was garlanded when Jackson scored his hat-trick from yet another Morton cross which proved that the English defenders had not been inoculated by experience.

England had been marginal in every sense, Kelly netting from a free kick in the final minute to deprive the Scottish supporters of the immeasurable satisfaction of a whitewash but the game had ascended into the realms of mythology some time before the final whistle was sounded by referee Willie Bell, a Scot who had the wit to delay the end of the contest until Jack Harkness was in possession.

The Scottish goalkeeper sagely stuffed the ball up his jersey and bolted for the dressing-room before the prize could be appropriated by fans in search of a relic. In the midst of a state of collective shock the English players displayed commendable grace when they suggested that the ball be presented to Alex Jackson in recognition of a performance of extraordinary accomplishment made even more remarkable by the fact that he was still in his teens. Eventually the match ball was donated to the Scottish Football Association who periodically allow it to be displayed like the national icon it is, inscribed with the immortal scoreline and the names of the team of 31 March 1928, the mesmerising Wembley Wizards. They had achieved a victory which was quintessentially Scottish, which is to say improbable and virtually unrepeatable.

They had been unfancied, even by their own people, to win the match. It was a sure spur to their ambition. They were a disparate collection of skills and tempers and in fact they played together only on that unforgettable afternoon in the rain but they had an instinctive mastery of their art which allowed them to make an ally of monsoon conditions. In the most resonant manner for their countrymen the little men had eclipsed the greater force and in so doing they roused the deep-rooted Scottish admiration for the triumph of guile over strength, the capacity Bruce had exemplified when he destroyed the cumbrous English warhorses with his lithe ponies at Bannockburn.

It was perfectly Scottish to revere the result because it represented a crushing demonstration of superiority over the single country which mattered, ignoring the fact that both Scotland and England had played at Wembley to avoid the wooden spoon in the Home Championships for that season. By their victory over England, remarkable and deserved though it had been, the Scots had not even placed themselves on top of a very small football heap but they had won the only competition of significance for them. As the witticism of the day had it: "The English believe they are superior to everyone else. The Scots know they are superior to the English." Not for the first time London was treated to an evening of uproar, although in those irretrievable days both factions were prepared to join in the mood of carnival without rancour.

The Scottish celebrations were extended and the trains which ferried the tartan campaigners back across the border were so many ecstasy expresses. To be fair, the Scots were not alone at that time in believing that England represented the standard by which excellence might be measured, although they were singular in supposing that ascendancy on the football field implied some kind of fulfilment in other areas. In any case, 1928 was the year in which a challenge to the old order was at last signalled across broader horizons.

★ ★ ★

When the Olympic Games were held in Amsterdam in 1982 FIFA, football's ruling body, voted to inaugurate a World Cup tournament as a more representative measure of excellence than the Olympic competition from which professional players were officially forbidden to take part. The first tournament, it was decided, would take place in 1930. In Barcelona in 1929 Uruguay won the right to stage the inaugural World Cup. The Netherlands, Italy, Spain and Sweden had all applied to host the first finals but none presented a more compelling case than the South American country, which was to celebrate a centenary of independence in 1930 and whose team had just become Olympic champions. To underline the seriousness of their desire to stage the finals the Uruguayans offered to pay the fares and accommodation costs of the visiting teams and to build a stadium to showcase the matches. It was a gracious and generous gesture and Uruguay's rivals for the honour withdrew their candidacies. Their goodwill did not extend to accepting invitations to play in South America and there was outright opposition to the venue from Austria, Czechoslovakia, Germany, Hungary and Switzerland, all of whom refused to travel. Eventually Belgium, France, Romania and Yugoslavia agreed to take part, although none of them could be said to be enthusiastic about the idea. The four British associations were ineligible because they had withdrawn from FIFA after a row about compensation for club players whose employers were naturally disinclined to pay them to cruise halfway around the world to play football in a faraway country of which they knew little.

Still, it was possible to make up four groups from the 13 teams which did attend and it was in Pool IV that Scotland was to register its claim to an unforeseen record in the World Cup. Pool IV contained three teams, the United States, Paraguay and Belgium, the Americans being the seeded team and therefore favourites to move into the semi-final stage of the tournament. The Americans' status was not so surprising as it would seem nowadays because the United States team was mainly composed of men who had played professional football in Britain and who had moved across the Atlantic when the Bethlehem Steel Corporation set up what was to prove to be an abortive league on the other side of the ocean. Half of the team were Scots – Andrew Auld, James Brown, James Gallacher, Bart McGhee and Alec Wood – most of whom had a background in Ayrshire junior football and whose physique and robust style prompted the French to label them as "the shotputters".

The United States World Cup team in 1930 – *Back row:* Alex Wood, Andy Auld, Robert Millar (coach); *Middle row:* James Gallacher, Bart McGee; *Front row:* James Brown.

DR HENRY DRUCKER

Dr Henry Drucker, formerly lecturer in politics at Edinburgh University, now at Oxford University, has been a keen observer of the Scottish obsession with football.

"Football in Scottish life is much more than a sport. It's really the arena in which Scotland and Scots assert themselves and play a role in international affairs. There is no genuine focus for Scottish life, no arena for the Scottish identity to be seen. So football, which is the most popular sport and the sport of many working-class people, particularly in the West of Scotland, has come to play this role.

"I think you would find that if Scotland were independent football could just be about football and Scots would treat it the way people in properly independent countries do. The West Germans and the French may be very good at football but they have other ways of assuring themselves that they really are important and as good as anybody else.

"The great intensity of feeling at Wembley is focused nowhere else because it's the English who are seen as the people who keep the Scots down, and again I think that's an expression of a lack of political focus which would not be felt in Wales, for example, because there are other ways to express Welshness – a quarter of the population are Welsh-speaking.

"In Scotland football dominates the cities which are real working-class centres, like Glasgow, Dundee and Aberdeen. Interestingly, football is not anything like so dominant in Edinburgh where rugby has a large following and that's because

Their strength was in defence but they possessed the Scottish gift for drawing opponents on to the counterpunch. To general surprise, their strategy was not predicated on mere kick and rush tactics and they demonstrated the traditional Scottish virtue of close passing and possession play to such an extent that they easily beat Paraguay 3–0 in the opening match of the group, and when Belgium were defeated by the same score the USA proceeded to the last four.

Sadly, their quixotic progress came to an emphatic halt when they were crushed by Argentina, although the first half of the match was competitive enough with the American team keeping the deficit down to 1–0 at the interval and netting afterwards through Brown who was operating on the right wing, but his effort was merely a token; the Argentinians scored another five goals, one of which so angered the American trainer that he ran on to the pitch to remonstrate with the referee. To dramatise the climax of his harangue he threw his medical bag on to the pitch, breaking a bottle of chloroform. The fumes overcame him and he had to be carted off and dumped on the touchline while Argentina proceeded on their way to the final which saw them beaten 4–2 by Uruguay. The 1930 World Cup had not been a representative tournament but the competition had established itself as a fixture.

If few people in Britain understood the significance the new competition would assume in future nobody could have guessed that by the time the Scots woke up to its importance there would only be the most remote chance of equalling the achievement of their countrymen Auld, Brown, Gallacher, McGhee and Wood in reaching a World Cup semi-final.

*   *   *

The happenings in Montevideo were easily eclipsed by domestic events in 1930, the year Scotland returned to Wembley for the first time since the Wizards match. In the intervening season they had recorded another idiosyncratic win over England. The Wizards had made use of torrential rain to advance their cause and at Hampden in 1929 their successors harnessed the wind to beat the English in the final minute of the game. Then, the Scots had been reduced to ten men when Alex Jackson dislocated his elbow in a collision with Ernie Blenkinsop and with the match scoreless in its closing moments Alec Cheyne took the ball for a walk down the right wing to waste time. The Aberdeen man, on his debut for Scotland, did enough to win a corner kick which he elected to take himself, delivering a curling back post ball which had almost reached the end of its flight when it was seized by a sudden twist of wind and carried into the net beyond the visiting defenders. There were 110,512 spectators in the ground and after a fractional pause to confirm that such an improbable finale had, in fact, given Scotland the victory they unleashed a shout which rattled the windows of the Victoria Infirmary half a mile away. Alex Jackson heard it and advised those nearby that Scotland had certainly won and in that moment the legend of the Hampden Roar was added to that of the confirmed Hampden Swirl.

In 1930, though, it was more a case of the Wembley Wake as England rehabilitated themselves with a 5–2 thrashing of Scotland by way of compensation for the humiliation they had endured two years before. A much more serious setback at the hands of the English occurred the following season when the Football League prohibited its clubs from releasing players for international duty with any country except England, a decree which provoked the Scots into a classic display of self-contradiction.

In the first of the Home Internationals they met Wales, who had been reduced to a pathetic state by the same Football League restriction on their eligible players. When it became known in Scotland that the Welsh would field a makeshift team including three amateur players the talk was of how many the Scots would score. One estimate suggested two dozen goals could not be ruled out of the question. Nobody paid much attention to the background rumble of bulldozers pushing mountains of humiliation into place ready to bury such conceits. Six minutes into the match Wales led by a spectacular volleyed goal by Bamford and although the aptly named Barney Battles equalised shortly before the interval there was no further scoring.

In reaction to a public response of stupefied shock the selectors retained only three players for the following match against Ireland in Belfast which ended in a goalless draw. Another purge was prescribed for the final international and the prevailing mood of pessimism was so black that it seemed that the Scottish players should make their way to Hampden in tumbrils. The English press regarded the match as little more than a formality. Under such circumstances the Scots' prospects naturally brightened and, willed on by a crowd of 129,810 whose exhortations must have reinforced the "swirl", they netted the opening goal after a scoreless first half. It actually resulted from a forceful miskick by the veteran Scottish winger Archibald which ricocheted from Blenkinsop and then Hibbs before falling to Stevenson who jabbed it across the line. Jimmy McGrory, whose international career sadly languished under the shadow of Hughie Gallacher, demonstrated his own knack of collecting vital goals when he put the match beyond England's reach with a powerful header after Alan Morton had presented one more of his millimetre perfect crosses from the left.

John Thomson kept goal for Scotland that day with an agility which was etched in the memory of that mammoth crowd. It was his last appearance for his country before he lost his life in the tragic collision with Sam English at Ibrox five months later. Davie Meiklejohn, the formidable Rangers captain, transferred his inspirational powers to the Scottish skipper's role and strenuously defied the English attempts to retrieve the match. By full time the victory was as complete as the team had unexpectedly proved to be and the Scottish players were as lauded after the match as they had been dismissed as no-hopers before it.

Hampden Park was Scotland's strength throughout the thirties. Four straight wins and one loss contrasted with three defeats, a win and a draw at Wembley but if the Scots were comparatively invincible in front of their behemoth support in Glasgow it was discovered that they did not travel so well. In 1931 they visited Vienna to be demolished 5-0 by Austria whose tactics were based on the precepts of the Scottish close-passing game as taught to them by Jimmy Hogan, a coach from Nelson in Lancashire who had preached the gospel of possession football and midfield skill before the First World War. He was to return to Austria in 1932 and his influence was decisive in creating the formidable Austrian *Wunderteam* which beat England in Vienna in 1936.

In the aftermath of the Second World War Scottish football presented a striking contrast between the health of the domestic game and a

Edinburgh is not altogether Scottish – it can be seen as a bit of Sussex which floated up and got tagged on to Linlithgow.

"I've had students who have never been out of Scotland except for football matches and I remember one man who got a very high-powered job in Westminster – who has done very well, incidentally – who came to me after he got the job and confessed that he'd never been to London except to see Scotland at Wembley.

"After the Union of Parliaments in 1707, the Church, educational system and Scots law all helped to unite Scotland but the distinctiveness of these institutions has declined. If there was some kind of British league I think that would be a terrible moment for Scotland."

Princess Elizabeth with Field Marshall Montgomery for the England-Scotland match at Wembley, February 1944. On the day, England gave it the full Monty, winning 6-2. This is regarded as an unofficial fixture and is, of course, considered meaningless north of the Border.

sequence of disappointments at international level. Seven of the first eight official internationals played in peacetime ended in defeats. One of these occurred in a match against Belgium in the Heysel Stadium where the pitch was understandably rugged following its use by the *Wehrmacht* as a tank compound, but although Scotland registered a 6-0 victory in Luxembourg in their next match more thoughtful native observers realised that the Scots were far short of the capacity to mount anything like a football *blitzkrieg* on the Continent.

The 1947-48 season was a nadir for the supporters who watched the team being convincingly beaten by the other three home countries and there was no respite on the summer tour with a further three reverses against Belgium, Switzerland and France. The Scottish players were understandably aggrieved by the antics of the Austrian referee when Switzerland scored the winning goal of a 2-1 victory – he leapt into the air and congratulated the goalscorer – but there could be no disguising the fact that Scotland had been overtaken by the revolution of the techniques and strategy which was transforming the expectations of numerous countries whose prospects had been entirely ignored by a blinkered administration and public.

It was now that victory in the annual encounter with England began to assume the nature of a mind-altering drug, as the SFA secretary George Graham obviously understood when he promised that if the players won the 1949 fixture at Wembley they would be transported to a seven-week tour of America on the *Queen Mary*, with the bonus of £50 spending money. Scotland survived a lengthy onslaught by England to run out 3-1 winners, with Laurie Reilly scoring the first of six goals he would put past England goalkeepers to supplement strikes by Jimmy Mason and Billy Steel in a match which was dominated by the vivacious performance of Jimmy Cowan, the Scottish goalkeeper. The American tour was satisfactory, despite an unscheduled 2-0 defeat by Belfast Celtic, and the following season George Graham used similar bait to induce the team to beat England at Hampden.

This time, however, the prize was of much greater importance than an undemanding sequence of friendlies in the USA. Anxious to secure the participation of British sides FIFA magnanimously offered to treat the Home Championship as a qualifying group for the World Cup finals to be held in Brazil in the summer of 1950 and was even prepared to extend the invitation to the top two countries. In a revealing display of priorities the SFA decreed that Scotland would only attend if they finished as champions and the team went into the Hampden match knowing that a draw would be sufficient to secure their tickets for South America. Rio receded when Bentley scored for England in the 63rd minute, and although Bauld beat Bert Williams with a stinging shot which looked likely to produce the equaliser it struck the crossbar and rebounded along with the SFA's haughty conditional acceptance of their place in the World Cup finals.

Despite pleas from English officials and players for the Scots to join them on the expedition to South America, George Graham remained immovable and England set off alone. With hindsight it is possible to believe that Graham inadvertently saved the Scots from participation in a fiasco. England began their campaign happily enough with a 2-0 defeat of Chile which seemed to augur well enough for their next fixture against the United States, who had been beaten 3-1 by Spain. However, the Spanish victory was deceptive because the Americans had led by a goal until ten minutes from time. It did not take a soothsayer to realise that they were very likely to tune their performance to an even higher pitch against England; the manager and captain of the United States were both Scots.

Bill Jeffrey, the manager, had emigrated in 1920 to find work on the railways, but his talent as a footballer led him to be employed by Penn State College where he was employed as a coach and a mechanics teacher. Eddie McIlvenney was a less probable inspiration, a player who had reached the summit of his career with Wrexham and who, when the Welsh Third Division club gave him a free transfer in 1948, not unnaturally decided that emigration was the only course compatible with his prospects. His career revived on the other side of the ocean, where Scottish professionals had traditionally provided the backbone of attempts to nourish interest in soccer and Jeffrey promoted him to the status of captain of the international side.

Against England he undertook his duties with the relish of a man who understood that destiny had presented him with an implausible chance to inscribe his name in the game's annals. Against an England side whose names read like a roll-call of schoolboys' heroes – Bentley, Finney, Mannion, Mortensen and Mullen – he oversaw the repeated repulse of their best efforts by an American defence which was surfing on adrenalin. Baffled, the English forwards began to overcomplicate their play and were inevitably caught too far upfield when a throw-in was conceded to the Americans. McIlvenney took it briskly and the ball made its way to his half-back colleague Bahr who struck a shot-cum-cross from the left. Williams, the English goalkeeper, appeared to have it covered when Gaetjens arrived to break its trajectory with his head. Some said afterwards that he had timed his leap admirably, others thought that the ball had done no more than ricochet from his skull. It was immaterial because the header sped past Williams and inflicted the most embarrassing defeat in England's history. The Americans were carried from the pitch by the admiring Brazilian spectators who retained their affection for the shock team of the tournament despite the United States' subsequent 5-2 defeat by Chile.

The lessons of inadequate preparation were not wasted on England and they were particularly memorised by Alf Ramsey, who played at full back against the USA. Perhaps it was no accident that he retained, until the end of his managerial career with England, a marked taste for victories over Scotland. The Scottish football authorities, however, were in no position to derive vicarious satisfaction even from such a happy occurrence as the defeat of their oldest rivals because unlike the United States they had not thought fit to appoint a national team manager to shape their own diverse resources into some kind of coherent and reliable unit.

★   ★   ★

In December 1950 Scotland set an unwelcome record when they were defeated by Austria at Hampden to become the first of the home countries to be beaten at home. The match was no classic, a patchy affair played on a pitch frozen virtually as hard as concrete and the single goal it produced was similarly scrappy when Melchior struck a shot without power and saw it go in off a post. But Hampden was no longer the Garden of Eden for Scotland in a world where others had digested the fruits of the knowledge of football which had long before seemed to belong exclusively to the Scots.

A further defeat by Austria was similarly ill-omened when Billy Steel found himself sent off with eight minutes to play in the Prater Stadium, the first Scottish player to be dismissed in an international. When the two countries next met, it was on more serious terms. In 1954 Scotland again qualified for the World Cup finals as runners-up in the Home Championship and this time the SFA decided to take part, even going so far as to create the unprecedented position of national team manager, a role which was filled by Andy Beattie, the manager of Huddersfield. It was also thought proper that Scotland should prepare for a month at Ayr but good intentions were undermined by a lack of good faith. Even before the team assembled at Ayr there was trouble behind the scenes and Beattie threatened to resign if he was not given a free hand by the Scottish selection committee.

The immediate problem was smoothed over by the time the official party left for Switzerland but the traditional Scottish taste for schismatic behaviour reasserted itself in a personality clash between Beattie and the autocratic SFA secretary who was now Sir George Graham. The selectors were accommodated in a hotel 200 yards from the team HQ and some idea of the prevailing climate can be got from the fact that whenever Beattie and Graham were obliged to meet, each refused to go to the other, preferring to rendezvous at a point midway between the bases. In such circumstances Scotland did well to restrict Austria to a 1-0 win in their opening match in Pool III and they were unlucky to be denied a late equaliser when Neil Mochan's shot was only smothered on the line at the second attempt by Schmied, the Austrian goalkeeper.

After the pleasing resolution shown in their first World Cup outing the Scottish effort now degenerated into farce on an operatic scale when they lined up to face Uruguay in the next match. Appropriately, it was preceded by an overture in the shape of the Uruguayan national anthem, a two-part job which took all of six minutes to play through. As they stood to attention during this grotesque interlude the Scottish players had plenty of scope for introspection. In the face of his rows with the SFA as well as dissension within the team, Andy Beattie had announced his intention of departing Switzerland, but not until after the Uruguay match – a decision he was soon to regret deeply.

The match kicked off in 100-degree heat for which the Scots were laughably ill-equipped. Tommy Docherty, then an aggressive half back with Preston, recently recollected the episode in typical fashion.

We had these big grey tracksuits which looked as though we had borrowed them from the team at Barlinnie and underneath that we wore the blue woolly jerseys with the thick collars and long sleeves and the big heavy badge. You would have thought they were going on an expedition to the Antarctic or something. And we saw these other teams like Uruguay with short Continental gear and low-cut boots and real quality kit while we were so disorganised it wasn't true.

When we played Uruguay we were absolutely tired out by the time they finished the national anthems. People said that when the game got started we looked like Highland cattle grazing but we looked as though we were standing around because they were knocking the ball about and sprinting. At half-time we just walked into the shower with our kit on and stayed there. We were glad when they scored because the radio people would go on to the pitch and interview them. They would talk about the build-up and how the goal was scored and of course we were quite pleased because it gave us a chance to get our wind back.

There was no shortage of opportunity for the Scottish players to adjust their breathing; Uruguay went on a rampage, scoring seven goals and administering the most thorough humiliation in the history of the Scottish game. Some of the livelier imaginations amongst the Scottish sports writers had suggested that the South Americans were vulnerable in defence where they were prone to leave gaps which the Scots could exploit. Scotland saw as much of the gaps as a maddened bull glimpses beyond the matador's swirling cape. The Scottish players staggered from the field in a state of profound shock, understanding fully for the first time the chasm – not so much of ability but of *attitude* – which yawned between them and the footballing nations they had for so long perceived as pupils. Uruguay had shown who were the masters now.

At home the recriminations were bitter but incredibly there was not only a complete failure to absorb the lessons of Switzerland but also a wilful refusal to accept the realities of the new order in football. In 1958 the World Cup finals were held in Sweden and again Scotland qualified for the latter stages. For the first time they had been required to display their credentials in a qualifying group which included foreign opposition in the formidable shape of Spain and Switzerland, emerging with six points from a possible eight and even taking time out to beat West Germany 3-1 in Stuttgart at a time when their hosts were reigning world champions.

The barometer had begun to fall sharply shortly before the departure for Sweden, however, and there was a demoralising 4-0 defeat by England at Hampden which produced the unaccustomed sight of bare patches on the terracings as thousands of home fans left early, unable to bear the torment of a beating which would have been greater but for the heroics of Tommy Younger in the Scottish goal. Scotland set off for the World Cup as the only qualifying country without a manager, although this time they were entitled to a degree of sympathy because the SFA had appointed Matt Busby on a part-time basis in January only to lose his services as a result of the Munich disaster the following month. Nevertheless, no attempt was made to find a replacement and the team was left to the guidance of the willing but clearly limited Scotland trainer Dawson Walker.

Billy Steel, the first Scot to be ordered off in an international.

To TOMMY DOCHERTY, one of The Sports Network's World Cup soccer analysts, there is no middle ground.

Everything is either "very, very good" or "a shambles" to the outspoken Scot, who's been in the game for 40 years–as a player, coach, manager and commentator.
Doc's frankness hasn't always endeared him to his employers, of which he's had many. Before turning to television, he served with something like 14 different teams.
"I've had more clubs than Jack Nicklaus," he likes to joke.

Tommy Docherty started Scotland on the way to the 1974 World Cup finals. In 1990 he was to be found in Toronto, dissecting the Italian finals in the habitual manner, here observed by the *Toronto Globe & Mail*.

Frank Haffey, "not a bad chanter", according to Denis Law.

The Scots were drawn to play in Pool II with France, Paraguay and Yugoslavia and met the latter in their opening match. The Slavs were highly rated and in the opening stages it looked as though they had started where Uruguay had left off. Scotland were ponderous and hindered by an injury to their left winger, Imlach of Nottingham Forest. A demoralising rout looked certain when Patakovic put Yugoslavia into an early lead but, as they had done against Austria in 1954, the Scottish players discovered an admirable resolve and Murray levelled the scores shortly after half-time. With 20 minutes to play they even seemed to have taken the lead when the Slav goalkeeper fumbled a cross and the ball rebounded from Mudie and over the line. The referee awarded a foul against Scotland and the match ended 1-1.

Paraguay were next and once again the Scots' intelligence failed to inform their strategy. The South Americans were not in the Uruguayan league and played physical football which should have suited Scotland. Inexplicably the Scots chose to field a comparatively slight team and lost by the odd goal in five to a side which had conceded seven goals to France, who were next to face Scotland in a match which gave rise to another dose of what-might-have-been speculation. The leader of the French attack, Just Fontaine, laid on the opening goal for Kopa but Hewie was offered the best possible opportunity to bring Scotland back into the match only to strike the post with a penalty kick. Fontaine himself scored next and Sammy Baird at last cracked the French defence with a drive which bounced favourably from a post. For the second time in succession, however, the Scots finished bottom of their group.

The knowledge that more thorough preparation might well have seen them proceed into the next stage of the competition was more galling than heartening. Even worse was the understanding, slowly to dawn over several years, that in the predatory world of international football the Scots were low in the food chain.

★   ★   ★

It was to take until 1974 before Scotland were to appear in another World Cup finals. The years wound on to reveal Brazil, England and Brazil again as world champions. Of these, the hardest to bear was England, at least for the Scottish supporters who had been thrown back on devotion to the annual fixture at Hampden or Wembley for the most powerful expression of their allegiance to the dark blue cause. As a ritual it sometimes offered all the joys of self-flagellation. In 1959 Andy Beattie was again in charge, having succeeded Matt Busby when the Manchester United manager found the national post too severe a strain on his depleted health. Beattie deployed a diminutive Scottish team at Wembley and saw them perform worthily but not quite well enough to thwart an England team for whom Billy Wright celebrated his 100th appearance, his career overlapping with that of the youthful Bobby Charlton whose contribution was the only goal of the match.

The youngster had mixed luck the following year in Glasgow when he missed a twice-taken penalty kick but succeeded with another spot award to guarantee a draw in a match which saw Leggat net for the home team. The Scottish goalkeeper, Frank Haffey, was at the centre of a contentious incident when the referee disallowed a goal claimed by England when Joe Baker charged him into the net. A year later, if it had been up to the Scottish support at Wembley, Haffey would have been charged again, preferably with treason after a display which eclipsed even the fiasco against Uruguay.

By then Scotland had a new manager in Ian McColl, who was not burdened like his predecessors by having to guide the national team as well as a club side but the situation was scarcely an improvement because McColl was still, at the age of 33, on Rangers' books as a player. For Wembley he selected another Scottish side which was short on inches, this time in the forward line, but the deficiencies were not to be found in attack on an afternoon when both defences were porous, Scotland's in the extreme. The visitors were 3-0 down before they began to assemble any kind of coherence and acquitted themselves reasonably to reach 3-2, but they were caught out by a swiftly taken Greaves free kick which allowed Douglas to extend the lead. Still the contest provided a monument to defensive frailty as the scoreline moved to 5-3 for England but it was the Scots who collapsed utterly as goal succeeded goal until the margin was mercifully halted at 9-3.

It was a performance which launched a thousand jokes about Scottish goalkeepers and although Frank Haffey was by no means responsible for all the havoc which afflicted his team, he gouged himself a niche in the demonology of Scottish football by an evident failure to grasp the extent of the calamity. When Denis Law reached the sanctuary of the dressing-room he was astounded to discover Haffey – who had a reputation as a passable chanter – singing in the bath. "The rest of us were trying to drown ourselves," says Law. "As a matter of fact, we were trying to drown *him* . . .". When the Scottish team bus ran the gauntlet of the tartan mob on Wembley Way after the match most of the players kept their heads below window level in order to minimise the barrage of missiles which bounced off the vehicle. When the cacophony of bottles and cans suddenly heightened to a life-threatening crescendo, Law looked up from his crouching position. Haffey, with a radiance which would have become the Queen Mother, was waving to the fans trying to claw him through the glass. He was even to be seen posing for TV cameras against the backdrop of Big Ben as it chimed nine times but there was no need to ask for whom the bell tolled. He never played for Scotland again and eventually went to Australia to perform for St George, Budapest, Hakoah and Sutherland FC, where he earned the reputation of an eccentric crowd-pleaser, sitting on his crossbar and jumping down whenever a goal threatened, which was roughly the opposite of his behaviour at Wembley. He was an amiable enough fellow, the big six-footer, and was able to savour a strange irony when his career with Celtic came to an end in October 1964. He was paid to keep goal in England, of all places, when Swindon Town had him on their books for a few months.

The Scottish supporters were wrenched from the depths of their humiliation at Wembley by an abrupt mood swing as the team entered an unusually consistent phase. Scotland came painfully close to qualifying for the 1962 World Cup finals in Chile when they recovered from a 4-0 defeat by Czechoslovakia in Bratislava to beat the Czechs 3-2 at Hampden, a result which led to a play-off in Brussels to see which of the two countries would proceed to South America. At full-time they were tied at 2-2 but it was the Czechs who possessed the extra resources for a 4-2 win which not only saw them into the latter stages of the tournament but carried them all the way to the final where they at last succumbed to the Brazilians.

For Scotland the failure to reach the 1966 finals in England was

Haffey, after England proved to be on song in their 9-3 rout of Scotland at Wembley in 1961.

especially harrowing. The 1961 thrashing had been followed by a fertile period against the Auld Enemy with three wins, a draw and one defeat, and the reverse was only by the odd goal in seven in a thrilling match at Hampden three months before England won the World Cup against West Germany at Wembley. The Scottish team which lost 4-3 on 2 April 1966 remains one to savour: Ferguson, Greig, Gemmell, Murdoch, McKinnon, Baxter, Johnstone, Law, Wallace, Bremner, Johnston. Their talents were not to grace the ultimate stage because Scotland, without the transcendent Baxter, had been beaten at home by Poland and in Naples by Italy in their qualifying group despite the best efforts of Jock Stein – in a temporary managerial capacity – to contain the debilitating effects of repeated injury problems.

The sound of grinding teeth was to be heard throughout Scotland as Bobby Moore (so irritatingly clean-cut) stepped up to receive the World Cup but when England proceeded unbeaten for the following nine months nemesis was directed towards them in a tartan cavalcade. No single performance of the international team is so enshrined in the modern Scottish memory as the 1967 display at Wembley when Scotland, inspired by Baxter's atavistic tactical advice – "Let's take the piss oot o' them" – responded by capering preposterously around the field. In the record books their feat is merely registered as a 3-2 victory but the goals were virtually irrelevant. What mattered to the Scottish support, transported to bliss for 90 minutes, was the utter disdain shown by Baxter, Law, Bremner and Gemmell for the English – and them world champions, too! – on their own midden. Each Scottish fan in the stadium that afternoon believed that this was the World Cup final which should have been. For the Scots it was Nirvana and

Baxter scores his first goal from the penalty spot against England in 1963.

Valhalla combined and only slightly diminished for being nine months behind schedule.

* * *

There was, however, to be no place in the sun of Mexico for the 1970 World Cup finals. Once more Scotland stumbled in their qualifying group, although this time they produced a splendid display against West Germany in Hamburg, losing the vital goal in a 3-2 defeat with only 11 minutes left to play, with Gemmell being sent off for retaliation almost at the final whistle. There was no relief in the European Championships which were at last widely accepted in 1972 as being second in importance to the World Cup. The Scots were to establish a pattern of consistent failure to qualify which increasingly contrasted with a new-found ability to reach the World Cup finals repeatedly, a sequence which began when the culminating stages of the tournament were hosted by West Germany in 1974. Tommy Docherty had been appointed temporary manager in 1971 in succession to Bobby Brown and he immediately injected the team with a shot of his characteristic aggression, mingling the discipline of a 4-3-3 formation with the old Scottish virtues of adventurous flank play and a sharp-tackling but creative midfield.

Docherty, who had been confirmed as manager on a full-time basis, resigned midway through the 1972-73 season, lured south by the greater financial appeal of Manchester United, and although there was considerable regret at his departure there is a case for the argument which suggests that as one of life's sprinters he had perhaps

Denis Law's goal against England in 1967.

passed the summit of his achievement with the national side. He was replaced by Willie Ormond, a man of a different kidney from the exuberant Doc. The contrast was so marked that many at the time felt that Scotland had erred on the side of caution, forgetting that as the left-wing component of the Famous Five, the Hibs forward line of happy memory for those who attended Easter Road in the 1950s, Ormond had been an adventurous attacker noted for his willingness to play where the knocks were hardest. He showed remarkable fortitude in recovering from three leg breaks and a fractured arm and he was capable of playing pugnaciously when the occasion required. As a manager he had overcome the confinement of limited resources with St Johnstone and, aided by his splendid ability to assess the worth of individual players to a fine tolerance, he guided the unfashionable Perth club into European football.

Moreover, he had played in Scotland's demeaning World Cup expedition to Switzerland in 1954 and was unlikely to permit a repeat performance in West Germany. First, though, the Scots had to complete their qualifying campaign successfully. He could hardly have imagined he would have to endure such a demoralising start to his reign when England, hoisting long downfield balls over a frosty Hampden pitch, administered a crushing 5-0 defeat in the SFA centenary celebration match on 14 February 1973. The Home

International series was similarly dispiriting when it brought a home defeat by Northern Ireland along with a further 1-0 reverse against England at Wembley. The following match was lost by the same score to Switzerland in Berne and when Brazil visited Glasgow for the SFA's second commemorative match they were no more kind to their hosts' morale than England had been and left Scotland with yet another 1-0 defeat to consider. Ormond, however, had used the fixtures wisely to test the strength of his squad and he was aware that the game which mattered had yet to come. When it arrived on the evening of 26 September 1973, it was to be one of the most memorable seen at Hampden in two decades.

Docherty had inflamed the Scots' desire to reach the 1974 finals with successive victories over Denmark in Copenhagen and Glasgow and when Czechoslovakia, the other contender in the group, were held to a 1-1 draw by the Danes in May, the way was open for Ormond's Scotland to qualify by beating the Czechs in the first of two encounters between the countries. When they met at Hampden it was a straightforward contest with the Scots sustaining waves of attack against a crammed visiting defence but, as so often happens in such circumstances, the aggressors were punished for their forward policy. Nehoda broke free shortly after the half-hour mark to direct a speculative shot which found the net although Ally Hunter, the Kilmarnock goalkeeper, got both hands to the ball in flight.

An ominous groan of woe was heard from the terracings at this point but the Scottish support responded to Hunter's evident unhappiness by chanting his name and urging the team to renew their assaults, a policy which was repaid when Jim Holton leapt to direct a header beyond several Czech defenders to beat Victor for the equaliser. The second half was played amidst a tumult of noise which reached a thunderous climax with 15 minutes left to play when Jordan, who had arrived as a substitute for Dalglish, exploited the Czechs' obvious aerial weakness to strike a winning goal which plunged the decaying stadium into some of the most raucous celebrations ever witnessed there.

Scotland lost the return in Bratislava by the only goal of the game but the outcome was academic and Scotland were able to plan for West Germany with two matches against the host nation. The first, played at Hampden, drew a pleasing tribute from the German manager, Helmut Schoen, after his side had been permitted a 1-1 draw with a late goal by Hoeness and a penalty kick taken too casually by Bremner. Schoen insisted that Scotland were the best side his team had encountered in a year which had seen the Germans play such illustrious opposition as Argentina, Brazil, Czechoslovakia, France and the USSR. In the Home Championship Northern Ireland won the opening match 1-0 but Ormond remedied a Scottish fault when he demanded speedier distribution from midfield and his players responded with satisfying 2-0 wins against Wales and England. Jimmy Johnstone chose to punctuate the two victories with his much publicised version of the North Atlantic Drift when he was propelled – willingly it must be stated – from the Scottish HQ at Largs into the Firth of Clyde in a dinghy with a single oar.

It had been decided that fine tuning for the finals could be had with matches in Belgium, where Scotland were beaten by a debatable penalty kick, and in Norway where Johnstone was again discovered in the drink, only this time in the bar of the team hotel in Oslo where he was imbibing late into the evening with Billy Bremner. A caucus amongst the SFA officials was for sending the pair home but Ormond

BOBBY CHARLTON

Bobby Charlton, whose playing career with Manchester United spanned 17 years from 1956 to 1973, and who won no fewer than 106 caps for England, principally as a centre-forward, was born in Ashington in Northumberland and first played against Scotland in 1958, beginning auspiciously with a 4-0 victory.

"I was brought up in the north-east of England about thirty or forty miles south of the Scottish border and living in that area we had a lot of affiliations with the Scots. For example, if someone asked if you were going to the Cup final you'd have to say 'Well, which one?'. It wasn't automatic that it was the FA Cup final because that was a six or seven hour drive if you were lucky enough to have a car and since the Scottish Cup final had crowds of 134,000 in those days it was almost as big an event in the north-east.

"The one thing about playing against the Scots was that you never, ever had a dull game, no matter what level it was at. I mean, I played for England schoolboys in a 0-0 draw with Scotland and I thought God bless us, that's competitive in the extreme for a schoolboy match, but it was something I came to expect and between you and me, it was a bloody nuisance if we lost because we would hear it until the following year.

"My philosophy was, if you play against the Scots put in your proper planning because it made life that little bit easier for the rest of the season. It meant more for the Scots to beat the English than it did for the English to beat the Scots, especially the year after we won the World Cup. If anybody had said to me who, out of all the teams in the world will come to Wembley and beat you, I would have said the Scots. And sure enough, it

pled their case successfully and collected his dividend when Bremner responded with rousing contributions during the finals.

In prospect, Scotland had an evens chance of proceeding from a group which found them in the company of Brazil, Yugoslavia and Zaire in Dortmund and Frankfurt and it was generally felt that a great deal hinged on how many they might be able to score in their opening match against the unknown Africans. As it turned out, Zaire had been coached diligently and during the opening stages they played attractive, effective football. After a period of readjustment Scotland came into the match and Lorimer hit one of his venomous drives to open up the scoring; the margin was doubled when Jordan, who had created the first goal, headed a second. With a fractional increase in luck the Scots could have won 4-0, Hay having struck the post and Lorimer the crossbar, and although they were criticised for having played cautiously against opposition which was not likely to be treated too leniently by the other teams in the group, Ormond had not forgotten the effects of playing in excessive heat in Switzerland 20 years earlier and drew back from urging his players towards a possibly damaging exhaustion in similar conditions in Dortmund.

In the second match Scotland encountered a Brazil team which played at the summit of their form and again they struggled in the first quarter of the match but, rallied by the unquenchable Bremner, it was the Scots who dominated and who might have scored on three occasions, the best chance falling to Bremner himself when he attempted to measure a close-range shot at the back post only to watch in anguish as the ball squirmed narrowly wide of the goal. The goalless draw was more than respectable but since Yugoslavia had run up a 9-0 scoreline against Zaire the Scots were now obliged to beat the Slavs if they were to progress.

This they could not do. They were forced to settle for a 1-1 draw when Jordan equalised in the final minute, although even then they were denied qualification by the slimmest of margins when Brazil scored their last goal late against a concussed goalkeeper in a 3-0 win over Zaire to edge into the next stage of the tournament. The Scots were out but affairs were plainly much better ordered than they had been in Switzerland or Sweden, and as it turned out Scotland were to be the only unbeaten country in the West German finals. Those who had followed their exploits at home demonstrated warm approval of the efforts of Ormond's squad by turning out in force for the arrival of the team plane in Glasgow; a crowd estimated at 10,000 greeted a group of players who were as talented a group as any collected together to perform in dark blue jerseys.

The euphoria continued into the following season but it was insufficient to ensure similar success in the European Championships, in which Scotland were beaten 2-1 at home by Spain after Tommy Hutchinson missed a penalty kick. For the return match in Valencia Ormond conscripted Charlie Cooke, the inspirational Chelsea player who had come to resemble King Arthur as a presence to be summoned during the hour of need. He obliged by constructing a goal in the first minute for Jordan but when Buchan handled on the line the referee awarded first a penalty kick and then a goal, and although the Scots could claim credit with a 1-1 draw their hopes in the tournament had greatly diminished. They flickered briefly with a 1-0 win over Denmark in Copenhagen but there was a recurrence of difficulties off the field when Billy Bremner, Arthur Graham, Joe Harper, Pat McCluskey and Willie Young were suspended by the SFA after getting themselves involved in a row in a Danish bar.

In official circles it was felt that Ormond had permitted discipline to become too lax and when Scotland were ultimately excluded from the European Championships by Spain's draw in Romania the manager's tenure was at a close. He was permitted to announce his resignation but it was the equivalent of handing him a pistol and inviting him to step outside and do the gentlemanly thing.

The obvious successor was Jock Stein but not for the first time he elected to stay at Celtic. It was a decision which he regretted in common with the rest of the country within two years. Thwarted in their attempt to enlist the most statesmanlike figure in Scottish football, the SFA turned to a radically different character. In so doing, they reflected the mood of a newly assertive and bombastic Scotland on the upward curve of one of its periodic revivals of nationalism. The Scottish National Party, campaigning on the effective but insubstantial slogan of "It's Scotland's Oil" – a reference to the recently developed mineral wealth of the North Sea – had achieved an unparalleled representation in Parliament and the country was in the mood to be sold visions of the glories to follow. With the hour came the salesman.

Ally McLeod inherited a team of skills and balance to which he added his singular brand of motivation, and it could not be denied that he was capable of convincing players to rise above themselves on decisive occasions, as he had shown during his spells in charge of Ayr United and Aberdeen. He had only one trophy to his credit, the least prestigious of the three domestic Scottish honours, the League Cup, which was won by Aberdeen. His progress had been too rapid to allow examination of the effect of adversity on his temperament or methods. In this, the SFA must be held responsible for the calamity which was soon to befall Scotland; they had ditched a cautious but prudent and successful manager in order to invest in what was fundamentally a speculation.

There was a case for a finely judged increase in Scottish aspiration after Ormond but McLeod expanded ambition in logarithmic leaps and critical mass was achieved in June 1977 when Scotland beat an unimpressive England side 2–1 at Wembley with goals from McQueen

was, because the supporters came down thinking 'If they're the world champions and we can beat them, that must mean that we're the best.'

"But with the Scots it's always peaks and troughs and never the sort of consistency which England had for a period of around eight or nine years. I don't want to be detrimental but I felt maybe we had other important fixtures while for Scotland there was only one, so that Wales could beat them, Ireland could beat them, and it didn't matter – so long as the English didn't beat them. If you went in unprepared against the Scots they would beat you simply because they had the passion and the desire and if you didn't match them in that, there could only be one outcome."

Wembley under a weight of Scottish celebration after the 2-1 win over England in 1977.

The law prevents the annexation of Trafalgar Square as a Scottish loch.

and Dalglish. The Scottish supporters celebrated the final whistle by promenading *en masse* across the Wembley turf and perching on top of the crossbars, which quickly fractured under the pressure. Ally McLeod had a swift opportunity to contemplate the force he had unleashed when he attempted to retreat to the sanctuary of the players' tunnel at full-time, only to be restrained by a security man who was disinclined to believe that McLeod was the Scotland team manager. Only when the England manager Don Revie intervened was McLeod permitted to reach the visitors' dressing-room where he was astounded to discover four Scottish supporters sharing the bath with the goalkeeper, Alan Rough.

In the aftermath of the Wembley frolics Scotland set off on a summer tour of South America which brought the team's first-ever win on the continent, a fine 4-2 victory over Chile. A 1-1 draw with Argentina followed but the match was marred when Willie Johnston was sent off early in the second half. Despite the player's tempestuous reputation he was defended by McLeod and most of the Scottish officials who believed that he was the victim of an injustice. Although the final tour game ended in a 2-0 defeat by Brazil in Rio the exercise had been a notable success which suggested that the Scots were well-equipped to conduct a serious campaign if they qualified for the finals of the 1978 World Cup in Argentina.

First, though, they had to overcome Wales in a fixture played at the unlikely venue of Anfield, chosen by Wales as their nominal home ground because Ninian Park had been restricted to a crowd limit of 10,000. The Welsh FA needed the money they would accrue from a capacity crowd at the Liverpool stadium and they were rewarded by an attendance of 50,800 on 12 October 1977. They were less gratified after an evening on which Scotland proceeded towards the finals after an unusually contentious match which swung towards the Scots when Joe Jordan rose with Davie Jones to contest a high cross ball. Both players raised their hands and one certainly touched the ball, the impression of M. Wurtz, the French referee, being that Jones was the culprit, an opinion he might have revised had he turned to see Jordan kissing his own fist in obvious self-congratulation.

Masson waited until the Welsh protests had evaporated and

converted the spot kick to ignite the customary scenes of dementia amongst the Tartan Army. Wales, however, had never been out of the match and Alan Rough was forced to make the kind of brilliant reflex save which was his greatest strength when he deflected a forceful Toshack shot on to the top of his crossbar. The *coup de grâce* was administered when Martin Buchan was put clear on the right to direct a delightful cross into the path of Dalglish whose sparkling header swept gloriously into the net to kill the frail Welsh hopes of a draw. Dalglish had achieved an unique distinction, that of scoring on his home ground a goal for the visiting team which proved to be decisive for his own side.

Aside from winning a Hampden friendly against Bulgaria, Scotland would travel to South America with only the Home Championship as late preparation, an odd hiatus which disguised the evidence that the team had, in fact, peaked too early and was in decline. By the time the matches against the other home countries demonstrated this important truth, it was too late to make any significant changes to the expedition plans. The three games were all played at Hampden, Scotland being unwilling to fulfil their fixture with Northern Ireland in Belfast because of the disorder in Ulster, but despite home advantage the Scots could only manage 1-1 draws with the Welsh and Irish and, worst of all, were beaten by England when Coppell scored the only goal of the match. Scotland suddenly seemed to be afflicted by eccentricity and it was in keeping with the tenor of their preparation that the scorer of their goals against Wales and Northern Ireland, Derek Johnstone, would not make an appearance in Argentina.

More alarmingly, McLeod had begun to make increasingly implausible predictions about the Scots' chances, encouraged by the fact that he was in charge of the only home country to be represented in the finals and he was not made wary by the extensive coverage given to his remark that if Scotland failed to return with the World Cup, there would always be the consolation of second or third place. Nor can it be said that he was unaware of the traps which awaited him. In an interview with the author of this volume, conducted shortly before he left for Argentina, McLeod was asked what, in his view, were the particular hazards which might derail his euphoric cavalcade. The national manager answered: "It isn't the likes of Argentina or West Germany which worry me. You have to motivate Scottish players for games against teams like Peru or Iran where we think we've got the game won before we start. They worry me a lot more than Holland, for example." Despite this uncanny preview of the calamity which was to come, McLeod was not prepared to limit the fantasy rations. Asked what he planned to do after the World Cup, he replied: "Retain it!"

The players, meanwhile, had become embroiled in a round of negotiations and disputes about their share of what was confidently expected to be a cash bonanza and there were times when the SFA appeared to be operating from a location somewhere in the Casbah. Most bizarre of all was the parade of Scotland's World Cup squad in an open-topped bus around Hampden, where they had so recently failed to win their previous three games. When the squad actually reached South America certain of the group were flattered to discover that as well as the Scottish sports writers who customarily travelled with the team they were to be attended by an additional retinue of newsmen, many of them English, which was taken to imply recognition of Scotland's achievement in being the only UK country to reach the finals.

Willie Johnston in disgrace,
Argentina 1978.

In fact, the supplementary reporters included a carrion element who guessed that Scotland might provide a diet of unorthodoxy which they were not averse to magnifying, insulated as they were by several thousand miles from the impact of their stories. The local press boys had even fewer scruples – the *Buenos Aires Daily Herald* well in front of the pack – and were quickly processing wild tales of drunken orgies amongst the Scottish players. The stories were picked up and retold – with additional lurid detail – by the South American press agencies, some of whom were able to provide pictures of Scottish footballers unashamedly posing in their strips, grinning through four-day growth, bottles in hand, repeating McLeod's more radical predictions through an alcoholic haze.

What the delighted Argentine press had stumbled upon was the phenomenon of Scottish supporters dressing as duplicates of the team, down to the players' names embroidered on the back of their jerseys. It was an illusion which short-circuited the Argentinian commandos deputed to guard the Scottish headquarters, who were present in serious numbers around the Sierras Hotel. The Rangers full back Sandy Jardine found himself in conversation in the hotel lounge with a Scottish fan who was contentedly downing serial beers in the presence of his heroes. When Jardine asked how the interloper had been permitted to pass through the armed cordon, the fan replied: "They just looked at the back of my strip so I suppose they thought I was Willie Donnachie." Some time later Donnachie, who in his capacity as a real-life Scotland defender had gone for an incognito stroll in civilian dress, was released from the Argentinian Army guardhouse to which he had been confined after being charged with impersonating a Scottish footballer.

By full-time in the first Group IV match with Peru, several of his team-mates could have been remanded on the same indictment. The momentum generated by McLeod's outrageous enthusiasm and willingness to believe his own propaganda lasted for just over an hour of the initial contest. Scotland had taken the lead when Quiroga, rated by the English sporting press as an honorary Scottish goalkeeper, deflected Rioch's shot towards Jordan who knocked it over the line but the Scots were unable to build on their early lead and Cueto brought the scores level shortly before the interval.

Nevertheless, Scotland were offered an opportunity to restore their lead when Diaz fouled Rioch to concede a penalty kick. Peru had not neglected their homework as Scotland had done and Quiroga moved to his right to save Masson's irresolute effort to convert. Thereafter the Scots lacked the energy to chase a game which moved out of their orbit when Cubillas strode forward to score two decisive goals.

McLeod's confidence was cruelly exposed as bluster but he did not deserve the next blow to fall upon his head. Willie Johnston and Kenny Dalglish had undergone the mandatory dope tests after the game; Johnston's had been declared positive. It transpired that he had taken pills described variously as remedies for hay fever or fatigue. Hay fever was thought more probable by those who had seen his display against Peru, which did not suggest reinforced energy. Johnston was sent away in ignominy and when he was put into a car at Buenos Aires airport with a spectacularly armed military escort he genuinely feared that he was being driven off to be shot. If he had been an Argentinian footballer he probably would have been despatched behind the hangars but instead he was flown to Paris to be met by his manager at West Brom, Ron Atkinson, who assured the player that he was now in a position to negotiate a sponsorship deal with Boots the Chemist. Johnston was never to play for his country again but at least he could reflect that his position could have been infinitely worse if Scotland had actually succeeded in beating Peru, in which case his transgression could have been punished by the penalty of a two-goal defeat against the Scots.

Meanwhile, back at the *rancho* the drug scare had an unlikely side effect. McLeod had collected every pill in his players' possession and on the way to a Scottish training session he halted the team bus and dumped his haul into a convenient field where several grazing horses quickly consumed the unaccustomed treat. When the bus made its return journey the Scottish players and officials were vastly amused to see the previously sedate horses frolicking around their pasture like spring lambs.

The incident provided rare comic relief, however, as morale continued to subside on a massive scale. In an attempt to reinstate some kind of normality McLeod persisted with the use of Masson and Rioch in midfield, two half-backs when at least one fresh attacking midfielder was required. McLeod's knowledge of Iran was not complete enough to merit the description of sketchy and most of what he did know had been gleaned from the Welsh manager Mike Smith, with a supplement from Andy Roxburgh who had watched them lose 3-0 to Holland in the other opening Group IV match. Iran had not been thought sufficiently dangerous to warrant a first-hand appraisal and the result was predictably farcical. McLeod had foreseen that overconfidence could prove Scotland's undoing in such a game but nobody could have accused Scotland of swagger in the aftermath of the fiasco against Peru. This time the Scots were utterly mediocre, emerging with an unmerited 1-1 draw in which the Iranians scored both goals, Eskandrian putting the ball past his own goalkeeper in a mistimed attempt to clear his penalty box. Danalfar equalised later.

Mocked by the South American press, reviled at home, the Scots were now ripe for reincarnation as a football team. McLeod at last brought the forceful Souness into his calculations and word reached the Scottish camp that they had been rated – perfectly reasonably – as no-hopers to beat the Dutch in their final group match. Conditions were almost perfect for a famous victory but the final motivation was only supplied when Rensenbrink put Holland into the lead. Scotland now needed to score four goals to qualify for the next stage of the World Cup. Souness began the move which permitted Dalglish to swivel and drive home the equaliser shortly before half-time. In the second half Souness was fouled in the box and Gemmill scored decisively from the penalty kick. The best was yet to come and when it arrived Scotland had, by general consent, created the goal of the finals. Dalglish lost possession on the right but Archie Gemmill ravenously gathered the loose ball and embarked on a devastating corkscrew sprint towards Jongbloed's goal, trailing stricken Dutch defenders in his wake. Gemmill's approach shot was as gorgeous as his approach work and it rasped past the astounded Dutch goalkeeper. In Scotland the impact of the goal staggered a television audience whose dutiful devotion had been soured by a profound sense of anger and betrayal. Was it possible, was it *thinkable* that Ally had somehow worked the miracle?

Although the home viewers could not know it, the manager was at that moment invoking help from above. At Gemmill's goal John Robertson of Nottingham Forest, a Scottish substitute, called out to

Graeme Souness found his international career at an end when he was dropped from the team to play Uruguay in 1986.

him: "Boss, somebody up there likes you!" For the first time since Masson's misplaced penalty kick McLeod was disposed to agree and immediately reverted to type. Johnny Rep fastened on to a misplaced clearance 30 yards out. As the Dutch player manoeuvred for position McLeod mentally urged him to attempt the unlikely shot. Rep obliged with a dipping drive for which Alan Rough was not apparently alert. The ball billowed into the net behind the aggrieved Scottish goalkeeper and Scotland, after their magnificent and unforeseen flurry, were on their way home.

The post-mortem was lengthy and debates about the causes and impact of 1978 continue to surface in Scotland yet. McLeod, who had admittedly been let down by some experienced players, was able to say with justification that until the game against Peru he had given Scots – and by no means only the football-minded section of the population – the finest 18 months that they had ever enjoyed. A century earlier he could have achieved the same result by distributing Winchester rifles and cheap whisky to the Apaches. When the final reckoning was presented to a nation which had colluded in the abdication of its critical faculties it was as though Watergate and Waterloo had combined as five million people reminded themselves about the doubts they had entertained and which somehow failed to materialise before Cubillas scored his first goal in Cordoba.

Still, the recriminations were surprisingly wholesome. In a score of countries – Italy leaps to mind – where national aspirations should in theory be satisfied by sovereignty rather than results on the football field, a returning team dismissed from the World Cup in such circumstances would have required armed police protection. In Scotland certain necessary perspectives were at last accommodated

Jock Stein approves Jordan's opening goal against the Soviet Union, 1982.

and football henceforth would be required to bear more realistic expectations.

The SFA was placed in a deliciously excruciating position. Having rewarded Willie Ormond for his decency with a degradingly shabby conclusion to his spell as manager, they had got what they wanted in Ally McLeod only to discover that they did not want what they got. Unwilling to dismiss him, if only for the satisfaction his sacking would afford the baiting press, they confirmed him in office by a casting vote and were greatly relieved when he decided to depart in any case.

His departure was entirely in character. Sitting in his office at Park Gardens some months after the return from Argentina, McLeod was surprised by a visit from his former employer, the Ayr United chairman John Ferguson. At Somerset Park Ferguson had displayed a paternal affection for McLeod but he avoided contact with his protégé when Aberdeen enticed him from Ayr. After a few awkwardly mumbled opening remarks Ferguson came to the point of his errand, namely, that if McLeod wished to return to Somerset Park a *rapprochement* would not be out of the question. The two men went for a meal together and within 48 hours Ally was back at his former desk in Ayr. He was gone like a comet sweeping back into the twilight after an incandescent dance around the sun.

Years later, he was to say of his meeting with John Ferguson: "I made my mind up very quick. We went for lunch and, you know, he didnae pay for it. It was me who took him . . .."

★   ★   ★

Jock Stein, his Celtic connection severed just before Scotland set off for Argentina in the summer of 1978, had been induced to take over the guidance of Leeds United but north of the border he was Scotland manager by acclaim, in popular desire if not in fact. Ally McLeod's removal to the Clyde coast permitted Stein's overdue accession to the Scottish post. As related in an earlier chapter, he oversaw the convalescence needed to restore a flayed national pride.

When Scotland next appeared in the World Cup finals, held in Spain in 1982, Stein immersed himself in the task of supervising propriety amongst players and pressmen alike. The balm of his reassuring presence extended to the Tartan Army, a source of a great deal of anxiety to the Spanish authorities prior to the tournament, largely because of their abiding recollection of the events of May 1972 when the aggrieved Rangers support at the Cup Winners' Cup final in Barcelona administered a rare beating to Franco's militia. With Scotland drawn to play in Group VI in the choice locations of Malaga and Seville it was felt that the anticipated descent of a massive Scottish support would be rendered volatile by exposure to local wine, some of which was on sale for the equivalent of 25 pence a bottle, although in varieties likely to appeal to connoisseurs of voltage rather than vintage.

The Scottish fans, with the delightful sense of self-mockery which they habitually display on trips abroad (England excepted), acknowledged their cartoon image with a brilliantly apt response which was displayed in Malaga's La Roselida stadium during the second group match. As Scotland and Russia took the field at the start of the match, their television audience was treated to the slogan "Alcoholism versus Communism", inscribed on a waving banner. By that time, however, the Spanish police had announced with relief that

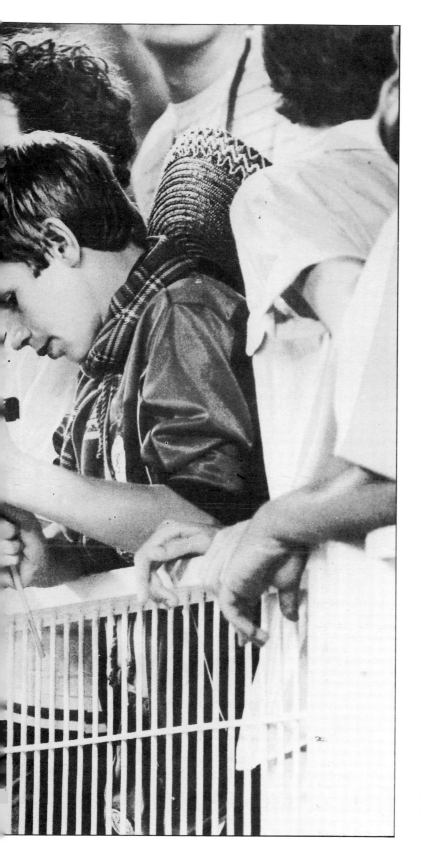

For Scottish supporters at the
World Cup, it has usually been
better to travel hopefully than to
arrive. Five consecutive
qualifications for the finals have
been followed by as many
first-round departures.

the Scots, many of whom had taken the opportunity to combine their supporters' activities with a family holiday in nearby Torremolinos or Benalmadena, had proved to be spectacularly well-behaved.

In such a climate of benevolent moderation it was almost possible to believe that the football was a subsidiary event, but only until the group matches released the old, familiar rituals of anxiety, acclaim and frustration. Scotland opened their campaign against New Zealand knowing, as they knew before Zaire eight years earlier, that superior goal difference could be the key to the elusive latter stage of the tournament. There would be no fatal underestimates in Scottish preparation this time, the fans believed, and someone demonstrated his reassurance with a banner bearing the message: "Don't worry – Ally McLeod Is In Blackpool!" Dalglish and Wark between them bore Scotland to a handsome 3-0 interval lead and the aura of Stein's professionalism permeated the terracings. But Act II heralded the return of accustomed spectres as the Kiwis scored twice before Robertson relieved the tension from a free kick set-piece and Archibald arrived to head a fifth.

In Seville three days later Scotland led briefly and thrillingly by Dave Narey's opportunist drive from 20 yards. The fact that Brazil then deposited four efforts in the net behind Alan Rough was disappointing but not disheartening, and a particularly pleasing feature of a searingly hot evening was the fraternisation of Scottish and Brazilian supporters throughout the city before and after the fixture. The streets of Seville witnessed a compelling fusion of culture on a remarkable night. Scottish players mingled their music with the hypnotic rhythms of Brazilian drums; the samba and the strathspey intertwined.

The final game, against the Soviet Union, brought Scotland to the old pass, the necessity for a victory to avoid departure from the competition on goal difference. Archibald prompted Jordan for the opening goal on the quarter hour mark, but after Chivadze's second-half equaliser Miller and Hansen lost possession when they collided in pursuit of a drifting wide ball and Shengalia was offered an open target, gratefully accepted. Scotland were effectively out of contention once more but Souness played the captain's part to the final moments, scoring the equaliser with a dynamic break from midfield finished by an accomplished low drive to make it 2-2. Again the Scots had found advancement in the World Cup marginally beyond their reach, but more importantly they had readjusted their focus, not so much to reduce aspiration as to contain the inevitable limitations of its achievement.

At the time of Jock Stein's untimely death in September 1985 he had steered Scotland to the brink of a fourth consecutive appearance in the finals, secured shortly afterwards under Alex Ferguson's guidance by a 2-0 win over Australia in Glasgow and a 0-0 draw in the return match in Melbourne. For their efforts on this tortuous route the Scottish players were rewarded with a place in the toughest pool in the Mexican finals the following year when they were drawn with West Germany, Denmark and Uruguay. The section was quickly christened the *Grupo del Muerte* – the Group of Death – although the journalist who coined this fanciful description owed less to the inspiration of tequila in Guadalajara than a shot of Talisker in Glasgow.

Straightforward ill-luck undermined Scotland at the outset when they lost 1-0 to a Danish team for whom Elkjaer scored. Aitken netted what appeared to be a perfectly legitimate goal only to be ruled offside by the referee whose decision was demonstrated to be badly at fault by

Dave Narey's 20-yard drive ("a toe-poke" – Jimmy Hill) gave Scotland the lead against Brazil in the Spanish World Cup finals of 1982. It could not be sustained and Scotland lost 4-1. It was a remarkable night off the field though.

video replays of the incident. Having lost narrowly to the team with a claim to being the best in Europe, the Scots were now scheduled to face Franz Beckenbauer's West Germany, destined to contest the final with Argentina. Strachan displayed compelling skills to open the scoring with a splendid angled drive but Voller equalised soon afterwards and when the Scots carelessly left Allofs unmarked immediately after the interval his shot proved to be the winner.

Since the tournament rules now provided for entry into the next stage for the best of the third-placed teams, Scotland could still reach the last 16 if they beat Uruguay in their final group match but the permutations of the fixture suggested that such an outcome would be improbable. Uruguay, under the direction of their coach Omar Borras, were a team soused in cynicism and required only to draw to move into the next round. Forty seconds into the match Batista lunged at Strachan in a tackle which might have amputated the Scottish player's legs. For this disgraceful assault he was quite correctly sent off by M. Quiniou, the French referee, but even with ten men the South American champions were adequate for the task of squandering as much time as possible without permitting football to be played and they secured the goalless draw which eliminated Scotland.

At the post-match press conference Uruguayan TV crews spat in the faces of Scottish pressmen, Omar Borras called the referee "a

An anxious Stein turns to his assistants on the Scottish bench as the Cardiff game draws to a close; at the final whistle he was struck down by a heart attack and died within minutes.

ANDY CAMERON

Andy Cameron, one of the best-loved Scottish comedians this century, has sustained a lifelong love affair with his two favourite teams, Rangers and Scotland. Despite his powerful allegiance to Ibrox, which he likes to refer to as The Stadium, he is held in sufficiently high regard by Celtic to have been featured as the main entertainment at the testimonial dinner given in honour of a Celtic captain, Roy Aitken.

"Apart from The Stadium I was a regular at one other ground when I was a boy. We went to Cathkin to see Third Lanark and me and my pals used to collect the beer bottles – this was in the days before they threw them. They just drank oot them and stuck them at their feet and we used to go over wi' the pram wheels and the big patched sheet bag and take them to the Old Quarry Bar, which was owned by two brothers, Davie and John Martin.

"John was deaf, so you couldnae get your money for the bottles because he couldnae see you over the top of the bar or hear you shouting 'Mister! Mister!' So you had to hope that Davie would hear you and come over and tell John why there was a bag of bottles on the counter. And that was how I earned my first coppers from football.

"I went down to Anfield when Scotland beat Wales before they qualified for Argentina. That was when the German player did a job for us, you know – Hans Jordan.

"So we were going to Argentina and I made the Ally's Army record which sold 236,000 copies and it got me on *Top of the Pops* twice with people like Generation X and The Jam, you know? And kids were coming up to me on *Top of the*

murderer" and Alex Ferguson declared that he wished the Danes and West Germans good luck in their attempt on the trophy but would not extend hopes for success to Uruguay. He added: "If Omar Borras defends his team he is sitting there lying, cheating and uttering a load of rubbish." Ernie Walker, the SFA secretary, was more succinct. He referred to the Uruguayans simply as "scum" and FIFA appeared to take a similar line, fining the South Americans 25,000 Swiss francs and threatening to eject them from the tournament if they did not improve their behaviour. In the event, Pasculli of Argentina did FIFA and the image of football a large favour by scoring the goal which sent Uruguay skulking back to Montevideo.

★   ★   ★

Alex Ferguson relinquished his part-time duties with the national team to return to his club job at Aberdeen, from where he soon afterwards moved south to inherit Manchester United from Ron Atkinson. His successor was Andy Roxburgh, the SFA's director of coaching, whose appointment had not been anticipated, although the author of this volume predicted his elevation to the manager's office on Radio 2 three days before it took place. It was announced that Roxburgh would assume the title of coach and after he stepped blinking out of the glare of the television arc lamps he set about the immense task of moulding the national team into a shape of his devising.

That he had a profound understanding of tactical thinking and vast knowledge of the world game was not in doubt – he had, after all, been the official FIFA observer in Brazil's section in the Mexico finals – but there were powerful reservations about his ability to cope with such a demanding task, especially since his involvement in club management had been confined to a spell at Clydebank. Indeed, shortly before his death Jock Stein remarked that Roxburgh, a former schoolteacher, had found the perfect outlet for his talents as director of coaching, adding: "We would never put him in the position of having to cope with the senior team. That isn't what he's happy at."

Ernie Walker thought differently, however, and his influence was sufficient to see Roxburgh appointed as full-time successor to Stein and Ferguson. At first he appeared to confirm the sceptics' misgivings, floundering somewhat as Scotland once more failed to qualify for the European Championships. A certain degree of callowness was exposed in the immediate aftermath of a stinging 4-1 defeat by Belgium in Brussels when TV viewers saw him retort sharply to a critical question with the words: "Well, I didn't ask for this job, you know".

★   ★   ★

By the time Scotland had to face the World Cup qualifying hurdles once more, Roxburgh had bedded himself into the job and the team embarked boldly on the task with a deserved 2-1 win over Norway in Oslo. There was a stumble in the next match when Yugoslavia came to Hampden and left with a 1-1 draw, but Scotland forged onwards to achieve nine points from a possible ten when a spirited 2-0 victory against France in Glasgow was sandwiched between home and away wins over Cyprus, although the decisive goal in Limassol was delayed until the seventh minute of stoppage time, rightly added by the East German referee to compensate for undisguised Cypriot time-wasting.

Roxburgh declined to consider the section as good as won, and warned: "We have done well so far, but the hardest part is yet to come." Unfortunately, such caution proved to be entirely well founded. After the summer break, Scotland travelled to Zagreb and succumbed 3-1 to a Yugoslav side whose cause was reinforced spectacularly by own goals from the Liverpool duo of Nicol and Gillespie. A month later in Paris, another bout of nervous defending saw a further own goal by Nicol contribute to a heavy 3-0 defeat.

Fortunately for the Scots, their final group match was at home to Norway and, even more happily, they required only a draw. When Ally McCoist put Scotland ahead with a well placed shot on the run, some of the strain was removed from the occasion. True to tradition, however, the Scottish supporters were obliged to endure a prolonged bout of torment when Jim Leighton permitted a speculative 35-yard shot to beat him in injury time before the final whistle at last soothed the torn nerves of the crowd.

Having thus qualified for the finals for a quite remarkable fifth time in succession, Scotland continued to be schizophrenic throughout the warm-up matches in the spring of 1990. From four home games there were two defeats, administered by the German Democratic Republic and Egypt, and a draw with Poland. Typically, the Scots' sole win was against Argentina, who unexpectedly made it to the World Cup final itself, and they completed their preparations with a narrow away win over Malta.

Although Andy Roxburgh correctly insisted that victories were not the main concern in the warm-up games, there was an alarming tendency for the defence to suffer self-inflicted wounds. By the time the Scots set off for Italy they had conceded five own goals in eight fixtures, while the scoring rate of the forwards had declined dramatically. In addition, the loss of Davie Cooper through injury, while the squad prepared in Malta, was to prove costly. It looked, too, as though Maurice Johnston would be forced to withdraw when he injured a stomach muscle in Malta, but the Rangers forward revived against the odds and was with the Scotland party which travelled to Genoa on June 6. It was temporary relief because the casualty rate would continue to rise at a worrying pace.

To reach the second stage for the first time, Scotland would have to gain at least three points from a section which also included Brazil, Sweden and Costa Rica. The consensus was that Brazil would win the section, with Sweden or Scotland, or both, moving on at the expense of Costa Rica who, it was universally considered, would blow themselves out after their opening match.

There were several miscalculations in this theory and it was perhaps of some comfort to the Scots when events proved that they were not the only people to guess the percentages wrongly. Scotland's history of débâcles against supposedly trifling opposition had been extended when Egypt administered a 3-1 beating shortly before the finals, in the first full international played at Pittodrie for 19 years. Costa Rica were nothing like as adventurous as Egypt, but in the Luigi Ferraris stadium on June 11 they proved capable of demolishing Scotland's fragile ambition.

It was a maddening afternoon for the Scottish management and the long-suffering battalions of the Tartan Army, over 15,000 strong, drawn up in their usual gaudy ranks in the stands. Scotland controlled lengthy tracts of possession but created little menace, particularly from midfield where Bett was patently lethargic and McStay ineffectual.

Pops and saying 'Can I have your autograph?' and I was signing and then they were saying 'Who are you?', and I was saying 'Whit?' "Anyway, the song sold so many copies and I put all the money from the single into an L.P. – financed it all myself – and the album came out the day after Iran drew 1-1 with Scotland. A man in Dundee did a roaring trade, selling it for a penny and giving you a hammer to smash it with. So there's about 30,000 lying about somewhere in Glasgow. I don't know where they got to. A garage in Clarkston, I think . . ."

The absence of Cooper, whose tantalising crosses would probably have disrupted the Costa Ricans, was now felt acutely.

Johnston did force an opening shortly before the interval, only to thrash a shot which required to be placed, permitting Conejo to deflect the ball one handed. At half-time it emerged that Gough could not continue, the victim of a recurrent foot injury, and the defence had to be rejigged with McKimmie replacing the Rangers player. Before the back line had composed itself, however, Costa Rica had scored.

A rare thrust soon after the break caught Scotland in disorder and Aitken, McPherson and McKimmie were neutralised as the ball sped on to Cayasso, free on the Scottish right. He composed himself to drag the ball wide of Leighton and steer it beyond the goalkeeper. It was virtually the sum total of Costa Rica's aggression on the day, but it was sufficient. Johnston slashed at another golden chance directly in front of goal, and there was nobody else of his calibre to share the burden of scoring.

The taste of ashes, Scotland's persistent contribution to the world football banquet, had not grown any more palatable with repetition. Some jeering and catcalls were aimed at the players at full-time but most of the fans trooped dejectedly away through the twisting streets of Genoa, their tartans turned to sackcloth yet again. They had made the journey in a mood of unaccustomed realism, well aware that the strictly limited flair and dash available to Roxburgh and his assistant Craig Brown had been withered by the effects of injuries and the familiar demands of the robust domestic season.

Depression was profound, the prospect barren and bleak, especially when it became apparent that the elegant Gillespie would not be fit to play against Sweden in the Luigi Ferraris stadium five days after the opening defeat. "We are in a daze," said Roxburgh. "We feel it every bit as painfully as the fans. We just cannot believe that we made nineteen chances to score and ended without a goal to show for it while Costa Rica were hardly up the field and came out with a win."

The coach returned to this litany daily, as though repetition might somehow change history. At this stage of the tournament, with England and the Republic of Ireland having produced pedestrian and cautious football in their opening matches, the British style of play was a target for ridicule, as much by its previous advocates as by a sardonic watching world. This was a slight on the Scottish approach to the finals which, for all its limitations, was a distinct departure from tradition, and in the warm-up matches before the finals the team had frequently deployed a five-man defence with up to three players taking turns as spare man.

In fact, Roxburgh had been keen to improve upon the experimental line-up seen in the friendly against Argentina, and would probably have used a sweeper in front of the back line if injuries had not restricted his options so severely. It was ironic, then, that Scotland should turn to the maligned domestic game for inspiration against Sweden. Both Roxburgh and the Swedish coach, Olle Nordin, had predicted that the match would take on the style of a British cup tie and, as matters turned out, it resembled even more closely the tenor and tempo of a Scottish Premier Division fixture, a contribution to these finals which, to the critics was the equivalent of turning up at an Armani fashion show in crimplene flared trousers.

The contest turned out to be at least as entertaining as many of those which had gone before and it was distinctly superior to a few; Italy's anaemic victory over the United States, to take a single example.

Andy Roxburgh and his assistant Craig Brown.

From a Scottish point of view it was the synthesis of will, energy and skill which proved most absorbing. Of these three, it was the latter which was scarcest in Roxburgh's inventory, but there were thrilling moments of force and fluency as Scotland relentlessly cornered their frustrated opponents.

Then there was application, a subject on which the Swedish defender Hysen, of Liverpool, had pronounced confidently a month earlier: "The Scots are not so much of a worry because they cannot run in the heat." The temperature in the Ferraris stadium was 70 degrees when the teams met but there was never any danger that the Scots would melt because when the sides emerged for their preparatory exercises, Scotland's most potent weapon was unleashed.

The cataracts of sound which swept down from the stands were astounding, even to those who were accustomed to the vivid manifestations of will which can be exerted by the Scottish supporters. Meditating on the scenes the following day, Roxburgh said: "It really was the most remarkable environment in which to play football and our supporters were truly magnificent. I thought it was astonishing to hear this morning that there was nobody arrested because when you get a crowd of that size anywhere in the world, you're liable to get at least one person arrested for something.

"For us, in some ways, that was the result which really mattered, because the supporters are representatives of the nation and we were very conscious before the match that we must do everything we could to live up to their standards and expectations."

The ceaseless exhortations of the Scottish supporters and the pattern of the match offered obvious parallels with the Grand Slam rugby union collision between Scotland and England three months before. Just as their rugby equivalents had done on that occasion, so the Scots launched themselves at their opponents from the start and secured the early lead which offered them the platform for ultimate victory.

McCall, who had been told to push up from midfield whenever the opportunity was offered, probed forward at a corner kick in the tenth minute and was first to reach McPherson's backward header to divert it over the line. It took Sweden 50 minutes to bring themselves back into the match because of the dominance of the Scottish midfield quartet of

The pain of following Scotland around the world is etched in tears on the face of this young supporter at the World Cup finals in 1982.

LAURIE REILLY

Laurie Reilly, a member of Hibernian's most accomplished forward line, known as the Famous Five, was born in Edinburgh on 28 October 1928. He joined Hibs as an outside-right, and although he also played on the other flank, it was as centre-forward that he made his name at Easter Road and with Scotland, for whom he was capped 38 times. His honours also include 13 appearances for the Scottish League and two championship medals with Hibs.

"I was brought up in the Gorgie area of Edinburgh, the Hearts end, and you learned your football just playing on the streets, which were a great breeding ground for players. I started off with a tennis ball and the bigger I got, the bigger the ball my Dad got me. When you played football at school you started off with a size three and I remember one Saturday we turned up and all of the threes were out so we got a four and we thought we were playing with a giant football. So you just grew up with a ball and you got accustomed to it.

"The Famous Five was one of those names which stuck to us as names do stick but the boys at the back played every bit as big a part in our success and deserved a lot of credit which they didn't get at the time. In the attack, Willie Ormond was an out and out raider, Gordon Smith used to fetch and carry, Bobby Johnston was the brains of the forward line, Eddie Turnbull was the workhorse and I was the luxury. I just put the ball in the net for them. None of us were ever coached much. In fact, Gordon Smith and I were speaking about this recently and we never, ever, were coached in our lifetime. We

Aitken, McLeod, McCall and Durie.

It was from that department that Scotland's second goal arrived, when McLeish and Fleck combined to send Aitken romping across the Swedish goalmouth, where Nilsson tripped the Scotland captain. Johnston whipped the penalty kick past Ravelli to score his ninth goal in World Cup contests and Scotland were almost home, but with fatigue embracing the players, the Tartan Army was forced to endure another of their periodic bouts of purgatory.

Stromberg, the Swedish substitute, ran on to a long ball to prod it past Leighton and if he had been brought on earlier he might have changed the outcome. As it was, Scotland survived to maintain a fragile grip on the tournament. As the supporters chorused in self mockery at the final whistle, to the tune of "Guantenamara": "Do it the hard way, we always do it the hard way".

$\star$ $\star$ $\star$

Which left Brazil, the adversaries of 1974 and 1982. A repeat of the 1974 result – a 0-0 draw in a match which Scotland dominated – was the probable key to the chance of proceeding into the next stage of the tournament. But the hard way had become harder still as injuries continued to fray the slender Scottish strength; Craig Levein, who had been viewed as a manifest asset, had to be ruled out because of a thigh strain, nor was Gillespie match fit. The suggestion, which had circulated amongst the Scottish support, that Andy Roxburgh had taken to telephoning Meccano every day for instructions, became less unlikely with each gloomy diagnosis of another casualty. And although Brazil, who had already qualified, were prepared to start without Muller, Branco and Mozer, the inclusion of Romario, Silas and Ricardo Rocha did not exactly suggest they were about to become debilitated.

Although the Scots were almost at the stage of conscripting the ball boys to guarantee a full team, there was always the question of whether Dr Jekyll or Mr Hyde would be included in this selection. As it turned out, it was Brazil who displayed the unforeseen side of their nature. It was not surprising that Scotland, in such an enfeebled state, failed to manage a single shot on goal from outside the penalty area, but for Brazil to do the same was almost beyond belief.

Nor were the South Americans much more efficient inside the box, where they contrived half a dozen shots. Only one had to be decisive, though, and it occurred nine minutes from full time, the result of a goalkeeping error by Jim Leighton. Dropped by Alex Ferguson from Manchester United's side for the FA Cup final replay with Crystal Palace shortly before the World Cup finals, Leighton had been retained in the Scottish goal by Andy Roxburgh and, in fairness, had not been culpable in either of the previous fixtures.

But on a night when the ball was made greasy by heavy rain, he failed to grasp a close range shot by Alimâo, so that the ball spun out of his control to be turned across the empty goalmouth towards Costa Luiz, otherwise known as Muller, who arrived at the far post to prod his shot across the line. Leighton was not alone in culpability. Gillespie was slow to react to the rebounding shot although, to be fair, the Liverpool man had only been employed as a substitute when McLeod had been forced to leave the field with concussion, and his reflexes were bound to be muted.

McStay, however, might have considered his part in carelessly conceding possession with a misplaced pass which began Brazil's scoring move, while McLeish missed Muller's crucial run on the blindside. In the last analysis, it was all irrelevant to the fact that Scotland were homeward bound again, although they had to wait until the next night for their dismissal to be confirmed when the Republic of Ireland drew with The Netherlands to take up the final remaining places in the second round.

The truth is that Scotland, limited in range and woefully troubled by fitness problems, gave what they could and probably rather more than could reasonably have been expected of them. At least the dogged, perpetually inspirational Scottish support had enjoyed, with the victory over Sweden, a moment of abandoned celebration.

Their departure was not without its ration of humour. It turned out that Murdo McLeod, who had been concussed when he absorbed a venomous free kick from Dunga full on the head, had managed to remain on the pitch for several minutes by persuading the Scottish physiotherapists that he was *compos mentis*. Doubts began to take root amongst his colleagues when McLeod asked them in which direction Scotland were supposed to be playing. "It wouldn't have been so bad," said McLeod, "but when I asked Stuart McCall he wasn't sure either. At one point I didn't know who we were playing against. It was the biggest night of my career and I haven't a clue what I was doing during most of it".

It could have been worse. McLeod was stationed behind the back post to meet one inswinging Brazilian cross ball and head it behind for a corner kick. As the ball had been delivered, his disordered senses very nearly persuaded him to put it behind Jim Leighton. "If it had gone in I would have been off up the field celebrating. I think it is safe to say it would have been an unforgettable episode for everybody except me."

★   ★   ★

There have been occasions when concussion would have seemed a blessing to Scots during the latter stages of the World Cup, but if the country's record has been an infuriating blend of promise and demoralisation, pointless achievement and dispiriting inability to achieve ordinary, plodding progress, it is worth applying other perspectives.

Scotland has participated in seven World Cup finals and five successive appearances were achieved via the qualification route, a record which is surpassed only by Italy and Mexico, and one which is quite extraordinary when it is measured against Scottish strengths. With a population which scarcely exceeds half that of London, Scotland has also seen four of its clubs reach a total of seven European trophy finals, winning on three occasions. Virtually all of the players involved were home based, while hardly any English team which has gone as far has done so without a quota of Scots, sometimes amounting to almost half of the side.

On the other hand, the 1990 World Cup finals did focus attention on the fact that the supply of top class Scottish players has dwindled alarmingly in recent years. It is not a consolation to note that the decline in class has been widespread and that the finals boasted scarcely a handful of footballers who would cause a neutral to go out of the way to watch them play. Why this should be is not clear, although it is certain that the standard of athleticism and fitness has increased dramatically in the past decade, leading to a greater equality

learned our football with that tennis ball against the school wall.

"The first time I saw Gordon Smith play was for the Hibs against the Hearts at Tynecastle when he was only 17 and I was in a tenement top flat looking on to the pitch from the window. Gordon scored three goals that day and he won me over right away.

"Many years ago, when I played alongside him in a game against Third Lanark, I watched Gordon running along the wing, keeping the ball up on his head and he kept it up six times. It was a credit to Third Lanark that they didn't hack him down because nowadays I can't see anybody being allowed to do that. It was something I only saw once in my lifetime and the supporters still speak of it yet – the old supporters. He was running up the hill, too, which was even more difficult."

of performance.

In Scotland's case, Andy Roxburgh believed that other factors had also been at work: "Until a generation ago, kids would happily play football in the streets until it was too dark to see the ball. Now they can stage matches on the home computer and if they did go out for a kick-about in the street, there is a good chance they would by run over by a juggernaut.

"Since the teachers' strike a few years ago, there has been a great falling-off of school football and a lot of the games which are played are ruined by adults taking too serious an interest and shouting at kids to close down available space and get wide on the overlap, when they should be encouraging youngsters just to go out and enjoy themselves and leave the heavy stuff until they're old enough to cope with it."

Some have been eager to blame the Premier Division, which forces teams to play each other four times a season, a frequency which increases when sides are drawn together in the cup competitions. It is also an odd feature of the ten-team league that it is played at what is almost certainly the fastest pace in Europe. Yet twenty years ago it was common for Scottish footballers moving to England to report problems in adjusting to a more rapid game south of the border.

However, in the 1980s the Premier Division also saw Aberdeen reach the Cup Winners' Cup final in 1983 and semi-final in 1984, while Dundee United made the semi-final of the European Cup in 1984 and the UEFA Cup final in 1987. All of which powerfully suggests that the dearth of talent is part of a recurring cycle.

At least Scotland has been at the same pass once or twice before. In 1951, the legendary Rangers and Scotland winger Alan Morton declared: "In Scotland today there is only one international eleven. Before the war, there were sufficient stars for several international teams." This was said three years before Scotland were humiliated 7-0 by Uruguay and, as one doleful newspaper asserted: "We used to be masters of football, teachers of the game. After this, there is nothing to look forward to, for Scotland is at the end of a road. The players of today cannot lace the boots of their predecessors, and as for the future, where are the young men who might offer us hope? Let us face facts and admit the modern game has seen the passing of our natural Scottish flair and the boys who might have carried our standard have few heroes to idolise."

Apparently that message was not absorbed by the likes of Law, Baxter, White, Bremner, Johnstone, Henderson, Greig or McNeill. It would be agreeable to suppose that our present forebodings have been similarly ignored by the class of 2000. In any case, each time we fill eleven dark blue jerseys and sweep them along on a tide of passionate longing, we become, in the absence of other outlets, a nation once again.

CHAPTER SIX

The Professional Supporter

MONEY MAY TALK but it had very little to say to football in Scotland before the Premier Division was born, and hardly raised its voice at all until the Scottish game cleaned up its act after 1980. In the stands and terracings the fans continued to clamour in the same old way, but it was the sound of lucrative deals being struck behind the scenes which sounded the keynote of Scottish football in the following decade.

There had always been cash in the sport. It was supplied by the paying customers, but where it went after it left their pockets was an enduring mystery. Before the abolition of the maximum wage in football it had certainly not been lavished on players' salaries and until the Ibrox disaster in 1971 the spectator facilities at most Scottish grounds were not so much primitive as primeval. As prosperity multiplied football's rival attractions, the game began to lose those followers who were less committed, and became a prey to those who should have been committed: the hooligans.

The need to spend substantial sums on stadium improvements and, increasingly in the 1980s, on players' rewards, meant that by the end of the decade business sponsors had emerged as the supporters who paid most of the bills. The robust health of the Scottish game led to a number of extremely lucrative commercial deals, the largest of which was the agreement by British Satellite Broadcasting to pay £12.25 million to the Scottish Football League and the Scottish Football Association for screening rights.

The League got £6 million for a three-year agreement which permitted BSB to show highlights of 60 matches plus a live match at each stage of the Skol Cup after the first round as well as 15 live league fixtures over the period. A year before the satellite deal B & Q, the DIY chain store company, sponsored the Scottish League for £1 million over two seasons, and in 1990 took up the option of injecting a further £612,000 plus ancillary sponsorships.

At the same time BBC Scotland and Scottish Television paid £1 million between them for screening rights for two seasons, while Alloa Breweries announced increased sponsorship of the Skol Cup, formerly the Scottish League Cup, but reconstituted as a highly successful early season tournament which had dispensed with replays and the sluggish home and away format which had once made it a ponderous competition.

Alloa Breweries' involvement began in season 1983-84 when the company paid £40,000 to sponsor the semi-finals and final, and the following year sponsorship of the entire tournament was obtained for £80,000. By 1990 this had doubled and a new three-year deal was revealed, worth around £750,000 in total. The Mitre company, meanwhile, agreed to supply 1,000 match balls over a three-year

Fans throng the street outside Firhill before a Partick Thistle-Rangers match in the late 1950s. Taken for granted for a century, the supporters disappeared as mysteriously as herring shoals by the middle of the 1970s.

period, a contribution worth £500,000. From the pools promoters came £1.7 million, for use of copyright, while bookmakers' levies and other sundries provided a further £200,000.

If the Scottish League in its centenary year had never enjoyed a more lucrative income, the SFA similarly persuaded its suitors to part with handsome dowries to marry football with commerce. Umbro, the sportswear manufacturers, invested £2.5 million over five years for the rights to manufacture and reproduce the Scottish international strips and tracksuits. BSB secured broadcast rights to selected Scottish Cup fixtures as well as international matches involving the Scotland side at home, in this case valued at £6.25 million over three years. BBC Scotland signed a four-year agreement for domestic TV and radio access and paid £4 million.

Nor was tradition held to be an obstacle to the inward wash of funds when in 1990 the Tennent Caledonian brewing concern paid £1.5 million for exclusive sponsorship rights for three seasons in the Scottish Cup. For the first time, the oldest trophy in professional football was rechristened as the Tennent's Scottish Cup and in a similarly unprecedented move it was decided to resolve the final by means of penalty kicks, which immediately proved necessary when Aberdeen and Celtic played out a goalless draw for two hours at Hampden, the northern club eventually winning when the spot kick ritual went to sudden death.

Much of the cash which is lavished on Scottish football percolates downwards to the game's small fry, but inevitably the bulk of sponsorship is distributed in the form of participation bonuses which favour the larger clubs in their frequent appearances in the later stages of competitions. If this tends to accelerate the growing gulf between rich and poor, nothing rewards the achievers so much as individual club sponsorship. In this area the most dazzling success belongs, inevitably, to Rangers, whose relationship with Scottish Brewers offers a textbook study in the mutual benefits to be derived from business investment in sport.

Scottish Brewers had become involved in large-scale football spending when they sponsored the Scottish Cup through their Younger's Tartan Special brand name between 1978 and 1980. In early rounds of the competition the return to the company was mainly in the form of perks such as a guaranteed allocation of tickets, but it was the final which made the enterprise worth while from a commercial point of view, because the SFA had taken the decision to permit live television coverage.

There was apprehension that live screening would bite into attendance figures but when Rangers defeated Aberdeen 2-1 in the 1978 final the crowd of 61,563 was an improvement of 7,000 on the previous season's Old Firm collision, which ended 1-0 in Celtic's favour. The following season was a different matter, when a transport strike in Glasgow kept the numbers down for a drab 0-0 draw between Rangers and Hibernian. The midweek replay was equally uninspiring and goalless and was watched by a meagre 33,508, and when matters dragged to a second replay the attendance fell to a dismal 30,602, resolved by an own goal by Duncan which gave Rangers a 3-2 victory in extra time.

With an Old Firm final in 1980, the crowd was bound to be swollen and, sure enough, more than 70,000 turned up. Unfortunately, this was the occasion when the cretinous element chose to stage a Donnybrook on the field after the final whistle signalled a 1-0 win for Celtic. The watching television audience, which had been the principal attraction for the sponsors, heard commentator Archie McPherson describe the brawl, and the resultant baton charge by mounted police, as resembling a scene from the film *Apocalypse Now*.

Considering that Parliament responded to the affair by enacting the Criminal Justice Scotland (1980) Act which banned the sale or consumption of alcohol at Scottish football matches, it would not have been surprising if Scottish Brewers had taken to subsidising something less prone to riotous intervention – the Highland Dancing Championships perhaps. The beer companies came under pressure from public criticism of their connection with sport at the same time as the SFA responded to the disfiguring of the tournament by raising the asking price for its sponsorship.

Three years with the Scottish Cup had cost Scottish Brewers £250,000, a sizeable sum by prevailing standards. When they allied themselves with football again six years later, the stakes had risen sharply but so had the rewards. In 1986, just after the epochal arrival of Graeme Souness at Ibrox, Rangers sounded out the company about the possibility of sponsoring the team. Previously, both Rangers and Celtic had been the subject of a linked deal with the double glazing manufacturers C. R. Smith and the received wisdom was that no commercial enterprise could afford to sponsor one half of the Old Firm alone, for fear that there would be a boycott of the product by

The arrival of Souness at Ibrox transformed Rangers into a sponsor's dream.

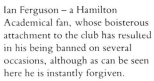

Ian Ferguson – a Hamilton
Academical fan, whose boisterous
attachment to the club has resulted
in his being banned on several
occasions, although as can be seen
here he is instantly forgiven.

aggrieved partisans of the opposition.

After some thought, Scottish Brewers decided that Rangers were worth an investment of £750,000 spread over three years. The company was known mainly for its ales and more traditional beers, at a time when the consumption of lager was rising sharply, particularly amongst younger drinkers, and the brewers were keen to increase their share of a lucrative market. The agreement stipulated that the Rangers strip would bear the brand name of McEwan's Lager.

It took four weeks for the impact to register and when it did, the effect was a marketing dream. The draught version of the lager was not greatly affected but the sale of McEwan's in cans doubled, forcing retailers to display it more prominently. One pub declined to stock Scottish Brewers' beer on the grounds that the Ibrox association had reduced takings, but this complaint was greeted with scepticism born of the fact that the licensee was well known for his devotion to the Parkhead cause.

In fact, Scottish Brewers were keen to negotiate a similar deal with Celtic for the same money, some of which was to be spent on reconstruction work at Parkhead. Predictably, Harp Lager, another of the company's products, was identified as having a sure appeal to Celtic supporters. Negotiations proceeded for some time, but were not ultimately brought to a conclusion.

However, with the Rangers deal Scottish Brewers had made a quantum leap in the lager market and results were so impressive that in 1987, a year after the original arrangement, the company exercised their option to renew the contract, which was due to expire in 1989. When David Murray bought the club late in 1988 he discovered that he had inherited a sponsor at a time when trading losses and the enormous recent spending on new players had pushed the club's overdraft to a level which was costing £1 million a year in interest charges alone.

Murray renegotiated in order to get cash in advance for a renewed contract which linked Scottish Brewers with Ibrox until 1996, with an option to extend the arrangement until 1999. When the deal was concluded Rangers were able to bank £5 million. A similar agreement with Admiral, the sportswear manufacturers, put £4 million into the Rangers account. Such an immense cash input permitted Rangers to announce in the summer of 1990 that their overdraft had been slashed from £11 million to £2 million, removing a debt which had threatened to torpedo the vast ambition of the new regime at Ibrox. Murray and Rangers gained an early financial advantage traded off against a highly promising potential return for Scottish Brewers and Admiral in later years.

Such deals represented an immense financial flow into the once sedate backwaters of the Scottish game; unforeseen cross currents were also produced. The brewery could not stipulate that the name of their product had to be duplicated on the Rangers strips which were available to the public, but those who bought the jerseys almost invariably wanted replicas of those worn by their heroes, so that in the first year of the sponsorship 100,000 customers were willing to pay around £20 each to extend the advertising of McEwan's Lager to public parks and indoor pitches throughout Scotland.

In an attempt to put a value on Rangers' presence, to use advertising industry jargon, Scottish Brewers monitored cuttings not only from Scotland, but Britain and elsewhere, but when the collection filled four filing cabinet drawers within the first year, the attempt was abandoned. "If we were talking in advertising terms about Rangers' presence in the international media," said Tony Belfield, the company's managing director, "we would have to assess it in telephone numbers. McEwan's lager is now our biggest product. We sell over 500,000 barrels of the draught lager and the cans account for more than half a million barrels and growing."

To put these figures into more graphic terms, in 1990 brewers were able to shift around 150 million pints of draught McEwan's and 36 million cans of the brand. Perhaps the most remarkable aspect about the exercise is the fact that the Rangers connection accounts for only 20 per cent of the company's spending on advertising and sponsorship. "But we certainly believe that with Rangers we have the most effective area of our sponsorship," Belfield said.

If the involvement of Scottish Brewers with Rangers is of obvious and remarkable mutual benefit, it must be said that such a profitable marriage was not on the cards before Graeme Souness arrived in 1986, for the simple reason that the brewery was not inclined to get involved with a football club which practised restrictions in its playing policy. To put it bluntly, Rangers had said since 1976 that they would not preclude the signing of Roman Catholic players, but it was only with the arrival of Souness that the old Ibrox taboo appeared likely to be broken.

Certain principles were established during the first sponsorship negotiations which ensured that there would be no problem about the signing of Catholics, or for that matter black players, although there had been no suggestion that Rangers operated any discrimination in that department. The arrival of Mark Walters and Maurice Johnston dispelled any lingering suspicion that Rangers had not truly been transformed.

In addition, there would have been considerably less enthusiasm on the brewery's part if Ibrox had not been transformed into a designer stadium and it was because Celtic Park did not offer the same standard of facilities that Scottish Brewers stipulated that a portion of sponsorship money would have to be spent on upgrading the stadium if a deal were to be struck.

The sponsorship of an individual team, particularly one which is likely to start every season as favourites to win every available domestic honour, offers certain ironic advantages, so that Rangers with the McEwan's Lager motif enjoyed particular success in the Skol Cup, underwritten by Scottish Brewers' trade rival, Alloa Breweries.

Of course, the use of football as a platform for the massive advertising of alcoholic drink has fuelled a continuing public debate about the merits of such an association, especially the notion that children insist on wearing replica jerseys bearing brand names. What is certain is that the income injected by the breweries was an indispensable ingredient in helping Scottish football to meet the need to pay higher wages in order to attract top-flight foreign players to supplement the home-grown variety.

It was also clear that, in any case, it would be close to impossible to find other sponsors whose investment and return would bear comparison with the drink makers, although Aberdeen did manage to secure a profitable deal with the Japanese video and hi-fi specialists, JVC. According to Tony Belfield, speaking after Scottish Brewers' renewed agreement with Rangers had been settled: "We are professional Rangers supporters and both ourselves and our competitors are professional football supporters.

The connection between Scottish football and the breweries was well known for decades. The difficulty lay in restructuring the image so that drink sponsorship became acceptable. Ironically, this was only achieved when alcohol was banned on the Scottish terracings.

"Our own interest, for example, extends to presence at every Premier Division ground except Tannadice, because Dundee United are sponsored by Belhaven, and we put £100,000 into subsidising the 28 First and Second Division clubs as well as money set aside for junior and amateur football and the Highland League. To put it bluntly, I don't know what Scottish football would do without the breweries – the drink trade. If they withdrew, the loss to Scottish football would be immense and irreplaceable."

Epilogue

Tom Fagan's lifetime service to Albion Rovers was rendered as a supporter, gatechecker, odd job man, director and chairman. He also served on the SFA Council and had a spell as an International Selector in the late '60s and early '70s. Variously a demolition contractor, car dealer and publican in his native Coatbridge, he was able to travel considerably during his periods as a football administrator. During the course of an interview with the author for BBC TV in October 1985, the conversation turned to an encounter which took place in Argentina in 1978 between Tom Fagan and Senor Joao Havelange, president of FIFA, the governing body of world football.

An Albion Rovers fixture, satisfying unfathomable needs.

RF: You asked Joao Havelange what he thought about Albion Rovers?
Fagan: I didn't ask him. He says, "Who are you?" I says, "Albion Rovers." He says, "Never heard of them." I said, "You ignorant bugger." But it was a natural thing. I mean, it wisnae him alone – there were other people never heard of Albion Rovers. You go the world over, they couldn't possibly know who Albion Rovers were.
RF: But you told them.
Fagan: Well, naturally. You've got to be telt, haven't you? Christ. Somebody asks who Neil Kinnock is and you've got to tell them who he is (laughs).
RF: Some chairmen have put half a million pounds into their clubs or whatever. What have you put into Albion Rovers, Tom?
Fagan: I've put my life into it, I've put my life. I've skint myself.

I had a good business, a great business, and just let it run right down. I left other people to run my business and it went away to hell. I was earning good money, five or six hundred quid on the Wednesday afternoon at the Glasgow market, I could do it easy. But you're committed to a thing, you like it and that was it. Committed.

RF: Suppose for the sake of argument football was banned in Scotland tomorrow. What would it mean to you and to the Scots?

Fagan: Oh, we would just emigrate (laughs), and go away somewhere else then, wouldn't we? Go where the game's getting played. I wouldnae go and watch that American football on a Sunday – that's the biggest rubbish I've ever seen in my life. Fellows wi' pads up here and about four hundred poun' of gear on them and they carry the ball for about fifty yards and it's recorded every time, how far they carry it. What a farce. I like the girls they have out in front. They'd be all right (laughs).

RF: There's only one game in Scotland for you, Tom?

Fagan: There's only one thing in Scotland, in my life, and that's football. Football . . . that's it.

Tom Fagan died in Monklands District Hospital on 29 September 1986, almost a year to the day after the conversation recorded above. Two seasons later, Albion Rovers achieved promotion to the First Division and ended a period in the bottom league which ran unbroken back to 1955-56.

Statistics

INTERNATIONAL MATCHES

SCOTLAND v ENGLAND

1872	Glasgow	Scotland 0	England 0
1873	The Oval	England 4	Scotland 2
1874	Glasgow	Scotland 2	England 1
1875	The Oval	England 2	Scotland 2
1876	Glasgow	Scotland 3	England 0
1877	The Oval	England 1	Scotland 3
1878	Glasgow	Scotland 7	England 2
1879	The Oval	England 5	Scotland 4
1880	Glasgow	Scotland 5	England 4
1881	The Oval	England 1	Scotland 6
1882	Glasgow	Scotland 5	England 1
1883	Sheffield	England 2	Scotland 3
1884	Glasgow	Scotland 1	England 0
1885	The Oval	England 1	Scotland 1
1886	Glasgow	Scotland 1	England 1
1887	Blackburn	England 2	Scotland 3
1888	Glasgow	Scotland 0	England 5
1889	The Oval	England 2	Scotland 3
1890	Glasgow	Scotland 1	England 1
1891	Blackburn	England 2	Scotland 1
1892	Glasgow	Scotland 1	England 4
1893	Richmond	England 5	Scotland 2
1894	Glasgow	Scotland 2	England 2
1895	Everton	England 3	Scotland 0
1896	Glasgow	Scotland 2	England 1
1897	Crystal Pal.	England 1	Scotland 2
1898	Glasgow	Scotland 1	England 3
1899	Birm'ham	England 2	Scotland 1
1900	Glasgow	Scotland 4	England 1
1901	Crystal Palace	England 2	Scotland 2
1902	Glasgow	Scotland 0	England 1
	(Ibrox disaster: Match declared unofficial)		
1902	Birmingham	England 2	Scotland 2
1903	Sheffield	England 1	Scotland 2
1904	Glasgow	Scotland 0	England 1
1905	Crystal Pal.	England 1	Scotland 0
1906	Glasgow	Scotland 2	England 1
1907	Newcastle	England 1	Scotland 1
1908	Glasgow	Scotland 1	England 1
1909	Crystal Pal.	England 2	Scotland 0
1910	Glasgow	Scotland 2	England 0
1911	Everton	England 1	Scotland 1
1912	Glasgow	Scotland 1	England 1
1913	Stamford Br.	England 1	Scotland 0
1914	Glasgow	Scotland 3	England 1
1915 16 17 18	Not Played		
1919*	Everton	England 2	Scotland 2
1919*	Glasgow	Scotland 3	England 4
1920	Hillsboro'	England 5	Scotland 4
1921	Glasgow	Scotland 3	England 0
1922	Birmingham	England 0	Scotland 1
1923	Glasgow	Scotland 2	England 2
1924	Wembley	England 1	Scotland 1
1925	Glasgow	Scotland 2	England 0
1926	Old Trafford	England 0	Scotland 1
1927	Glasgow	Scotland 1	England 2
1928	Wembley	England 1	Scotland 5
1929	Glasgow	Scotland 1	England 0
1930	Wembley	England 5	Scotland 2
1931	Glasgow	Scotland 2	England 0
1932	Wembley	England 3	Scotland 0
1933	Glasgow	Scotland 2	England 1
1934	Wembley	England 3	Scotland 0
1935	Glasgow	Scotland 2	England 0
1936	Wembley	England 1	Scotland 1
1937	Glasgow	Scotland 3	England 1
1938	Wembley	England 0	Scotland 1
1939	Glasgow	Scotland 1	England 2
1940 41 42 43 44 45	Not Played		
1946*	Glasgow	Scotland 1	England 0
1947	Wembley	England 1	Scotland 1
1948	Glasgow	Scotland 0	England 2
1949	Wembley	England 1	Scotland 3
1950†	Glasgow	Scotland 0	England 1
1951	Wembley	England 2	Scotland 3
1952	Glasgow	Scotland 1	England 2
1953	Wembley	England 2	Scotland 2
1954†	Glasgow	Scotland 2	England 4
1955	Wembley	England 7	Scotland 2
1956	Glasgow	Scotland 1	England 1
1957	Wembley	England 2	Scotland 1
1958	Glasgow	Scotland 0	England 4
1959	Wembley	England 1	Scotland 0
1960	Glasgow	Scotland 1	England 1
1961	Wembley	England 9	Scotland 3
1962	Glasgow	Scotland 2	England 0
1963	Wembley	England 1	Scotland 2
1964	Glasgow	Scotland 1	England 0
1965	Wembley	England 2	Scotland 2
1966	Glasgow	Scotland 3	England 4
1967	Wembley	England 2	Scotland 3
1968	Glasgow	Scotland 1	England 1
1969	Wembley	England 4	Scotland 1
1970	Glasgow	Scotland 0	England 0
1971	Wembley	England 3	Scotland 1
1972	Glasgow	Scotland 0	England 1
1973	Wembley	England 1	Scotland 0
1974	Glasgow	Scotland 2	England 0
1975	Wembley	England 5	Scotland 1
1976	Glasgow	Scotland 2	England 1
1977	Wembley	England 1	Scotland 2
1978	Glasgow	Scotland 0	England 1
1979	Wembley	England 3	Scotland 1
1980	Glasgow	Scotland 0	England 2
1981	Wembley	England 0	Scotland 1
1982	Glasgow	Scotland 0	England 1
1983	Wembley	England 2	Scotland 0
1984	Glasgow	Scotland 1	England 1
1985	Glasgow	Scotland 1	England 0
1986	Wembley	England 2	Scotland 1
1987	Glasgow	Scotland 0	England 0
1988	Wembley	England 1	Scotland 0
1989	Glasgow	Scotland 0	England 2

Scotland won 40, England 42, drawn 24
Scotland 168 goals, England 183 goals
* Unofficial 'victory' matches, and not included in analyses

SCOTLAND v WALES

1876	Glasgow	Scotland 4	Wales 0
1877	Wrexham	Wales 0	Scotland 2
1878	Glasgow	Scotland 9	Wales 0
1879	Wrexham	Wales 0	Scotland 3
1880	Glasgow	Scotland 5	Wales 1
1881	Wrexham	Wales 1	Scotland 5
1882	Glasgow	Scotland 5	Wales 0
1883	Wrexham	Wales 0	Scotland 3
1884	Glasgow	Scotland 4	Wales 1
1885	Wrexham	Wales 1	Scotland 8
1886	Glasgow	Scotland 4	Wales 1
1887	Wrexham	Wales 0	Scotland 2
1888	Edinburgh	Scotland 5	Wales 1
1889	Wrexham	Wales 0	Scotland 0
1890	Paisley	Scotland 5	Wales 0
1891	Wrexham	Wales 3	Scotland 4
1892	Edinburgh	Scotland 6	Wales 1
1893	Wrexham	Wales 0	Scotland 8
1894	Kilmarnock	Scotland 5	Wales 2
1895	Wrexham	Wales 2	Scotland 2
1896	Dundee	Scotland 4	Wales 0
1897	Wrexham	Wales 2	Scotland 2
1898	Motherwell	Scotland 5	Wales 2
1899	Wrexham	Wales 0	Scotland 6
1900	Aberdeen	Scotland 5	Wales 2
1901	Wrexham	Wales 1	Scotland 1
1902	Greenock	Scotland 5	Wales 1
1903	Cardiff	Wales 0	Scotland 1
1904	Dundee	Scotland 1	Wales 1
1905	Wrexham	Wales 3	Scotland 1
1906	Edinburgh	Scotland 0	Wales 2
1907	Wrexham	Wales 1	Scotland 0
1908	Dundee	Scotland 2	Wales 1
1909	Wrexham	Wales 3	Scotland 2
1910	Kilmarnock	Scotland 1	Wales 0
1911	Cardiff	Wales 2	Scotland 2
1912	Tynecastle	Scotland 1	Wales 0
1913	Wrexham	Wales 0	Scotland 0
1914	Glasgow	Scotland 0	Wales 0
1915 16 17 18 19	Not played		
1920	Cardiff	Wales 1	Scotland 1
1921	Aberdeen	Scotland 2	Wales 1
1922	Wrexham	Wales 2	Scotland 1
1923	Paisley	Scotland 2	Wales 0
1924	Cardiff	Wales 2	Scotland 0
1925	Tynecastle	Scotland 3	Wales 1
1926	Cardiff	Wales 0	Scotland 3
1927	Glasgow	Scotland 3	Wales 0
1928	Wrexham	Wales 2	Scotland 2
1929	Ibrox	Scotland 4	Wales 2
1930	Cardiff	Wales 2	Scotland 4
1931	Ibrox	Scotland 1	Wales 1
1932	Wrexham	Wales 2	Scotland 3
1933	Edinburgh	Scotland 2	Wales 5
1934	Cardiff	Wales 3	Scotland 2
1935	Aberdeen	Scotland 3	Wales 2
1936	Cardiff	Wales 1	Scotland 1
1937	Dundee	Scotland 1	Wales 2
1938	Cardiff	Wales 2	Scotland 1
1939	Edinburgh	Scotland 3	Wales 2
1940 41 42 43 44	Not played		
1945*	Glasgow	Scotland 2	Wales 0
1946	Wrexham	Wales 3	Scotland 1
1947	Glasgow	Scotland 1	Wales 2
1948	Cardiff	Wales 1	Scotland 3
1949†	Glasgow	Scotland 2	Wales 0
1950	Cardiff	Wales 1	Scotland 3
1951	Glasgow	Scotland 0	Wales 1
1952	Cardiff	Wales 1	Scotland 2
1953†	Glasgow	Scotland 3	Wales 3
1954	Cardiff	Wales 0	Scotland 1
1955	Glasgow	Scotland 2	Wales 0
1956	Cardiff	Wales 2	Scotland 2
1957	Glasgow	Scotland 1	Wales 1
1958	Cardiff	Wales 0	Scotland 3
1959	Glasgow	Scotland 1	Wales 1
1960	Cardiff	Wales 2	Scotland 0
1961	Glasgow	Scotland 2	Wales 0
1962	Cardiff	Wales 2	Scotland 3
1963	Glasgow	Scotland 2	Wales 1
1964	Cardiff	Wales 3	Scotland 2
1965	Glasgow	Scotland 4	Wales 1
1966	Cardiff	Wales 1	Scotland 1
1967	Glasgow	Scotland 3	Wales 2
1969	Wrexham	Wales 3	Scotland 5
1970	Glasgow	Scotland 0	Wales 0
1971	Cardiff	Wales 0	Scotland 0
1972	Glasgow	Scotland 1	Wales 0
1973	Wrexham	Wales 0	Scotland 2
1974	Glasgow	Scotland 2	Wales 0
1975	Cardiff	Wales 2	Scotland 2
1976	Glasgow	Scotland 3	Wales 1
1976†	Glasgow	Scotland 1	Wales 0
1977	Wrexham	Wales 0	Scotland 0
1977†	Liverpool	Wales 0	Scotland 2
1978	Glasgow	Scotland 1	Wales 1
1979	Cardiff	Wales 3	Scotland 0
1980	Glasgow	Scotland 1	Wales 0
1981	Swansea	Wales 2	Scotland 0
1982	Glasgow	Scotland 1	Wales 0
1983	Cardiff	Wales 0	Scotland 2
1984	Glasgow	Scotland 2	Wales 1
1985†	Glasgow	Scotland 0	Wales 1
1985†	Cardiff	Wales 1	Scotland 1

Scotland won 60, Wales 18, drawn 23
Scotland 238 goals, Wales 111 goals
* Unofficial 'victory' match, and not included in analyses

SCOTLAND v IRELAND

1884	Belfast	Ireland 0	Scotland 5
1885	Glasgow	Scotland 8	Ireland 2
1886	Belfast	Ireland 2	Scotland 7
1887	Glasgow	Scotland 4	Ireland 1
1888	Belfast	Ireland 2	Scotland 10
1889	Glasgow	Scotland 7	Ireland 0
1890	Belfast	Ireland 1	Scotland 4
1891	Glasgow	Scotland 2	Ireland 1
1892	Belfast	Ireland 2	Scotland 3
1893	Glasgow	Scotland 6	Ireland 1
1894	Belfast	Ireland 1	Scotland 2
1895	Glasgow	Scotland 3	Ireland 1
1896	Belfast	Ireland 3	Scotland 3
1897	Glasgow	Scotland 5	Ireland 1
1898	Belfast	Ireland 0	Scotland 3
1899	Glasgow	Scotland 9	Ireland 1
1900	Belfast	Ireland 0	Scotland 3
1901	Glasgow	Scotland 11	Ireland 0
1902	Belfast	Ireland 1	Scotland 5
1903	Glasgow	Scotland 0	Ireland 2
1904	Dublin	Ireland 1	Scotland 1
1905	Glasgow	Scotland 4	Ireland 0
1906	Dublin	Ireland 0	Scotland 1
1907	Glasgow	Scotland 3	Ireland 0
1908	Dublin	Ireland 0	Scotland 5
1909	Glasgow	Scotland 5	Ireland 0
1910	Belfast	Ireland 1	Scotland 0
1911	Glasgow	Scotland 2	Ireland 0
1912	Belfast	Ireland 1	Scotland 4
1913	Dublin	Ireland 1	Scotland 2
1914	Belfast	Ireland 1	Scotland 4
1915 16 17 18	Not played		
1919*	Glasgow	Scotland 2	Ireland 1
1919*	Belfast	Ireland 0	Scotland 0
1920	Glasgow	Scotland 3	Ireland 0
1921	Belfast	Ireland 0	Scotland 2
1922	Glasgow	Scotland 2	Ireland 1
1923	Belfast	Ireland 0	Scotland 1
1924	Glasgow	Scotland 2	Ireland 0
1925	Belfast	Ireland 0	Scotland 3
1926	Glasgow	Scotland 4	Ireland 0
1927	Belfast	Ireland 0	Scotland 2
1928	Glasgow	Scotland 0	Ireland 1
1929	Belfast	Ireland 3	Scotland 7
1930	Glasgow	Scotland 3	Ireland 1
1931	Belfast	Ireland 0	Scotland 0
1932	Glasgow	Scotland 3	Ireland 1
1933	Belfast	Ireland 0	Scotland 4
1934	Glasgow	Scotland 1	Ireland 2
1935	Belfast	Ireland 2	Scotland 1
1936	Edinburg	Scotland 2	Ireland 1

1937	Belfast	Ireland 1	Scotland 3
1938	Aberdeen	Scotland 1	Ireland 1
1939	Belfast	Ireland 0	Scotland 2
1940 41 42 43 44 45	Not played		
1946*	Belfast	Ireland 2	Scotland 3
1946	Glasgow	Scotland 0	Ireland 0
1947	Belfast	Ireland 2	Scotland 0
1948	Glasgow	Scotland 3	Ireland 2
1949†	Belfast	Ireland 2	Scotland 8
1950	Glasgow	Scotland 6	Ireland 1
1951	Belfast	Ireland 0	Scotland 3
1952	Glasgow	Scotland 1	Ireland 1
1953†	Belfast	Ireland 1	Scotland 3
1954	Glasgow	Scotland 2	Ireland 2
1955	Belfast	Ireland 2	Scotland 1
1956	Glasgow	Scotland 1	Ireland 0
1957	Belfast	Ireland 1	Scotland 1
1958	Glasgow	Scotland 2	Ireland 2
1959	Belfast	Ireland 0	Scotland 4
1960	Glasgow	Scotland 5	Ireland 2
1961	Belfast	Ireland 1	Scotland 6
1962	Glasgow	Scotland 5	Ireland 1
1963	Belfast	Ireland 2	Scotland 1
1964	Glasgow	Scotland 3	Ireland 2
1965	Belfast	Ireland 3	Scotland 2
1966	Glasgow	Scotland 2	Ireland 1
1967	Belfast	Ireland 1	Scotland 0
1969	Glasgow	Scotland 1	Ireland 1
1970	Belfast	Ireland 0	Scotland 1
1971	Glasgow	Scotland 0	Ireland 1
1972	Glasgow	Ireland 0	Scotland 2
1973	Glasgow	Scotland 1	Ireland 2
1974	Glasgow	Ireland 1	Scotland 0
1975	Glasgow	Scotland 3	Ireland 0
1976	Glasgow	Ireland 0	Scotland 3
1977	Glasgow	Scotland 3	Ireland 0
1978	Glasgow	Ireland 1	Scotland 1
1979	Glasgow	Scotland 1	Ireland 0
1980	Belfast	Ireland 1	Scotland 0
1981†	Glasgow	Scotland 1	Ireland 1
1981	Glasgow	Scotland 2	Ireland 0
1981†	Belfast	Ireland 0	Scotland 0
1982	Belfast	Ireland 1	Scotland 1
1983	Glasgow	Scotland 0	Ireland 0
1983	Belfast	Ireland 2	Scotland 0

Scotland won 60, Ireland 15, drawn 16
Scotland 253 goals, Ireland 81 goals
* Unofficial 'victory' matches, and not included in analyses.

SCOTLAND v ARGENTINA

1977	Buenos Aires	Argentina 1	Scotland 1
1979	Glasgow	Scotland 1	Argentina 3
1990	Glasgow	Scotland 1	Argentina 0

SCOTLAND v AUSTRALIA

1985†	Glasgow	Scotland 2	Australia 0
1985†	Melbourne	Australia 0	Scotland 0

SCOTLAND v AUSTRIA

1931	Vienna	Austria 5	Scotland 0
1933	Glasgow	Scotland 2	Austria 2
1937	Vienna	Austria 1	Scotland 1
1950	Glasgow	Scotland 0	Austria 1
1951	Vienna	Austria 4	Scotland 0
1954†	Zurich	Scotland 0	Austria 1
1955	Vienna	Austria 1	Scotland 4
1956	Glasgow	Scotland 1	Austria 1
1960	Vienna	Austria 4	Scotland 1
1963	Glasgow	Scotland 4	Austria 1
	(Match abandoned 10 minutes before time)		
1968†	Glasgow	Scotland 2	Austria 1
1969†	Vienna	Austria 2	Scotland 0
1978‡	Vienna	Austria 3	Scotland 2
1979‡	Glasgow	Scotland 1	Austria 1

SCOTLAND v BELGIUM

1946	Glasgow	Scotland 2	Belgium 2
1947	Brussels	Belgium 2	Scotland 1
1948	Glasgow	Scotland 2	Belgium 0
1951	Brussels	Belgium 0	Scotland 5
1971‡	Liege	Belgium 3	Scotland 0
1971‡	Aberdeen	Scotland 1	Belgium 0
1974	Bruges	Belgium 2	Scotland 1
1979‡	Brussels	Belgium 2	Scotland 0
1979‡	Glasgow	Scotland 1	Belgium 3
1982‡	Brussels	Belgium 3	Scotland 2
1983‡	Glasgow	Scotland 1	Belgium 1
1987‡	Brussels	Belgium 4	Scotland 1
1987‡	Glasgow	Scotland 2	Belgium 0

SCOTLAND v BRAZIL

1966	Glasgow	Scotland 1	Brazil 1
1972	Rio	Brazil 1	Scotland 0
1974†	Frankfurt	Scotland 0	Brazil 0
1977	Rio	Brazil 2	Scotland 0
1982†	Seville	Brazil 4	Scotland 1
1987	Glasgow	Scotland 0	Brazil 2
1990	Turin	Scotland 0	Brazil 1

SCOTLAND v BULGARIA

1978	Glasgow	Scotland 2	Bulgaria 1
1986‡	Glasgow	Scotland 0	Bulgaria 0
1987‡	Sofia	Bulgaria 0	Scotland 1

SCOTLAND v CANADA

1983	Vancouver	Canada 0	Scotland 2
1983	Edmonton	Canada 0	Scotland 3
1983	Toronto	Canada 0	Scotland 2

SCOTLAND v CHILE

1977	Santiago	Chile 2	Scotland 4
1989	Glasgow	Scotland 2	Chile 0

SCOTLAND v COLUMBIA

1988	Glasgow	Scotland 0	Columbia 0

SCOTLAND v COSTA RICA

1990†	Genoa	Scotland 0	Costa Rica 1

SCOTLAND v CYPRUS

1968†	Nicosia	Cyprus 0	Scotland 5
1969†	Glasgow	Scotland 8	Cyprus 0
1989†	Limassol	Cyprus 2	Scotland 3
1989†	Glasgow	Scotland 2	Cyprus 1

SCOTLAND v CZECHOSLOVAKIA

1937	Prague	C'slovakia 1	Scotland 3
1938	Glasgow	Scotland 5	C'slovakia 0
1961†	Bratislava	C'slovakia 4	Scotland 0
1961†	Glasgow	Scotland 3	C'slovakia 2
1961†	Brussels	Scotland 2	C'slovakia 4
	(extra-time required – score after 90 minutes, 2-2)		
1972	Porto Alegre	Scotland 0	C'slovakia 0
1973†	Glasgow	Scotland 2	C'slovakia 1
1973†	Bratislava	C'slovakia 1	Scotland 0
1976	Prague	C'slovakia 2	Scotland 0
1977†	Glasgow	Scotland 3	C'slovakia 1

SCOTLAND v DENMARK

1951	Glasgow	Scotland 3	Denmark 1
1952	Copenhagen	Denmark 1	Scotland 2
1968	Copenhagen	Denmark 0	Scotland 1
1970‡	Glasgow	Scotland 1	Denmark 0
1971‡	Copenhagen	Denmark 1	Scotland 0
1972†	Copenhagen	Denmark 1	Scotland 4
1972†	Glasgow	Scotland 2	Denmark 0
1975‡	Copenhagen	Denmark 0	Scotland 1
1975‡	Glasgow	Scotland 3	Denmark 1
1986†	Neza	Scotland 0	Denmark 1

SCOTLAND v EGYPT

1990	Aberdeen	Scotland 1	Egypt 3

SCOTLAND v FINLAND

1954	Helsinki	Finland 1	Scotland 2
1964†	Glasgow	Scotland 3	Finland 1
1965†	Helsinki	Finland 1	Scotland 2
1976	Glasgow	Scotland 6	Finland 0

SCOTLAND v FRANCE

1930	Paris	France 0	Scotland 2
1932	Paris	France 1	Scotland 3
1948	Paris	France 3	Scotland 0
1949	Glasgow	Scotland 2	France 0
1950	Paris	France 0	Scotland 1
1951	Glasgow	Scotland 1	France 0
1958†	Orebro	Scotland 1	France 2
1984	Marseilles	France 2	Scotland 0
1989†	Glasgow	Scotland 2	France 0
1989†	Paris	France 3	Scotland 0

SCOTLAND v GERMANY

1929	Berlin	Germany 1	Scotland 1
1936	Glasgow	Scotland 2	Germany 0

SCOTLAND v FEDERAL REPUBLIC OF GERMANY

1957	Stuttgart	W. Germany 1	Scotland 3
1959	Glasgow	Scotland 3	W. Germany 2
1964	Hanover	W. Germany 2	Scotland 2
1969†	Glasgow	Scotland 1	W. Germany 1
1969†	Hamburg	W. Germany 3	Scotland 2
1974	Frankfurt	W. Germany 2	Scotland 1
1986‡	Queretaro	W. Germany 2	Scotland 1

SCOTLAND v GERMAN DEMOCRATIC REPUBLIC

1974	Glasgow	Scotland 3	E. Germany 0
1977	E. Berlin	E. Germany 1	Scotland 0
1982‡	Glasgow	Scotland 2	E. Germany 0
1983‡	Halle	E. Germany 2	Scotland 1
1985	Glasgow	Scotland 0	E. Germany 0
1990	Glasgow	Scotland 0	E. Germany 1

SCOTLAND v HOLLAND

1929	Amsterdam	Holland 0	Scotland 2
1938	Amsterdam	Holland 1	Scotland 3
1959	Amsterdam	Holland 1	Scotland 2
1966	Glasgow	Scotland 0	Holland 3
1968	Amsterdam	Holland 0	Scotland 0
1971	Amsterdam	Holland 2	Scotland 1
1978†	Mendoza	Scotland 3	Holland 2
1982	Glasgow	Scotland 2	Holland 1
1986	Eindhoven	Holland 0	Scotland 0

SCOTLAND v HUNGARY

1938	Glasgow	Scotland 3	Hungary 1
1954	Glasgow	Scotland 2	Hungary 4
1955	Budapest	Hungary 3	Scotland 1
1958	Glasgow	Scotland 1	Hungary 1
1960	Budapest	Hungary 3	Scotland 3
1980	Budapest	Hungary 3	Scotland 1
1987	Glasgow	Scotland 0	Hungary 0

SCOTLAND v ICELAND

1984†	Glasgow	Scotland 3	Iceland 0
1985†	Reykjavik	Iceland 0	Scotland 1

SCOTLAND v IRAN

1978†	Cordoba	Scotland 1	Iran 1

SCOTLAND v ISRAEL

1981†	Tel Aviv	Israel 0	Scotland 1
1981†	Glasgow	Scotland 3	Israel 1
1986	Tel Aviv	Israel 0	Scotland 1

SCOTLAND v ITALY

1931	Rome	Italy 3	Scotland 0
1965†	Glasgow	Scotland 1	Italy 0
1965†	Naples	Italy 3	Scotland 0
1988	Perugia	Italy 2	Scotland 0

SCOTLAND v LUXEMBOURG

1947	Luxembourg	Luxembourg 0	Scotland 6
1986‡	Glasgow	Scotland 3	Luxembourg 0
1987‡	Luxembourg	Luxembourg 0	Scotland 0

SCOTLAND v MALTA

1988	Ta'Qali	Malta 1	Scotland 1
1990	Ta'Qali	Malta 1	Scotland 2

SCOTLAND v NEW ZEALAND

1982†	Malaga	Scotland 5	New Zealand 2

SCOTLAND v NORWAY

1929	Oslo	Norway 3	Scotland 7
1954	Glasgow	Scotland 1	Norway 0
1954	Oslo	Norway 1	Scotland 1
1963	Bergen	Norway 4	Scotland 3
1963	Glasgow	Scotland 6	Norway 1
1974	Oslo	Norway 1	Scotland 2
1978‡	Glasgow	Scotland 3	Norway 2
1979‡	Oslo	Norway 0	Scotland 4
1988†	Oslo	Norway 1	Scotland 2
1989†	Glasgow	Scotland 1	Norway 1

SCOTLAND v PARAGUAY

1958†	Norrkoping	Scotland 2	Paraguay 3

SCOTLAND v PERU

1972	Glasgow	Scotland 2	Peru 0
1978†	Cordoba	Scotland 1	Peru 3
1979	Glasgow	Scotland 1	Peru 1

SCOTLAND v POLAND

1958	Warsaw	Poland 1	Scotland 2
1960	Glasgow	Scotland 2	Poland 3
1965†	Chorzow	Poland 1	Scotland 1
1965†	Glasgow	Scotland 1	Poland 2
1980	Poznan	Poland 1	Scotland 0
1990	Glasgow	Scotland 1	Poland 1

SCOTLAND v PORTUGAL

1950	Lisbon	Portugal 2	Scotland 2
1955	Glasgow	Scotland 3	Portugal 0
1959	Lisbon	Portugal 1	Scotland 0
1966	Glasgow	Scotland 0	Portugal 1
1971‡	Lisbon	Portugal 2	Scotland 0
1971‡	Glasgow	Scotland 2	Portugal 1
1975	Glasgow	Scotland 1	Portugal 0
1978‡	Lisbon	Portugal 1	Scotland 0
1980‡	Glasgow	Scotland 4	Portugal 1
1980†	Glasgow	Scotland 0	Portugal 0
1981†	Lisbon	Portugal 2	Scotland 1

SCOTLAND v ROMANIA

1975‡	Bucharest	Romania 1	Scotland 1
1975‡	Glasgow	Scotland 1	Romania 1
1986	Glasgow	Scotland 3	Romania 0
1990‡	Glasgow	Scotland 2	Romania 1

SCOTLAND v REPUBLIC OF IRELAND

1961†	Glasgow	Scotland 4	Ireland 1
1961†	Dublin	Ireland 0	Scotland 3

SCOTTISH FOOTBALL LEAGUE ATTENDANCE FIGURES

SEASON 1964/65

First Division	League Cup	League Championship	Total
Aberdeen	38,577	138,738	177,315
Airdrieonians	5,646	62,405	68,051
Celtic	109,001	310,829	419,830
Clyde	11,704	78,053	89,757
Dundee	31,996	204,469	236,465
Dundee United	32,279	153,864	186,143
Dunfermline Athletic	36,485	71,309	82,587
Falkirk	11,278	71,309	82,587
Heart of Midlothian	34,775	271,584	306,359
Hibernian	29,983	235,037	265,020
Kilmarnock	30,944	167,230	198,174
Morton	36,949	167,834	204,783
Motherwell	13,485	83,810	97,295
Partick Thistle	42,721	102,107	144,828
Rangers	127,616	494,511	622,127
St Johnstone	23,405	95,706	119,111
St Mirren	31,905	86,278	118,183
Third Lanark	6,746	45,920	52,666
	655,495	2,908,508	3,564,003

Second Division	League Cup	League Championship	Total
Albion Rovers	3,271	9,585	12,856
Alloa	2,498	12,543	15,041
Arbroath	5,516	16,806	22,322
Ayr United	10,750	18,609	29,359
Berwick Rangers	4,641	17,120	21,761
Brechin City	1,146	7,985	9,131
Cowdenbeath	1,251	7,481	8,732
Dumbarton	9,141	18,888	28,029
East Fife	22,171	23,985	46,156
East Stirlingshire	9,686	37,157	46,843
Forfar Athletic	3,579	11,346	14,925
Hamilton Academical	5,202	24,065	29,267
Montrose	2,979	13,292	16,271
Queen of the South	9,887	48,606	58,493
Queen's Park	3,291	17,185	20,476
Raith Rovers	8,895	16,597	25,492
Stenhousemuir	1,326	4,558	5,884
Stirling Albion	2,552	31,393	33,945
Stranraer	3,619	13,587	17,206
	111,401	350,788	462,189

Semi-Final Tie
Rangers v Dundee United	39,584	*Total*	4,026,192
Celtic v Morton	54,818	*League Cup Semi-Final Ties*	94,402
	94,402	*League Cup Final Tie*	91,424

Final Tie
Celtic v Rangers	91,424	*Grand Total* 4,212,018

SCOTLAND v YUGOSLAVIA
1955	Belgrade	Yugoslavia 2	Scotland 2
1956	Glasgow	Scotland 2	Yugoslavia 0
1958†	Vasteras	Scotland 1	Yugoslavia 1
1972	Belo Horizonte	Scotland 2	Yugoslavia 2
1974†	Frankfurt	Scotland 1	Yugoslavia 1
1984	Glasgow	Scotland 6	Yugoslavia 1
1988†	Glasgow	Scotland 1	Yugoslavia 1
1989†	Zagreb	Yugoslavia 3	Scotland 1

SCOTLAND v ZAIRE
1974	Dortmund	Scotland 2	Zaire 0

CENTENARY CELEBRATION MATCHES
1973	Glasgow	Scotland 0	England 5
1973	Glasgow	Scotland 0	Brazil 1
1973	Glasgow	Scotland 1	W. Germany 1

† World Cup
‡ European Championship

1963	Dublin	Ireland 1	Scotland 0
1969	Dublin	Ireland 1	Scotland 1
1986‡	Dublin	Ireland 0	Scotland 0
1987‡	Glasgow	Ireland 1	Scotland 0

SCOTLAND v SAUDI ARABIA
1988	Riyadh	Saudi Arabia 2	Scotland 2

SCOTLAND v SPAIN
1957†	Glasgow	Scotland 4	Spain 2
1957†	Madrid	Spain 4	Scotland 1
1963	Madrid	Spain 2	Scotland 6
1965	Glasgow	Scotland 0	Spain 0
1974‡	Glasgow	Scotland 1	Spain 2
1975‡	Valencia	Spain 1	Scotland 1
1982	Valencia	Spain 3	Scotland 0
1984†	Glasgow	Scotland 3	Spain 1
1985†	Seville	Spain 1	Scotland 0
1988	Madrid	Spain 0	Scotland 0

SCOTLAND v SWEDEN
1952	Stockholm	Sweden 3	Scotland 1
1953	Glasgow	Scotland 1	Sweden 2
1975	Gothenburg	Sweden 1	Scotland 1
1977	Glasgow	Scotland 3	Sweden 1
1980†	Stockholm	Sweden 0	Scotland 1
1981†	Glasgow	Scotland 2	Sweden 0
1990†	Genoa	Scotland 2	Sweden 1

SCOTLAND v SWITZERLAND
1931	Geneva	Switzerland 2	Scotland 3
1946	Glasgow	Scotland 3	Switzerland 1
1948	Berne	Switzerland 2	Scotland 1
1950	Glasgow	Scotland 3	Switzerland 1
1957†	Basle	Switzerland 1	Scotland 2
1957†	Glasgow	Scotland 3	Switzerland 2
1973	Berne	Switzerland 1	Scotland 0
1976	Glasgow	Scotland 1	Switzerland 0
1982‡	Berne	Switzerland 2	Scotland 0
1983‡	Glasgow	Scotland 2	Switzerland 2

SCOTLAND v TURKEY
1960	Ankara	Turkey 4	Scotland 2

SCOTLAND v URUGUAY
1954†	Basle	Scotland 0	Uruguay 7
1962	Glasgow	Scotland 2	Uruguay 3
1983	Glasgow	Scotland 2	Uruguay 0
1986†	Neza	Scotland 0	Uruguay 0

SCOTLAND v USA
1952	Glasgow	Scotland 6	USA 0

SCOTLAND v USSR
1967	Glasgow	Scotland 0	USSR 2
1971	Moscow	USSR 1	Scotland 0
1982†	Malaga	USSR 2	Scotland 2

First Division

First Division	League Cup	League Championship	Total
Aberdeen	51,355	140,951	192,306
Celtic	103,447	409,734	513,181
Clyde	19,006	66,643	85,649
Dundee	61,185	153,155	214,340
Dundee United	52,031	149,315	201,346
Dunfermline Athletic	20,837	121,885	142,692
Falkirk	13,543	75,124	88,667
Hamilton Academical	6,020	53,260	59,260
Heart of Midlothian	54,075	192,748	246,823
Hibernian	34,165	198,288	232,453
Kilmarnock	31,854	137,223	169,077
Morton	19,815	110,802	130,620
Motherwell	31,662	87,621	119,283
Partick Thistle	14,423	116,825	131,248
Rangers	122,743	415,497	538,240
St Johnstone	13,774	84,418	98,192
St Mirren	17,260	82,170	99,430
Stirling Albion	5,116	71,771	76,887
	672,334	2,672,380	3,339,694

Second Division

Second Division	League Cup	League Championship	Total
Airdrieonians	16,444	30,785	47,229
Albion Rovers	2,995	14,511	17,506
Alloa	6,764	10,244	17,008
Arbroath	4,209	21,515	25,724
Ayr United	18,263	66,723	84,986
Berwick Rangers	4,762	15,235	19,997
Brechin City	1,419	6,903	8,322
Cowdenbeath	1,564	7,111	8,675
Dumbarton	3,095	19,461	22,556
East Fife	5,964	18,569	24,533
East Stirlingshire	2,933	7,575	10,508
Forfar Athletic	1,194	6,974	8,168
Montrose	2,018	14,678	16,696
Queen of the South	8,207	42,543	50,750
Queen's Park	2,643	11,671	14,314
Raith Rovers	21,823	19,948	41,771
Stenhousemuir	555	4,827	5,382
Stranraer	3,476	12,352	15,828
Third Lanark	4,064	14,807	18,871
	112,392	346,432	458,834

Semi-Final Ties

Celtic v Hibernian	46,074		Total
Rangers v Kilmarnock	54,702	100,776	League Cup Semi-Final Ties
Celtic v Hibernian Replay		51,023	League Cup Semi-Final Replay

Final Tie

Celtic v Rangers		107,609	League Cup Final Tie

Celtic v Hibernian Replay 51,023

107,609 Grand Total

4,057,926

First Division	League Cup	League Championship	Total
Aberdeen	47,436	190,323	237,759
Airdrieonians	7,971	80,140	88,111
Ayr United	23,937	78,428	102,365
Celtic	132,959	528,396	661,355
Clyde	22,503	78,847	101,350
Dundee	25,215	153,610	178,825
Dundee United	23,588	124,820	148,408
Dunfermline Athletic	37,034	105,251	142,285
Falkirk	11,352	75,844	87,193
Heart of Midlothian	32,991	173,192	206,183
Hibernian	51,958	209,464	261,402
Kilmarnock	45,085	132,310	177,395
Motherwell	11,935	94,259	106,194
Partick Thistle	14,837	107,371	122,208
Rangers	130,241	485,743	615,984
St Johnstone	12,586	85,103	97,689
St Mirren	26,188	72,702	98,890
Stirling Albion	19,141	60,962	80,103
	676,957	2,836,762	3,513,699

Second Division

Second Division	League Cup	League Championship	Total
Albion Rovers	1,897	12,192	14,089
Alloa	2,613	13,553	16,166
Arbroath	4,661	23,436	28,097
Berwick Rangers	2,792	14,866	17,658
Brechin City	1,954	7,599	9,553
Clydebank	3,586	29,350	32,936
Cowdenbeath	3,035	10,447	13,482
Dumbarton	3,147	13,762	16,909
East Fife	5,162	28,114	33,276
East Stirlingshire	1,324	7,770	9,094
Forfar Athletic	2,530	9,468	11,998
Hamilton Academical	2,636	19,370	22,006
Montrose	4,245	14,025	18,270
Morton	24,485	72,655	97,140
Queen of the South	7,513	31,570	39,083
Queen's Park	1,923	13,924	15,847
Raith Rovers	3,729	52,138	55,867
Stenhousemuir	406	5,124	5,530
Stranraer	2,487	13,435	15,922
Third Lanark	3,165	12,864	16,029
	83,290	405,662	488,952

Semi-Final Ties

Celtic v Airdrieonians	36,967		Total
Rangers v Aberdeen	38,620	75,587	League Cup Semi-Final Ties
		38,086	League Cup Semi-Final Replay

Final Tie

Celtic v Rangers		94,582	League Cup Final Tie

Rangers v Aberdeen Replay 38,086

4,002,651

94,582 Grand Total

4,210,906

First Division	League Cup	League Championship	Total
Aberdeen	66,786	170,947	237,733
Airdrieonians	6,606	64,453	71,059
Celtic	197,443	533,337	730,780
Clyde	5,801	65,834	71,635
Dundee	35,771	134,488	170,259
Dundee United	51,683	102,551	154,234
Dunfermline Athletic	15,040	124,594	139,634
Falkirk	10,225	83,850	94,075
Heart of Midlothian	14,510	182,036	196,546
Hibernian	29,479	195,079	224,558
Kilmarnock	31,645	88,993	120,638
Morton	20,378	104,124	124,502
Motherwell	8,067	82,789	90,856
Partick Thistle	8,115	120,544	128,659
Raith Rovers	5,197	95,952	101,149
Rangers	195,819	594,655	790,474
St Johnstone	14,695	76,382	91,077
Stirling Albion	6,858	49,207	56,065
	724,118	2,869,815	3,593,933

Second Division

Second Division	League Cup	League Championship	Total
Albion Rovers	1,363	10,978	12,341
Alloa	2,531	11,859	14,390
Arbroath	5,152	26,620	31,772
Ayr United	21,251	40,852	62,103
Berwick Rangers	4,759	10,530	15,289
Brechin City	808	5,948	6,756
Clydebank	9,293	19,941	29,234
Cowdenbeath	1,699	6,937	8,636
Dumbarton	3,517	15,872	10,389
East Fife	15,067	25,479	40,546
East Stirlingshire	978	87,214	88,192
Forfar Athletic	829	10,239	11,068
Hamilton Academical	3,400	12,176	15,576
Montrose	2,052	11,651	13,703
Queen of the South	6,861	35,241	42,102
Queen's Park	5,719	17,722	23,441
St Mirren	7,983	62,571	70,554
Stenhousemuir	266	4,192	4,458
Stranraer	2,965	7,748	10,713
	96,495	423,770	520,263

Semi-Final Ties

Celtic v Morton	45,662		Total
Dundee v St Johnstone	17,812	63,474	League Cup Semi-Final Ties

Final Tie

Celtic v Dundee		66,660	League Cup Final Tie

4,114,196

63,474

66,660 Grand Total

4,244,330

SEASON 1968/69

First Division	League Cup	League Championship	Total
Aberdeen	50,260	192,836	243,096
Airdrieonians	13,983	73,216	87,199
Ayr United	7,164	56,904	64,068
Celtic	175,981	590,576	766,557
Clyde	14,678	77,146	91,824
Dundee	24,344	119,058	143,402
Dundee United	22,933	141,226	164,159
Dunfermline Athletic	22,305	109,177	131,482
Falkirk	13,020	86,637	99,657
Heart of Midlothian	26,623	182,171	208,794
Hibernian	31,263	184,190	215,453
Kilmarnock	16,389	129,178	145,567
Morton	40,581	99,262	139,843
Partick Thistle	58,155	106,009	164,164
Raith Rovers	12,949	106,076	119,025
Rangers	137,891	555,630	693,521
St Johnstone	12,318	90,754	103,072
St Mirren	9,406	160,316	169,722
	690,243	3,060,362	3,750,605

Second Division	League Cup	League Championship	Total
Albion Rovers	4,139	10,044	14,183
Alloa	1,675	12,776	14,451
Ayr United	18,475	48,723	67,198
Berwick Rangers	2,722	7,684	10,406
Brechin City	813	5,774	6,587
Clydebank	3,687	14,809	18,496
Cowdenbeath	1,969	8,099	10,068
Dumbarton	3,218	14,388	17,606
East Fife	13,093	25,153	38,246
East Stirlingshire	1,548	17,694	19,242
Forfar Athletic	2,025	13,483	15,508
Hamilton Academical	13,061	14,596	27,657
Montrose	3,314	9,180	12,494
Motherwell	10,265	48,000	58,265
Queen's Park	3,026	14,883	17,909
St Johnstone	12,318	30,183	42,501
Stenhousemuir	515	5,147	5,662
Stirling Albion	3,477	21,575	25,052
Stranraer	6,488	12,556	19,044
	105,828	334,747	440,575

Semi-Final Ties
Celtic v Clyde 34,676 — Total 4,191,180
Hibernian v Dundee 19,504 — *League Cup Semi-Final Ties* 54,180
54,180 — *League Cup Final Tie* 74,240

Final Tie
Celtic v Hibernian 74,240 — *Grand Total* 4,317,600

SEASON 1969/70

First Division	League Cup	League Championship	Total
Aberdeen	74,288	177,418	251,706
Airdrieonians	42,694	61,755	104,449
Ayr United	14,985	137,303	152,288
Celtic	186,398	564,195	750,593
Clyde	6,121	67,234	73,355
Dundee	28,418	118,085	146,503
Dundee United	19,579	141,552	161,131
Dunfermline Athletic	23,300	109,620	132,920
Heart of Midlothian	25,528	190,128	215,656
Hibernian	39,495	223,178	262,673
Kilmarnock	11,488	103,610	115,058
Morton	37,715	81,295	119,010
Motherwell	29,791	115,794	145,585
Partick Thistle	10,294	96,975	107,269
Raith Rovers	36,624	63,318	99,942
Rangers	126,033	571,774	697,807
St Johnstone	25,134	106,924	132,058
St Mirren	18,888	115,836	134,724
	756,733	3,045,994	3,802,727

Second Division	League Cup	League Championship	Total
Albion Rovers	1,938	5,734	7,672
Alloa	1,374	25,215	26,589
Arbroath	5,898	23,558	29,456
Berwick Rangers	1,329	16,124	17,453
Brechin City	1,478	5,914	7,392
Clydebank	4,267	13,177	17,444
Cowdenbeath	1,585	39,497	41,082
Dumbarton	12,732	21,067	33,799
East Fife	6,213	21,834	28,047
East Stirlingshire	2,486	13,017	15,503
Falkirk	13,094	69,014	82,918
Forfar Athletic	3,945	11,447	15,392
Hamilton Academical	1,439	9,246	10,685
Montrose	2,484	12,161	14,645
Queen of the South	9,894	38,326	48,220
Queen's Park	2,794	11,642	14,436
Stenhousemuir	697	6,230	6,927
Stirling Albion	5,486	19,413	24,899
Stranraer	3,001	9,303	12,304
	82,944	371,919	454,863

Semi-Final Ties
Celtic v Ayr United 35,110 — Total 4,257,590
St Johnstone v Motherwell 19,576 — *League Cup Semi-Final Ties* 54,686
54,686 — *League Cup Semi-Final Replay* 47,831
Celtic v Ayr United Replay 47,831 — *League Cup Final Tie* 73,067

Final Tie
Celtic v St Johnstone 73,067 — *Grand Total* 4,433,174

SEASON 1970/71

First Division	League Cup	League Championship	Total
Aberdeen	38,940	250,044	288,984
Airdrieonians	9,055	71,717	80,772
Ayr United	17,497	112,548	130,045
Celtic	150,803	534,817	685,620
Clyde	18,010	57,070	75,080
Cowdenbeath	10,883	56,944	67,827
Dundee	38,653	120,879	159,532
Dundee United	23,714	112,599	136,313
Dunfermline Athletic	23,691	117,267	140,958
Falkirk	10,936	108,003	118,939
Heart of Midlothian	46,135	198,348	244,483
Hibernian	81,089	173,661	254,750
Kilmarnock	13,743	90,476	104,219
Morton	22,011	75,075	97,086
Motherwell	27,610	99,901	127,511
Rangers	168,473	491,548	660,021
St Johnstone	10,375	117,506	127,881
St Mirren	10,104	105,256	115,360
	721,722	2,893,659	3,615,381

Second Division	League Cup	League Championship	Total
Albion Rovers	2,157	9,296	11,453
Alloa	3,315	19,326	22,641
Arbroath	4,568	25,139	29,707
Berwick Rangers	3,096	9,496	12,592
Brechin City	916	5,931	6,847
Clydebank	4,878	24,751	29,629
Cowdenbeath	25,494	28,797	54,291
East Fife	6,064	52,391	58,455
East Stirlingshire	—	8,761	8,761
Forfar Athletic	1,103	12,726	13,829
Hamilton Academical	1,360	12,868	14,228
Montrose	3,565	16,160	19,725
Partick Thistle	18,496	12,847	31,343
Queen of the South	6,774	25,441	32,215
Queen's Park	922	12,722	13,644
Raith Rovers	5,618	35,543	41,161
Stenhousemuir	575	7,592	8,167
Stirling Albion	3,587	15,219	18,806
Stranraer	3,716	17,560	21,276
	96,204	352,566	448,770

Semi-Final Ties
Rangers v Cowdenbeath 31,987 — Total 4,064,151
Celtic v Dumbarton 32,903 — *League Cup Semi-Final Ties* 64,890
64,890 — *League Cup Final Tie* 101,000

Final Tie
Rangers v Celtic 101,000 — *Grand Total* 4,230,041

Parkhead – traditional football ground in a traditional setting, but its huge terracings became a liability after the Hillsborough Disaster in 1989.

Kenny Dalglish and John Greig lead the Old Firm out to battle in 1976.

Maurice Johnston is booked for running
behind the Celtic goal to celebrate
with ecstatic (and incredulous)
Rangers supporters. Repentance
does not appear to be written on
his expression.

First Division	League Cup	League Championship	Total
Aberdeen	54,361	305,881	360,242
Airdrieonians	13,631	91,446	105,077
Ayr United	37,614	128,384	165,998
Celtic	130,144	531,094	661,208
Clyde	8,253	61,773	70,026
Dundee	27,019	136,343	163,362
Dundee United	20,195	115,021	135,216
Dunfermline Athletic	25,469	115,672	141,141
East Fife	12,541	96,291	108,832
Falkirk	41,171	113,947	155,118
Heart of Midlothian	26,908	190,333	217,241
Hibernian	66,299	238,973	305,272
Kilmarnock	12,329	97,182	109,511
Morton	25,124	84,101	109,225
Motherwell	12,709	102,027	114,736
Partick Thistle	26,601	172,927	199,528
Rangers	125,774	445,386	571,160
St Johnstone	23,855	105,360	129,215
	689,967	3,132,141	3,822,108

Second Division	League Cup	League Championship	Total
Albion Rovers	1,693	9,267	10,960
Alloa	4,497	17,689	22,186
Arbroath	7,858	35,678	43,356
Berwick Rangers	2,047	9,577	11,624
Brechin City	1,016	9,352	10,368
Clydebank	16,118	24,025	40,143
Cowdenbeath	3,030	27,699	30,729
Dumbarton	4,300	57,911	62,211
East Stirlingshire	1,348	10,633	11,981
Forfar Athletic	2,258	20,211	22,469
Hamilton Academical	1,489	16,135	17,624
Montrose	4,290	23,912	28,202
Queen of the South	6,870	39,224	46,094
Queen's Park	2,045	14,532	16,577
Raith Rovers	11,808	41,124	52,932
St Mirren	15,769	68,686	84,455
Stenhousemuir	2,218	8,001	10,219
Stirling Albion	9,065	31,369	40,434
Stranraer	4,414	19,216	23,630
	102,133	484,241	586,374

Semi-Final Ties
Partick Thistle v Falkirk 20,291 — Total 4,408,482
Celtic v St Mirren 29,488 — League Cup Semi-Final Ties 49,779
49,779 — League Cup Final Tie 62,740

Final Tie
Partick Thistle v Celtic 62,740 — 62,740 Grand Total 4,521,001

First Division	League Cup	League Championship	Total
Aberdeen	70,040	233,456	303,496
Airdrieonians	2,455	82,543	107,094
Arbroath	13,514	61,030	74,644
Ayr United	21,394	108,681	130,575
Celtic	97,384	452,303	549,687
Dumbarton	20,418	98,132	118,550
Dundee	61,461	134,024	195,485
Dundee United	12,587	117,722	130,309
East Fife	25,868	83,350	109,218
Falkirk	13,501	87,159	100,660
Heart of Midlothian	18,414	173,614	192,028
Hibernian	50,030	273,702	323,732
Kilmarnock	9,092	76,310	85,402
Morton	9,209	72,056	81,265
Motherwell	20,061	88,855	108,916
Partick Thistle	20,508	125,773	146,281
Rangers	94,244	466,976	561,220
St Johnstone	25,582	80,420	106,002
	608,458	2,816,106	3,424,564

Second Division	League Cup	League Championship	Total
Albion Rovers	1,852	7,660	9,512
Alloa	5,735	15,332	21,067
Berwick Rangers	6,999	8,352	15,351
Brechin City	1,343	7,886	9,229
Clyde	5,040	31,677	36,717
Clydebank	12,239	23,355	35,594
Cowdenbeath	4,251	22,282	26,533
Dunfermline Athletic	7,625	75,947	83,572
East Stirlingshire	2,772	11,310	14,082
Forfar Athletic	2,190	18,144	20,334
Hamilton Academical	3,000	31,938	34,938
Montrose	3,508	21,526	25,034
Queen of the South	10,833	23,756	34,589
Queen's Park	3,229	11,033	14,262
Raith Rovers	5,956	37,705	43,661
St Mirren	23,371	53,619	76,990
Stenhousemuir	6,862	12,152	19,014
Stirling Albion	15,269	36,342	51,611
Stranraer	12,995	17,747	30,742
	135,069	467,763	602,832

Semi-Final Ties
Celtic v Aberdeen 39,682 — Total 4,027,396
Hibernian v Rangers 46,518 — League Cup Semi-Final Ties 86,200
86,200 — League Cup Final Tie 71,696

Final Tie
Hibernian v Celtic 71,696 — Grand Total 4,185,292

First Division	League Cup	League Championship	Total
Aberdeen	52,425	147,163	199,588
Arbroath	14,258	52,776	67,034
Ayr United	18,279	103,911	122,190
Celtic	164,421	420,957	585,378
Clyde	9,520	51,084	60,604
Dumbarton	18,656	75,174	93,830
Dundee	28,889	118,113	147,002
Dundee United	14,028	92,959	106,987
Dunfermline Athletic	17,277	98,351	115,628
East Fife	11,240	61,397	72,637
Falkirk	21,110	73,817	94,927
Heart of Midlothian	32,374	199,457	231,831
Hibernian	63,321	243,768	307,089
Morton	9,803	48,268	58,071
Motherwell	38,733	107,257	145,990
Partick Thistle	12,128	112,510	124,638
Rangers	167,056	380,058	547,114
St Johnstone	14,882	65,542	80,424
	708,400	2,452,562	3,160,962

Second Division	League Cup	League Championship	Total
Airdrieonians	9,016	49,645	58,661
Albion Rovers	7,048	10,727	17,775
Alloa	2,362	15,919	18,281
Berwick Rangers	3,045	12,000	15,045
Brechin City	1,087	7,918	9,005
Clydebank	1,696	23,062	24,758
Cowdenbeath	4,223	14,211	18,434
East Stirlingshire	4,053	14,346	18,399
Forfar Athletic	2,461	10,757	13,218
Hamilton Academical	6,269	41,826	48,095
Kilmarnock	17,330	65,507	82,837
Montrose	3,820	16,942	20,762
Queen of the South	4,015	36,102	40,117
Queen's Park	2,371	10,152	12,523
Raith Rovers	9,420	710	41,190
St Mirren	15,043	40,814	55,857
Stenhousemuir	2,652	8,102	10,754
Stirling Albion	8,945	23,243	32,188
Stranraer	2,195	18,064	20,259
	107,051	451,107	558,158

Semi-Final Ties
Dundee v Kilmarnock ??,??? — Total 3,719,120
Celtic v Rangers ??,??? — League Cup Semi-Final Ties ??,???
 — League Cup Final Tie 27,974

Final Tie
Dundee v Celtic 27,974 — 27,974 Grand Total ?,???,???

SEASON 1974/75

First Division

	League Cup	League Championship	Total
Aberdeen	23,497	165,143	188,640
Airdrieonians	10,037	74,824	84,861
Arbroath	6,198	48,856	55,054
Ayr United	16,606	98,601	115,207
Celtic	77,112	387,170	464,282
Clyde	5,913	55,186	61,099
Dumbarton	9,347	73,832	83,179
Dundee	28,280	124,704	152,984
Dundee United	23,312	112,698	136,010
Dunfermline Athletic	16,810	81,974	98,784
Heart of Midlothian	40,239	207,820	248,059
Hibernian	64,045	233,254	297,299
Kilmarnock	19,944	119,367	139,311
Morton	7,363	56,093	63,456
Motherwell	16,466	99,157	115,623
Partick Thistle	17,106	104,314	121,420
Rangers	104,919	558,534	663,453
St Johnstone	16,780	72,128	88,908
	503,974	2,673,655	3,177,629

Second Division

	League Cup	League Championship	Total
Albion Rovers	2,357	9,868	12,225
Alloa	3,034	12,153	15,187
Berwick Rangers	1,496	9,915	11,411
Brechin City	930	8,345	9,275
Clydebank	3,720	22,522	26,242
Cowdenbeath	2,365	13,786	16,151
East Fife	3,763	35,192	38,955
East Stirlingshire	2,112	22,145	24,257
Falkirk	17,498	49,736	67,234
Forfar Athletic	1,722	10,839	12,561
Hamilton Academical	6,209	44,350	50,559
Meadowbank Thistle	3,178	12,857	16,035
Montrose	2,983	25,303	28,286
Queen of the South	5,098	35,610	40,708
Queen's Park	2,670	10,394	13,064
Raith Rovers	4,558	29,681	34,239
St Mirren	9,167	45,521	54,688
Stenhousemuir	1,084	8,576	9,660
Stirling Albion	3,944	23,688	27,632
Stranraer	2,990	15,175	18,165
	80,878	445,656	526,534
			3,704,163

Semi-Final Ties
Celtic v Airdrieonians 19,330 — Total
Hibernian v Falkirk 19,876 — League Cup Semi-Final Ties 39,206 — 39,206
39,206 — League Cup Final Tie

Final Tie
Celtic v Hibernian 53,838 — Grand Total 53,838 — 3,797,207

SEASON 1975/76

Premier Division

	League Cup	League Championship	Total
Aberdeen	29,403	211,928	241,331
Ayr United	14,360	124,106	138,466
Celtic	85,955	505,179	591,134
Dundee	14,351	157,814	172,165
Dundee United	13,851	137,100	150,951
Heart of Midlothian	33,975	228,179	262,154
Hibernian	38,115	248,345	286,460
Motherwell	29,939	172,351	202,290
Rangers	87,099	551,660	638,759
St Johnstone	6,991	86,171	93,162
	354,039	2,422,833	2,776,872

First Division

	League Cup	League Championship	Total
Airdrieonians	17,348	32,667	50,015
Arbroath	5,265	22,049	27,314
Clyde	15,158	18,433	33,591
Dumbarton	16,957	27,775	44,732
Dunfermline Athletic	11,117	32,347	43,464
East Fife	5,962	23,792	29,754
Falkirk	6,855	32,809	39,664
Hamilton Academical	6,619	25,697	32,316
Kilmarnock	10,044	55,110	65,154
Montrose	9,015	21,700	30,715
Morton	2,630	18,887	21,517
Partick Thistle	21,420	62,934	84,354
Queen of the South	13,166	28,880	42,046
St Mirren	6,865	48,073	54,938
	148,421	451,153	599,574

Second Division

	League Cup	League Championship	Total
Albion Rovers	1,526	5,225	6,751
Alloa	1,000	11,750	12,750
Berwick Rangers	1,422	4,213	5,635
Brechin City	732	4,425	5,157
Clydebank	9,942	18,079	28,021
Cowdenbeath	3,879	9,367	13,246
East Stirlingshire	1,908	7,227	9,135
Forfar Athletic	2,416	7,644	10,060
Meadowbank Thistle	1,211	6,016	7,227
Queen's Park	1,931	7,853	9,784
Raith Rovers	7,396	26,829	34,225
Stenhousemuir	6,511	5,622	12,133
Stirling Albion	6,180	14,706	20,886
Stranraer	4,185	11,435	15,620
	50,239	140,391	190,630
			3,567,076

Semi-Final Ties
Rangers v Montrose 20,318 — Total
Celtic v Partick Thistle 31,421 — League Cup Semi-Final Ties 51,739 — 51,739
51,739 — League Cup Final Tie

Final Tie
Rangers v Celtic 55,706 — Grand Total 55,706 — 3,674,521

SEASON 1976/77

Premier Division

	League Cup	League Championship	Total
Aberdeen	41,872	248,357	290,229
Ayr United	14,339	121,524	135,863
Celtic	49,936	505,126	555,062
Dundee United	21,717	128,294	150,011
Heart of Midlothian	44,254	210,519	254,773
Hibernian	35,259	180,057	215,316
Kilmarnock	13,683	105,283	118,966
Motherwell	18,364	129,068	147,432
Partick Thistle	11,705	113,164	124,869
Rangers	92,344	390,456	482,800
	343,473	2,131,848	2,475,321

First Division

	League Cup	League Championship	Total
Airdrieonians	9,722	35,142	44,864
Arbroath	10,242	26,128	36,370
Clydebank	27,935	57,856	85,791
Dumbarton	10,156	27,263	37,419
Dundee	16,134	85,836	101,970
East Fife	4,935	31,546	36,481
Falkirk	9,944	31,600	41,544
Hamilton Academical	6,289	36,164	42,453
Montrose	12,272	29,612	41,884
Morton	3,832	39,175	43,007
Queen of the South	5,352	37,633	42,985
Raith Rovers	5,123	44,383	49,506
St Johnstone	9,531	32,181	41,712
St Mirren	10,315	121,891	132,206
	141,782	636,410	778,192

Second Division

	League Cup	League Championship	Total
Albion Rovers	10,814	7,942	18,756
Alloa	3,479	23,005	26,484
Berwick Rangers	980	7,601	8,581
Brechin City	1,086	6,545	7,631
Clyde	3,388	12,790	16,178
Cowdenbeath	2,301	11,434	13,735
Dunfermline Athletic	4,531	31,450	35,981
East Stirlingshire	1,521	9,800	11,321
Forfar Athletic	1,944	12,558	14,502
Meadowbank Thistle	742	11,479	12,221
Queen's Park	2,239	12,114	14,353
Stenhousemuir	922	8,532	9,454
Stirling Albion	10,364	28,708	39,072
Stranraer	2,817	24,903	27,720
	47,128	208,861	255,989
			3,509,502

Semi-Final Ties
Aberdeen v Rangers 20,990 — Total
Celtic v Heart of Midlothian 21,706 — League Cup Semi-Final Ties 42,696 — 42,696
42,696 — League Cup Final Tie

Final Tie
Aberdeen v Celtic 69,679 — Grand Total 69,679 — 3,621,877

Premier Division

	League Cup	League Championship	Total
Aberdeen	36,791	290,078	326,869
Ayr United	4,854	111,527	116,381
Celtic	49,201	532,218	581,419
Clydebank	4,940	80,716	85,656
Dundee United	19,438	151,394	170,832
Hibernian	4,585	173,643	178,228
Motherwell	20,494	148,237	168,731
Partick Thistle	2,535	150,862	153,397
Rangers	46,408	505,497	551,905
St Mirren	32,845	212,268	245,113
	222,091	2,356,440	2,578,531

First Division

	League Cup	League Championship	Total
Airdrieonians	1,839	24,642	26,481
Alloa	858	29,040	29,898
Arbroath	4,821	35,826	40,647
Dumbarton	1,572	36,957	38,529
Dundee	11,483	127,860	139,343
East Fife	545	35,317	35,862
Hamilton Academical	6,907	38,837	45,744
Heart of Midlothian	25,119	187,395	212,514
Kilmarnock	5,119	53,840	58,959
Montrose	2,144	25,675	27,819
Morton	8,309	80,035	88,344
Queen of the South	12,438	31,516	43,954
St Johnstone	10,941	39,950	50,891
Stirling Albion	10,089	43,221	53,310
	102,184	790,111	892,295

Second Division

	League Cup	League Championship	Total
Albion Rovers	1,030	10,051	11,081
Berwick Rangers	720	20,824	21,544
Brechin City	419	8,497	8,916
Clyde	912	18,843	19,755
Cowdenbeath	1,646	16,670	18,316
Dunfermline Athletic	13,008	36,158	49,166
East Stirlingshire	868	12,502	13,370
Falkirk	2,759	35,549	38,308
Forfar Athletic	8,942	21,049	29,991
Meadowbank Thistle	469	9,551	10,020
Queen's Park	1,337	12,625	13,962
Raith Rovers	1,542	36,245	37,787
Stenhousemuir	3,362	8,923	12,285
Stranraer	2,764	21,343	24,107
	39,778	268,830	308,608

Semi-Final Ties

Rangers v Forfar Athletic	12,799	Total
Celtic v Heart of Midlothian	18,840	League Cup Semi-Final Tie
	31,639	League Cup Final Tie

Final Tie

Rangers v Celtic	60,168	Grand Total

Total	3,779,434
League Cup Semi-Final Tie	31,639
League Cup Final Tie	60,168
Grand Total	3,871,241

Premier Division

	League Cup	League Championship	Total
Aberdeen	69,605	255,082	324,687
Celtic	89,888	455,445	545,333
Dundee United	12,648	163,817	176,465
Heart of Midlothian	6,729	194,961	201,690
Hibernian	2,693	176,296	205,989
Morton	17,403	142,693	160,096
Motherwell	2,714	139,323	161,037
Partick Thistle	2,789	143,391	146,180
Rangers	97,357	461,299	556,656
St Mirren	30,779	192,492	223,221
	373,605	2,324,799	2,703,404

First Division

	League Cup	League Championship	Total
Airdrieonians	3,514	27,749	31,263
Arbroath	5,964	23,831	29,795
Ayr United	12,332	63,860	76,192
Berwick Rangers	2,045	23,530	25,576
Clyde	4,060	31,728	35,788
Clydebank	3,471	22,536	26,007
Dumbarton	2,698	113,440	126,138
Hamilton Academical	5,333	40,066	45,399
Kilmarnock	6,047	57,628	63,675
Montrose	7,852	17,355	25,207
Queen of the South	1,295	23,414	24,709
Raith Rovers	3,942	35,096	39,038
St Johnstone	1,500	35,781	37,281
Stirling Albion	1,619	22,721	24,330
	71,663	538,735	610,398

Second Division

	League Cup	League Championship	Total
Albion Rovers	4,333	8,159	12,492
Alloa	2,539	16,377	18,916
Berwick Rangers	2,938	19,796	22,734
Brechin City	1,645	9,681	11,326
Cowdenbeath	691	13,644	14,335
Dunfermline Athletic	1,896	48,990	50,886
East Fife	919	18,637	19,556
East Stirlingshire	249	8,933	9,182
Falkirk	8,248	42,623	50,871
Forfar Athletic	5,916	20,477	26,393
Meadowbank Thistle	1,576	8,820	10,496
Queen's Park	804	9,046	9,850
Stenhousemuir	357	8,366	8,723
Stranraer	2,104	16,242	18,346
	34,315	249,791	284,106

Semi-Final Ties

Rangers v Celtic	47,549	Total
Aberdeen v Hibernian	21,052	League Cup Semi-Final Ties
	68,601	League Cup Final Tie

Final Tie

Rangers v Aberdeen	53,205	Grand Total

Total	3,597,908
League Cup Semi-Final Ties	68,601
League Cup Final Tie	53,205
Grand Total	3,719,514

Premier Division

	League Cup	League Championship	Total
Aberdeen	53,201	232,989	296,190
Celtic	62,782	512,987	575,769
Dundee	15,372	169,807	185,179
Dundee United	16,581	182,972	199,553
Hibernian	7,854	172,160	180,014
Kilmarnock	18,471	125,442	143,913
Morton	16,828	144,925	161,753
Partick Thistle	6,310	130,909	137,219
Rangers	37,580	367,287	404,867
St Mirren	7,532	186,172	93,704
	242,511	2,225,650	2,468,161

First Division

	League Cup	League Championship	Total
Airdrieonians	2,570	52,658	55,228
Arbroath	2,174	22,306	24,480
Ayr United	10,319	53,087	63,406
Berwick Rangers	1,251	30,303	31,554
Clyde	5,071	19,569	24,640
Clydebank	1,150	24,189	25,339
Dumbarton	1,087	24,444	25,531
Dunfermline Athletic	1,792	49,337	51,129
Hamilton Academical	11,305	40,634	51,939
Heart of Midlothian	6,081	114,695	121,496
Motherwell	2,017	53,691	55,708
Raith Rovers	12,468	46,808	59,276
St Johnstone	9,381	42,664	52,045
Stirling Albion	8,402	25,573	33,975
	75,788	599,958	675,746

Second Division

	League Cup	League Championship	Total
Albion Rovers	3,521	7,920	11,441
Alloa	1,696	12,714	14,410
Brechin City	446	11,720	12,166
Cowdenbeath	1,383	10,482	11,865
East Fife	2,355	15,159	17,514
East Stirlingshire	413	12,911	13,324
Falkirk	8,583	38,175	46,758
Forfar Athletic	2,628	21,621	43,049
Meadowbank Thistle	1,023	8,567	9,590
Montrose	2,028	13,999	16,027
Queen of the South	1,748	20,369	22,117
Queen's Park	2,372	9,236	11,608
Stenhousemuir	1,218	7,861	9,079
Stranraer	2,238	14,718	16,956
	31,652	205,452	237,104

Semi-Final Ties

Dundee United v Hamilton	????	Total
Aberdeen v Morton	????	League Cup Semi-Final Ties

League Cup Final Tie

Dundee Utd v Aberdeen	27,299	League Cup Final Tie
Dundee Utd v Aberdeen Replay	28,984	League Cup Final Tie Replay
		Grand Total

Total	5,601,011
League Cup Semi-Final Ties	????
League Cup Final Tie	27,299
League Cup Final Tie Replay	28,984
Grand Total	?,???,???

SEASON 1980/81

Premier Division	League Cup	League Championship	Total
Aberdeen	43,020	221,674	264,694
Airdrieonians	2,983	89,368	92,351
Celtic	53,619	411,053	464,672
Dundee United	32,048	138,891	170,939
Heart of Midlothian	9,575	139,653	149,228
Kilmarnock	7,660	81,119	88,779
Morton	2,253	108,070	110,323
Partick Thistle	17,164	98,660	115,824
Rangers	43,983	329,904	373,887
St Mirren	9,708	141,464	151,172
	222,013	1,759,856	1,981,869

First Division	League Cup	League Championship	Total
Ayr United	22,177	46,638	68,815
Berwick Rangers	1,188	18,769	19,957
Clydebank	4,274	17,416	21,690
Dumbarton	831	13,889	14,720
Dundee	27,808	99,024	126,832
Dunfermline Athletic	3,034	47,117	50,151
East Stirlingshire	430	23,564	23,994
Falkirk	1,594	40,597	42,191
Hamilton Academical	9,293	39,345	48,638
Hibernian	11,889	89,207	101,096
Motherwell	5,166	47,939	53,105
Raith Rovers	3,709	50,244	53,953
St Johnstone	1,379	49,304	50,683
Stirling Albion	5,622	18,099	23,721
	98,394	601,152	699,546

Second Division	League Cup	League Championship	Total
Albion Rovers	1,457	6,626	8,083
Alloa	1,750	14,625	16,375
Arbroath	2,855	13,236	16,091
Brechin City	527	12,955	13,482
Clyde	1,896	10,267	12,163
Cowdenbeath	1,238	10,647	11,885
East Fife	2,028	9,653	11,681
Forfar Athletic	3,897	16,585	20,482
Meadowbank Thistle	298	7,136	7,434
Montrose	1,548	8,690	10,238
Queen of the South	2,198	23,702	25,900
Queen's Park	1,937	15,624	17,561
Stenhousemuir	829	5,422	6,251
Stranraer	683	11,007	11,690
	23,141	166,175	189,316

Semi-Final Ties
Dundee United v Celtic 14,517
Celtic v Dundee United 19,700
Ayr United v Dundee 6,801
Dundee v Ayr United 9,438
League Cup Semi-Final Ties 50,456

Final Tie
Dundee United v Dundee 24,466 League Cup Final Tie 24,466

Total 2,870,731
League Cup Semi-Final Ties 50,456
League Cup Final Tie 24,466
Grand Total 2,945,653

SEASON 1981/82

Premier Division	League Cup	League Championship	Total
Aberdeen	51,454	204,485	255,939
Airdrieonians	6,708	68,772	75,480
Celtic	60,477	408,928	469,405
Dundee	19,196	136,268	155,464
Dundee United	33,593	169,489	203,082
Hibernian	24,156	134,018	158,174
Morton	15,131	69,692	84,823
Partick Thistle	6,280	92,108	98,388
Rangers	78,896	295,195	374,091
St Mirren	39,191	125,185	164,376
	335,082	1,704,140	2,039,222

First Division	League Cup	League Championship	Total
Ayr United	8,636	45,078	53,714
Clydebank	1,724	17,729	19,453
Dumbarton	1,130	10,197	11,327
Dunfermline Athletic	4,706	36,677	41,383
East Stirlingshire	817	12,025	12,842
Falkirk	5,150	39,000	44,150
Hamilton Academical	11,366	25,631	36,997
Heart of Midlothian	23,088	97,989	121,077
Kilmarnock	6,407	52,187	58,594
Motherwell	7,268	63,028	70,296
Queen of the South	3,669	22,590	26,259
Queen's Park	2,449	18,470	20,919
Raith Rovers	11,125	33,451	44,576
St Johnstone	18,498	37,190	55,688
	106,033	512,242	618,275

Second Division	League Cup	League Championship	Total
Albion Rovers	490	7,263	7,753
Alloa	2,642	13,372	16,014
Arbroath	3,443	12,514	15,975
Berwick Rangers	3,883	15,927	19,810
Brechin City	6,006	12,909	18,975
Clyde	1,607	10,195	11,802
Cowdenbeath	944	7,221	8,165
East Fife	1,030	10,048	11,078
Forfar Athletic	8,261	22,914	31,175
Meadowbank Thistle	715	5,506	6,220
Montrose	1,296	7,077	8,373
Stenhousemuir	535	6,152	6,687
Stirling Albion	2,476	9,574	12,050
Stranraer	1,745	11,004	12,749
	35,133	151,675	186,808

Semi-Final Ties
St Mirren v Rangers 5,113
Rangers v St Mirren 23,359
Dundee United v Aberdeen 13,824
Aberdeen v Dundee United 20,137
League Cup Semi-Final Ties 62,433

Final Tie
Rangers v Dundee United 53,795 League Cup Final Tie 53,795

Total 2,844,305
League Cup Semi-Final Ties 62,433
League Cup Final Tie 53,795
Grand Total 2,960,533

SEASON 1982/83

Premier Division	League Cup	League Championship	Total
Aberdeen	40,799	279,618	320,417
Celtic	54,207	427,311	481,518
Dundee	12,039	142,725	154,764
Dundee United	43,706	200,401	244,107
Hibernian	20,501	127,956	148,457
Kilmarnock	13,293	62,341	75,634
Morton	6,318	76,261	82,579
Motherwell	9,768	117,168	126,936
Rangers	62,638	318,253	380,891
St Mirren	13,216	107,822	121,038
	276,485	1,859,856	2,136,341

First Division	League Cup	League Championship	Total
Airdrieonians	8,895	31,413	40,308
Alloa	5,543	23,798	29,341
Ayr United	3,851	24,882	28,733
Clyde	3,337	16,185	19,522
Clydebank	9,465	17,707	27,172
Dumbarton	2,138	13,839	15,977
Dunfermline Athletic	8,631	28,309	36,940
Falkirk	4,402	29,682	34,084
Hamilton Academical	3,025	21,083	24,108
Heart of Midlothian	47,855	118,158	166,013
Partick Thistle	9,201	43,761	52,962
Queen's Park	2,138	19,016	21,154
Raith Rovers	4,407	28,188	32,595
St Johnstone	6,977	58,858	65,835
	119,856	474,879	594,744

Second Division	League Cup	League Championship	Total
Albion Rovers	707	5,334	6,041
Arbroath	6,482	13,915	20,397
Berwick Rangers	1,841	11,036	12,877
Brechin City	2,254	13,426	15,680
Cowdenbeath	1,926	6,139	8,065
East Fife	1,523	11,145	12,668
East Stirlingshire	1,143	4,280	5,423
Forfar Athletic	3,847	17,757	21,604
Meadowbank Thistle	539	10,372	10,911
Montrose	666	6,524	7,190
Queen of the South	2,523	13,772	16,295
Stenhousemuir	728	6,508	7,236
Stirling Albion	2,514	11,573	14,087
Stranraer	1,058	8,928	9,986
	27,751	140,709	168,460

Semi-Final Ties
Celtic v Dundee United 19,149
Dundee United v Celtic 15,522
Rangers v Hearts 22,548
Hearts v Rangers 18,993
League Cup Semi-Final Ties 76,212

Final Tie
Celtic v Rangers 55,372 League Cup Final Tie 55,372

Total 2,899,545
League Cup Semi-Final Ties 76,212
League Cup Final Tie 55,372
Grand Total 3,031,129

SEASON 1983/84

Premier Division	League Championship	League Cup	Total
Aberdeen	322,645	65,694	388,339
Celtic	331,025	71,368	402,393
Dundee	133,958	19,919	153,877
Dundee United	196,089	36,752	232,841
Heart of Midlothian	214,459	19,963	234,422
Hibernian	150,011	13,587	163,598
Motherwell	100,184	7,657	107,841
Rangers	395,920	73,703	469,623
St Johnstone	87,466	10,394	97,860
St Mirren	88,192	13,371	101,563
	2,019,949	322,408	2,352,357

First Division	League Championship	League Cup	Total
Airdrieonians	21,918	9,667	31,585
Alloa	14,663	5,377	20,040
Ayr United	27,038	1,264	28,302
Brechin City	14,815	2,620	17,435
Clyde	13,056	802	13,858
Clydebank	16,739	6,974	23,713
Dumbarton	16,537	760	17,297
Falkirk	36,638	1,815	38,453
Hamilton Academical	20,113	1,075	21,188
Kilmarnock	25,810	13,346	39,156
Meadowbank Thistle	10,757	4,132	14,889
Morton	35,289	5,157	40,446
Partick Thistle	48,385	1,959	50,344
Raith Rovers	19,991	3,117	23,108
	321,749	58,065	379,814

Second Division	League Championship	League Cup	Total
Albion Rovers	7,021	520	7,541
Arbroath	11,095	591	11,686
Berwick Rangers	10,611	1,580	12,191
Cowdenbeath	6,956	3,043	9,999
Dunfermline Athletic	20,703	2,618	23,321
East Fife	15,595	2,307	17,902
East Stirlingshire	4,673	186	4,859
Forfar Athletic	21,436	2,459	23,895
Montrose	5,725	1,254	6,979
Queen of the South	15,754	6,383	22,137
Queen's Park	9,885	702	10,587
Stenhousemuir	6,764	306	7,070
Stirling Albion	10,823	644	11,467
Stranraer	9,037	441	9,478
	156,078	23,034	179,112

Semi-Final Ties
Dundee United v Rangers 14,569 — *Total* 2,911,283
Rangers v Dundee United 37,180 — *League Cup Semi-Final Ties* 112,985
Celtic v Aberdeen 41,169 — *League Cup Final Tie* 66,369
Aberdeen v Celtic 20,067
112,985

Final Tie
Rangers v Celtic 66,369 — *Grand Total* 3,090,637

SEASON 1984/5

Premier Division	League Championship	League Cup	Total
Aberdeen	285,786	—	285,786
Celtic	374,893	—	374,893
Dumbarton	62,125	2,500	64,625
Dundee	151,897	15,231	167,128
Dundee United	191,983	39,987	231,970
Heart of Midlothian	203,483	19,673	223,156
Hibernian	133,652	6,337	139,989
Morton	62,397	—	62,397
Rangers	377,330	33,403	410,733
St Mirren	106,242	2,384	108,626
	1,949,788	119,515	2,069,303

First Division	League Championship	League Cup	Total
Airdrieonians	28,820	14,817	43,637
Ayr United	31,283	2,052	33,335
Brechin City	14,549	1,245	15,794
Clyde	16,803	—	16,803
Clydebank	20,513	—	20,513
East Fife	22,267	—	22,267
Falkirk	35,135	—	35,135
Forfar Athletic	23,884	—	23,884
Hamilton Academical	24,708	—	24,708
Kilmarnock	27,028	849	27,877
Meadowbank Thistle	11,123	6,755	17,878
Motherwell	47,666	—	47,666
Partick Thistle	36,685	—	36,685
St Johnstone	26,321	1,130	27,451
	366,785	26,348	393,633

Second Division	League Championship	League Cup	Total
Albion Rovers	8,437	348	8,785
Alloa	18,245	—	18,245
Arbroath	9,717	—	9,717
Berwick Rangers	8,620	—	8,620
Cowdenbeath	9,982	15,133	25,115
Dunfermline Athletic	46,576	10,067	56,643
East Stirlingshire	7,760	217	7,977
Montrose	11,872	—	11,872
Queen of the South	11,975	2,304	14,279
Queen's Park	10,324	—	10,324
Raith Rovers	16,963	906	17,869
Stenhousemuir	8,620	—	8,620
Stirling Albion	10,205	927	11,132
Stranraer	8,987	463	9,450
	188,283	30,365	218,648

Semi-Final Ties
Hearts v Dundee United 10,541 — *Total* 2,681,584
Dundee United v Hearts 13,468 — *League Cup Semi-Final Ties* 40,644
Rangers v Meadowbank 13,184 — *League Cup Final Tie* 44,698
Meadowbank v Rangers 3,451
40,644

Final Tie
Rangers v Dundee United 44,698 — *Grand Total* 2,766,926

SEASON 1985/86

Premier Division	League Championship	League Cup	Total
Aberdeen	257,871	45,573	303,444
Celtic	456,023	9,292	465,315
Clydebank	66,033	1,065	67,098
Dundee	161,108	—	161,108
Dundee United	195,162	26,137	221,299
Heart of Midlothian	291,564	4,478	296,042
Hibernian	164,428	42,249	206,677
Motherwell	100,293	2,996	103,289
Rangers	452,634	50,626	503,260
St Mirren	115,295	3,435	118,730
	2,260,411	185,851	2,446,262

First Division	League Championship	League Cup	Total
Airdrieonians	26,666	—	26,666
Alloa	15,138	2,010	17,148
Ayr United	28,852	—	28,852
Brechin City	12,639	790	13,429
Clyde	18,044	—	18,044
Dumbarton	22,236	—	22,236
East Fife	17,416	—	17,416
Falkirk	47,171	—	47,171
Forfar Athletic	16,297	7,282	23,579
Hamilton Academical	31,819	15,402	47,221
Kilmarnock	38,981	—	38,981
Montrose	13,882	1,952	15,834
Morton	25,118	5,159	30,277
Partick Thistle	37,351	—	37,351
	351,610	32,595	384,205

Second Division	League Championship	League Cup	Total
Albion Rovers	7,871	—	7,871
Arbroath	11,633	—	11,633
Berwick Rangers	11,755	598	12,353
Cowdenbeath	10,496	—	10,496
Dunfermline Athletic	54,577	2,581	57,158
East Stirlingshire	6,327	458	6,785
Meadowbank Thistle	10,720	442	11,162
Queen of the South	28,711	7,516	36,227
Queen's Park	11,141	505	11,646
Raith Rovers	19,504	—	19,504
St Johnstone	19,138	6,509	25,647
Stenhousemuir	12,212	—	12,212
Stirling Albion	12,103	954	13,057
Stranraer	9,643	2,090	11,733
	225,831	21,653	247,484

Semi-Final
Dundee United v Aberdeen 20,119 — *Total* 3,077,951
Aberdeen v Dundee United 12,585 — *League Cup Semi-Final Ties* 89,896
Hibernian v Rangers 17,916 — *League Cup Final Tie* 40,065
Rangers v Hibernian 39,276
89,896

Final Tie
Aberdeen v Hibernian 40,065 — *Grand Total* 3,207,912

SEASON 1986/87

Premier Division

Premier Division	League Cup	League Championship	Total
Aberdeen	38,581	277,099	315,680
Celtic	24,558	556,835	581,393
Clydebank	875	69,997	70,872
Dundee	3,851	165,286	169,137
Dundee United	—	229,508	229,508
Falkirk	—	138,033	138,033
Hamilton Academical	4,697	93,254	97,951
Heart of Midlothian	7,028	319,690	326,718
Hibernian	13,571	201,386	214,957
Motherwell	7,357	118,753	126,110
Rangers	33,712	795,343	829,055
St Mirren	—	129,040	129,040
	134,230	3,094,224	3,228,454

First Division

First Division	League Cup	League Championship	Total
Airdrieonians	—	31,460	31,460
Brechin City	499	13,487	13,986
Clyde	1,197	20,121	21,318
Dumbarton	746	23,691	24,437
Dunfermline Athletic	6,161	91,182	97,343
East Fife	8,835	27,497	36,332
Forfar Athletic	1,338	19,300	20,638
Kilmarnock	3,553	41,767	45,320
Montrose	—	14,259	14,259
Morton	2,097	42,496	44,593
Partick Thistle	1,346	38,640	39,986
Queen of the South	3,802	38,336	42,138
	29,574	402,236	431,810

Second Division

Second Division	League Cup	League Championship	Total
Albion Rovers	961	9,936	10,897
Alloa	—	11,545	11,545
Arbroath	738	9,506	10,244
Ayr United	3,680	31,057	34,737
Berwick Rangers	—	7,216	7,216
Cowdenbeath	411	7,288	7,699
East Stirlingshire	—	6,898	6,898
Meadowbank Thistle	402	7,807	8,209
Queen's Park	—	10,222	10,222
Raith Rovers	—	27,281	27,281
St Johnstone	—	20,412	20,412
Stenhousemuir	—	7,304	16,756
Stirling Albion	9,452	13,767	13,767
Stranraer	582	10,494	11,076
	16,226	180,733	196,959

Total 3,857,223
Skol Cup Semi-Final Ties 71,790
Skol Cup Final 74,219
Grand Total 4,003,232

Semi-Final Ties
Celtic v Motherwell 26,541
Rangers v Dundee United 45,249
Total 71,790

Final Tie
Celtic v Rangers 74,219

SEASON 1987/88

Premier Division

Premier Division	Skol Cup	Fine Fare League Championship	Total
Aberdeen	41,205	296,123	337,328
Celtic	13,711	730,388	744,099
Dundee	19,867	189,096	208,963
Dundee United	6,075	230,168	236,243
Dunfermline Athletic	17,705	203,384	221,089
Falkirk	—	146,503	146,503
Heart of Midlothian	20,899	365,929	386,828
Hibernian	10,383	254,977	265,360
Morton	1,899	108,533	110,432
Motherwell	15,304	146,511	161,815
Rangers	40,920	848,493	889,413
St Mirren	3,507	162,499	166,006
	191,475	3,682,604	3,874,079

First Division

First Division	Skol Cup	Fine Fare League Championship	Total
Airdrieonians	—	31,116	31,116
Clyde	—	23,120	23,120
Clydebank	—	23,397	23,397
Dumbarton	9,429	18,402	27,831
East Fife	—	21,570	21,570
Forfar Athletic	—	16,268	16,268
Hamilton Academical	—	44,957	44,957
Meadowbank Thistle	3,255	16,143	19,398
Kilmarnock	—	40,610	40,610
Partick Thistle	—	43,393	43,393
Queen of the South	2,003	28,200	30,203
Raith Rovers	7,902	46,402	54,304
	22,589	353,578	376,167

Second Division

Second Division	Skol Cup	Fine Fare League Championship	Total
Albion Rovers	536	6,806	7,342
Alloa	—	11,393	11,393
Arbroath	735	11,153	11,888
Ayr United	2,378	53,125	55,503
Berwick Rangers	467	8,962	9,429
Brechin City	—	9,487	9,487
Cowdenbeath	315	5,351	5,666
East Stirlingshire	2,240	6,718	8,958
Montrose	—	7,988	7,988
Queen's Park	1,410	12,203	13,613
St Johnstone	1,313	38,916	40,229
Stenhousemuir	394	6,809	7,203
Stirling Albion	11,737	15,208	26,945
Stranraer	390	9,362	9,752
	21,915	203,481	225,396

Total 4,475,642
Skol Cup Semi-Final Ties 67,873
Skol Cup Final Tie 71,961
Grand Total 4,615,476

SEASON 1988/89

Premier Division

Premier Division	Skol Cup	Fine Fare League Championship	Total
Aberdeen	9,139	253,928	263,067
Celtic	44,153	570,830	614,983
Dundee	8,794	168,328	177,122
Dundee United	21,140	230,940	252,080
Hamilton Academical	—	89,615	89,615
Heart of Midlothian	10,474	276,614	287,088
Hibernian	33,004	250,132	283,136
Motherwell	—	130,567	130,567
Rangers	73,806	705,393	779,199
St Mirren	5,970	151,172	157,142
	206,480	2,827,519	3,033,999

First Division

First Division	Skol Cup	Fine Fare League Championship	Total
Airdrieonians	3,239	44,751	47,990
Ayr United	—	70,828	70,828
Clyde	14,699	22,961	37,660
Clydebank	581	30,995	31,576
Dunfermline Athletic	21,700	132,480	154,180
Falkirk	2,751	71,854	74,605
Forfar Athletic	—	23,248	23,248
Kilmarnock	1,523	47,270	48,793
Meadowbank Thistle	7,566	16,119	23,685
Morton	3,131	39,723	42,854
Partick Thistle	3,890	51,030	54,920
Queen of the South	—	19,735	19,735
Raith Rovers	—	43,199	43,199
St Johnstone	—	55,965	55,965
	59,080	670,158	729,238

Second Division

Second Division	Skol Cup	Fine Fare League Championship	Total
Albion Rovers	592	11,223	11,815
Alloa	1,157	11,568	12,725
Arbroath	—	9,511	9,511
Berwick Rangers	—	7,706	7,706
Brechin City	1,363	8,963	10,326
Cowdenbeath	363	5,989	6,352
Dumbarton	2,203	10,124	12,327
East Fife	2,396	12,547	14,943
East Stirlingshire	430	5,424	5,854
Montrose	—	7,370	7,370
Queen's Park	734	12,184	12,918
Stenhousemuir	281	7,423	7,704
Stirling Albion	—	12,838	12,838
Stranraer	—	14,652	14,652
	9,519	137,522	147,041

B&Q League Championship 3,635,199
Skol Cup 275,079
Skol Cup Semi-Final Ties 72,104
Skol Cup Final Tie 72,122
Grand Total 4,054,504

SEASON 1989/90

	Skol Cup	B & Q League Championship	Total
Premier Division			
Aberdeen	20,929	278,005	298,934
Celtic	20,074	515,087	535,161
Dundee	3,021	159,906	162,927
Dundee United	7,041	192,935	199,976
Dunfermline Athletic	14,407	197,804	212,211
Heart of Midlothian	32,245	282,490	314,735
Hibernian	26,723	192,690	219,413
Motherwell	—	155,372	155,372
Rangers	31,762	691,839	723,601
St Mirren	4,754	137,627	142,381
	160,956	2,803,755	2,964,711
First Division			
Airdrieonians	1,320	45,895	47,215
Albion Rovers	2,384	23,812	26,196
Alloa	—	21,142	21,142
Ayr United	2,616	50,854	53,470
Clyde	—	19,948	19,948
Clydebank	765	21,229	21,994
Falkirk	9,046	58,186	67,232
Forfar Athletic	—	19,165	19,165
Hamilton Academical	11,837	33,042	44,879
Meadowbank Thistle	—	13,821	13,821
Morton	11,821	31,434	43,255
Partick Thistle	—	75,565	75,565
Raith Rovers	—	31,986	31,986
St Johnstone	—	117,316	117,316
	39,789	563,395	603,184
Second Division			
Arbroath	671	9,989	10,660
Berwick Rangers	1,643	9,900	11,543
Brechin City	1,179	12,260	13,439
Cowdenbeath	391	5,505	5,896
Dumbarton	9,069	11,529	20,598
East Fife	858	13,224	14,082
East Stirlingshire	—	5,994	5,994
Kilmarnock	3,903	64,940	68,843
Montrose	—	7,992	7,992
Queen of the South	1,046	14,008	15,054
Queen's Park	997	11,812	12,809
Stenhousemuir	—	10,571	10,571
Stirling Albion	492	14,166	14,658
Stranraer	735	15,771	16,506
Total Total	20,984	207,661	228,645

B&Q League Championship 3,574,811
Skol Cup 221,729
Skol Cup Semi-Final Ties 87,010
Skol Cup Final Tie 61,190
Grand Total 3,944,740

INDEX

(Figures in italic type represent illustrations)